Joyce as Theory

Joyce as Theory is the first book-length examination of James Joyce to argue he can be read as a theorist. Joyce is not just a favorite case study of literary theory; he wrote about how we make meaning, and to what effect. The present volume traces his hermeneutics in those narratives in *Finnegans Wake* which deal with textual production and interpretation, showing that the *Wake*'s difficulty exemplifies Joyce's theoretical stance. All reading involves responding to problems we cannot quite fathom.

This preoccupation places Joyce alongside Jacques Derrida and Jacques Lacan. *Joyce as Theory* revives debates on theory with a linguistic focus, laying open misconceptions that have muddled attempts to be over and done with this kind of thought. It demonstrates that Derrida and Lacan, almost exclusively presented as rivals, converge on a common position. It opposes the myth of linguistic theory as a formalist approach, instead showing that Joyce, Derrida, and Lacan give us a hermeneutic ethics alert to how meaning-making impacts our lived experience. And it challenges the notion that theory imposes matters alien to Joyce, demonstrating that it is an appreciation of Joyce's arguments in *Finnegans Wake* that generates a theoretical perspective.

Joyce as Theory is essential reading for researchers and students in Joyce studies, continental philosophy, literary theory, and modernist literature.

Gabriel Renggli was educated in French-speaking Switzerland, Dublin, and York. He received his PhD in English from the University of York in 2016. His publications include work on James Joyce, Jacques Derrida, Gilles Deleuze, liberation theology, and Jorge Luis Borges, examining various overlaps between fiction, hermeneutics, ontology, and ethics. He lives in Zurich.

Routledge Studies in Twentieth-Century Literature

Ernest Hemingway and the Fluidity of Gender
A Socio-Cultural Analysis of Selected Works
Tania Chakravertty

The Life and Works of Korean Poet Kim Myŏng-sun
The Flower Dream of a Woman Born Too Soon
Jung Ja Choi

Boasian Verse
The Poetic and Ethnographic Work of Edward Sapir, Ruth Benedict, and Margaret Mead
Philipp Schweighauser

Valencian Folktales
Enric Valor
Translated by Paul Scott Derrick and Maria-Lluïsa Gea-Valor

The Postwar Counterculture in Novels and Film
On the Avenue of the Mystery
Gary Hentzi

Authors and Art Movements of the Twentieth Century
Painterly Poetics
Declan Lloyd

Joyce as Theory
Hermeneutic Ethics in Derrida, Lacan, and *Finnegans Wake*
Gabriel Renggli

For more information about this series, please visit: www.routledge.com/Routledge-Studies-in-Twentieth-Century-Literature/book-series/RSTLC

Joyce as Theory
Hermeneutic Ethics in Derrida, Lacan, and *Finnegans Wake*

Gabriel Renggli

NEW YORK AND LONDON

First published 2023
by Routledge
605 Third Avenue, New York, NY 10158

and by Routledge
4 Park Square, Milton Park, Abingdon, Oxon, OX14 4RN

Routledge is an imprint of the Taylor & Francis Group, an informa business

© 2023 Gabriel Renggli

The right of Gabriel Renggli to be identified as author of this work has been asserted in accordance with sections 77 and 78 of the Copyright, Designs and Patents Act 1988.

All rights reserved. No part of this book may be reprinted or reproduced or utilised in any form or by any electronic, mechanical, or other means, now known or hereafter invented, including photocopying and recording, or in any information storage or retrieval system, without permission in writing from the publishers.

Trademark notice: Product or corporate names may be trademarks or registered trademarks, and are used only for identification and explanation without intent to infringe.

ISBN: 978-1-032-42153-7 (hbk)
ISBN: 978-1-032-42155-1 (pbk)
ISBN: 978-1-003-36141-1 (ebk)

DOI: 10.4324/9781003361411

Typeset in Sabon
by Newgen Publishing UK

for my parents

Contents

Acknowledgments		viii
Introduction		1
1	Reading What Is Not There	37
2	The Penman and the Critic	73
3	Tower of Babel	107
4	Making Do	142
	Concluding Remarks: The Uses of Difficulty	169
	Works Cited	180
	Index	190

Acknowledgments

I am grateful to Derek Attridge, who lent this book his patient and generous support when it was still a PhD thesis, written under somewhat unusual circumstances. At the University of York, I also thank Lawrence Rainey and Matthew Campbell, who provided feedback on drafts of various chapters. I greatly appreciate Luke Thurston's feedback on the entire thesis. Completing this manuscript would not have been possible without the hospitality and friendship of Boriana "Bobby" Alexandrova, Nick and Catherine Wolterman, Christine Gmür, Izzy Isgate, and James Keal.

I thank the Swiss embassy in Ireland, the University of York's F. R. Leavis Fund, and the Trieste Joyce Summer School for funding that enabled me to attend various events, and Johns Hopkins University Press for permission to reproduce material previously published in *Modernism/ modernity*.

In Zurich, I thank Fritz Senn and the entire James Joyce Foundation, who do marvelous work in providing scholars and enthusiasts of every ilk with the perfect surroundings in which to follow their calling. Some material used in Chapter 1 of this volume was presented at the Foundation's 2019 James Joyce Workshop, and I am grateful to all workshop participants for their feedback. Elena Baeva and Nora Keller played oh so many boardgames with me and helped me through some difficult times. Sarah d'Episcopo and Stephen Carlin commented on the book proposal.

I wish to thank my parents, Anita and Raimund, who got all of this started when they bought me my first comic book some 30 years ago, and then children's literature, and then the classics. You see where that kind of thing can lead to.

Finally, huge thanks are due to my partner, Jialu Zhu. I am so lucky to be a part of your life, and to know you are a part of mine!

Introduction

James Joyce is a theorist. In *Finnegans Wake*, he develops a hermeneutic philosophy that bears the hallmarks of what, in the latter half of the twentieth century, came to be called "literary theory." *Joyce as Theory* proposes to examine the *Wake*'s comments, at the level of meta-textual narrative, on signification and its limits. *Finnegans Wake* has a great deal to say about reading and writing, and about the complications that plague them. This is not to repeat the critical chestnut according to which the *Wake* is an account of its own creation or a manual to its own interpretation. Joyce asks of language a number of questions whose significance is in no way limited to his own text.

To examine these propositions, *Joyce as Theory* draws on the work of philosopher Jacques Derrida and of psychoanalyst Jacques Lacan. In demonstrating how their thinking on language resonates with Joyce's, helping us understand the sophistication of Joyce's inquiry, I will argue two additional points in support of my main one. First, contrary to the overwhelming majority of readings of Lacan and Derrida, I will show that their positions converge on a shared understanding of signification. When it comes to the repetitions of the signifier, Derrida is far more interested in the search for stability and the impact of various forms of authority than he is often made out to be. When it comes to the letter, the phallus, or the real, Lacan is far more concerned with relational networks and constructs than is suggested by superficial readings of that terminology. Lacan's and Derrida's thought can be revisited and the results of such reconsideration can be seen to meet somewhere between the mirage impressions – Derrida the relativist, Lacan the dogmatist – that lead debates about them astray. The matter is not helped by the fact that Derrida and Lacan were oddly deficient at reading each other. As Joyce intimates when he makes the twins Shem and Shaun the blueprint of all historical conflict, it is often the one most resembling you that you are prone to judge most harshly.

Secondly, as I will argue in this Introduction, a return to these two early exponents of theory (I use the term in a broad sense, for reasons I will

DOI: 10.4324/9781003361411-1

2 *Introduction*

presently discuss) is not an anachronistic strategy, but an approach well suited to Joyce's ideas about unreadability as well as to an appreciation of these ideas' undiminished relevance today. Joyce's hermeneutics in *Finnegans Wake* is concerned with the fact that our languages are hardly perfect tools. Time and again, we confront gaps in our expressive capacities. This theme parallels a shared concern of Derrida's and Lacan's, who also accentuate the extent to which language is shaped, even constituted, by its limitations and who examine the psychological and social effects of this constitution. The unreadability of *Finnegans Wake* has similar – similarly practical and pressing – implications.

Bringing this kind of theory to *Finnegans Wake* is not a new procedure. Key texts relating Joyce to Derrida or to Lacan include Alan Roughley's *Reading Derrida Reading Joyce* (1999), Christine van Boheemen-Saaf's *Joyce, Derrida, Lacan, and the Trauma of History* (1999), Luke Thurston's *James Joyce and the Problem of Psychoanalysis* (2004), Peter Mahon's *Imagining Joyce and Derrida* (2007), Sheldon Brivic's *Joyce Through Lacan and Žižek* (2008), the essay collection *Derrida and Joyce: Texts and Contexts* (2013) edited by Andrew Mitchell and Sam Slote, Daniel Bristow's *Joyce and Lacan* (2017), and Colette Soler's *Lacan Reading Joyce* (2018). It will become apparent, as I engage with some of these texts over the course of my argument, that critical enterprises can draw on significant affinities between theory and Joyce's writing, particularly *Finnegans Wake*. We can trace theory's debts to Joyce, provide theoretical models for reading Joyce, or use Joyce's works to exemplify theoretical discussions. But it will also become clear that we can go beyond what the extant studies achieve, by shifting emphasis away from the *Wake* as an object-text on which or with which theories of interpretation can be seen to work, towards a theoretically informed articulation of the *Wake*'s own hermeneutics.

I should add that in examining the correspondences between Joyce, Derrida, and Lacan, I will discuss effects that occur in all language: in virtually any activity of reading or writing, speaking or listening. All three authors I consider address the very division between expression and its outside. This may seem an unreasonably large claim to make, but the underlying idea is a simple one few of my readers will contest: over the course of human history (as opposed to human myth) no language has ever been perfect. In this view, fault-lines are part of any meaning-production, however contextualized – though, to be clear, the manifestations of these fault-lines differ vastly, and various understandings of them are strongly context-bound. In other words, the *Wake* is not only a text signifying certain things. It also reflects on what it means to signify, *in general*, and it partly does so by way of its own impenetrability. Joyce confronts us with opacity, but like Lacan and Derrida, he maintains that opacity is a constitutive feature of all signifying systems. Thus, on the one hand, *Joyce as Theory* makes a contribution to *Finnegans Wake* criticism, where some

Introduction 3

aspects of the *Wake*'s questioning of language have gone insufficiently examined. On the other hand, these aspects will lead me to a theoretical analysis of signification – as opposed to a theoretical analysis of *Finnegans Wake* – since they show Joyce himself to be venturing a theory of the inexpressible.

The *Wake* asks us how we come to terms with what remains unassimilable. This involves the ethical demand made by unreadability, and more generally, by alterity. As my title and subtitle indicate, the theory put forward in *Finnegans Wake* involves an ethics. One of the things the present study argues is that the *Wake*'s ethics is inextricably linked to its hermeneutics. In charting my project in this Introduction, the first issue I want to address is therefore literary theory's relationship to ethics. I will now sketch an overview of theory that is preliminary to (but contextualizes) the presentation of my own approach to Joyce, Derrida, and Lacan. This sketch outlines why a hermeneutic position – a theory of sense-making – can already imply a certain ethical position. In particular, it is addressed to those readers who may feel uncomfortable with the idea of calling Joyce a theorist, or sceptical at the thought of privileging a relationship between theory and ethics. I will attempt to convince these readers of the validity of my approach by giving an overview of some of theory's key concerns, rather than assuming familiarity and indeed agreement with theoretical protocols.

How is it possible for theory to concern itself with ethics, if ethical relevance requires an applicability that sits uneasily with what may appear as theory's self-absorbed, unpractical nature? The response I want to develop is that this view of literary theory is a misapprehension. This argument is far from new, but in view of theory's persistently bad reputation (more about this in the next subsection) the point bears repeating, and doing so helps situate my own contribution. I should clarify that I use "theory" quite sweepingly. To some extent, this is inevitable, as the term gathers together distinct methodologies in a somewhat ill-defined manner. Yet, as Jonathan Culler notes, "the theoretical movements that introductions identify – such as structuralism, deconstruction, feminism, psychoanalysis, Marxism, and new historicism – have a lot in common. This is why people talk about 'theory' and not just about particular theories" (xi). Any generalisation that lumps together such diverse schools of thought risks imprecision. Still, there is something like theory's overarching project. Culler gives another useful pointer when he writes that literary "theory is not the theory *of literature*. If you had to say what 'theory' is the theory *of*, the answer would be something like 'signifying practices'" (43). I will follow Culler's proposition, using "literary theory," or "theory" for short, to refer to a thought interested in the production of meaning in literature and beyond. This thought's central concern, from the origins of theory right up to today, is that *objectivity* is a dangerous and politically fraught notion.

4   *Introduction*

Why Theory?

Allow me to begin with a personal anecdote. On 15 November 2014, the Faculty of Arts and Humanities of my alma mater, the University of Fribourg (Switzerland), conferred an honorary doctorate on Judith Butler for their work in fields such as gender studies, embodied subjectivity, and social politics. The decision was surrounded by controversy. Opposition to honoring Butler originated with a number of Catholic organizations outside the university as well as with parts of the university's Faculty of Theology. For instance, a member of the academic staff is cited by the Fribourg newspaper *La Liberté* as having stated that he "ne souscrit ni au 'gender' ni à la remise de ce doctorat" (qtd. in Zoellig), which I would translate as: "subscribes neither to 'gender [studies]' nor to the conferral of this doctorate." In the end, the ceremony took place as planned, but Butler's plenary address on the evening of 14 November, which I attended, was overshadowed by protests outside the lecture theatre.

Although I am troubled by the need that was displayed on this occasion to see one's own idea of gender upheld as an objective norm, the protesters unwittingly did a marvelous job of debunking the myth that theory is not serious. This myth has it that with its failure to accept facts which won't change no matter how much you debate them (such as the biological facts that may well be on the minds of those who do not subscribe to gender studies), and with its penchant to value poetic language over clarity, theory abandons knowledge of the world and even refuses to talk sense. The need to protest Butler tells a different story. Does their work feature counterintuitive ideas and defamiliarizing terminology? Yes. Is it cut off from reality? Not if the panic of these protesters is any indication to go by. Evidently, a theorist is well capable of getting their ideas across: both to audiences inspired by these ideas and to audiences *deeply* worried that those inspired might act on these ideas, bringing about real change in the world. As one of the members of the awarding committee, François Gauthier, puts it in an article about the event: with Butler, "la pensée émane de la vie dont elle doit, par méthode, se distancier – mais seulement pour y retourner" (§ 5): "the thought derives from life, from which it must distance itself through methodology – but only in order to return to it."

If some who take issue with theoretical approaches would venture that literary theory gets caught up in questions of discourse and interpretation to the detriment of facts and real-life phenomena, we need to recall that the first thing argued by theory is that there is no such thing as pure discourse. Any signifying gesture positions us in an abundance of (historical, political, etc.) frameworks. That is why theory is so skeptical of any notion of untainted objectivity. Theory maintains that these frameworks are never simply given. They are the product of decisions and of conventions, of the whole complex machinery through which we acquire knowledge and produce meaning. The line between "discourse"

Introduction 5

and "things" is thus irrevocably blurred, which is why theory holds that there is an irreducible complexity to our conceptualising of, engaging with, and communicating about things (say, about gender). This attitude is not a denial of factual reality. It reminds us that any expression of facts is also a selection, a framing, an editing, etc. of facts. What is more, all of these activities end up impacting the reality we are trying to describe. As Butler puts it with regard to our bodies: "To claim that discourse is formative is not to claim that it originates, causes, or exhaustively composes that which it concedes; rather, it is to claim that there is no reference to a pure body which is not at the same time a further formation of that body" (*Bodies* xix).

This complexity is what any metaphysics of presence dilutes when it maintains that relating to the factuality of the world is, or should be, straightforward. At that point, it is the purportedly practical attitude that skips over real-life difficulties. Inversely, theory is ideally situated to contribute to real-life considerations. For theory examines the very link between discourses and world, that is to say: discourses' formative and often all-too-concrete influence on our lives. Misreadings of this attitude, however, have been a consistent feature of theory's reception, especially of one infamous statement in Derrida's *Of Grammatology*. Untold damage has been done by the English translation of Derrida's dictum, "*il n'y a pas de hors-texte*" (158) as "*There is nothing outside of the text*" (158). Rendered thus, the phrase is an open invitation to reify or idolize whatever text one happens to be reading, and to declare the rest of the world inexistent. This misapprehension of what Derrida was saying soon became a widely circulated idea of deconstruction's agenda, giving rise to the myth of theory as a solipsistic, inconsequential toying around with textual fragments.

In 1979, a mere three years after *Of Grammatology* was translated into English, the very first issue of the *London Review of Books* states: "We are not in favour of the current fashion for the 'deconstruction' of literary texts, for the elimination of the author from his work" (ctd. in Shatz 4). Ten years later, in 1989, the idea that deconstruction is essentially an unmooring of meaning is taken up by Slavoj Žižek, who in *The Sublime Object of Ideology* differentiates the Lacanian approach from Derrida's aim "to deconstruct every substantial identity, to denounce behind its solid consistency an interplay of symbolic overdetermination" (78). Žižek's criticism is informed by two incorrect assumptions that have since widely come to define the reception of theory in general (including, ironically, that of Lacan) and of Derrida's work in particular. One: that Derrida *reduces* everything to language (any solid consistency or identity is disavowed). And two: that Derrida *randomizes* the operations of language (meaning is the free interplay of signifiers). The presence of these ideas can subsequently be traced, for instance, in Joyce studies. Another ten years further down the line, the idea that deconstruction cannot think anything outside language accounts for the contrast between Derrida and

6   Introduction

Lacan presented in Christine von Boheemen-Saaf's *Joyce, Derrida, Lacan, and the Trauma of History* (1999), which opposes "the Derridian tenet that there is 'nothing outside the text' " to "the presence of that which language cannot accommodate" (36). Ten years later again, Declan Kiberd requires neither citation nor explication to declare, in his 2009 *Ulysses and Us*: " 'theory' is rarely concerned with linking analysis to real action in the world" (10). And in 2010, Finn Fordham criticizes the notion of "reality as purely textual," asserting that "unlike Derrida, I aim to hold on to the notion that experience is relevant" (*I Do* 60).

Despite vastly different contexts and goals, what all of these examples have in common is that by conceiving of theory in general, or deconstruction in particular, as abstract, purely textual, essentially disinterested in the world, they misrepresent theory's capacity to explore the connections between world and discourse. Derrida never wrote that there is nothing outside of the text. That statement is a translation of "il n'y a rien en dehors du texte." Derrida, however, wrote "il n'y a pas de hors-texte:" there is no outside-the-text, there is no outside that is not text, there is nothing that escapes discursive frameworks of meaning-production. Of his example, Rousseau's *Confessions*, Derrida explains that "in what one calls the real life of these existences 'of flesh and bone,' beyond and behind what one believes can be circumscribed as Rousseau's text, there has never been anything but writing; [...] the 'real' supervening, and being added only while taking on meaning from a trace" (159) – that is, from the differential structure of signification, as I will elaborate in Chapter 1. Derrida emphasizes that the world itself comes to us filtered through discourse and discursively generated concepts, through cultural frameworks, historical perspectives, etc. We will never quite experience the world Rousseau experienced. So not only is Derrida saying (and most emphatically so) that our writing and reading are situated in real-life contexts. He is saying that any interest we take in the real world has to wrestle with this discursive mediation.

The interaction between world and discourse, far from confining us to some solipsistic textual space lost to the world, means that "world" cannot simply be delineated as a solid basis of existence, but is formed by many activities into a polyvalence of worlds. In turn, "discourse" cannot be limited to a representation of these worlds, because it is itself one of those formative activities, impacting what it codifies. (I will return to this idea when I argue that a text's formal attributes can at the same time constitute ethical attributes.) One of the things literary theory argues on the basis of the world–discourse interaction is that literature constitutes an activity in the world, not a secluded realm of its own. Not only do the production and consumption of literature draw on real-life modes of making sense; they participate in the negotiations that may question and develop these modes. The influence runs both ways; texts and their interpretations are part of how a society *makes* its existing order.

Introduction 7

In this view, looking at discourses – including their formal aspects and their manifestation as literature – is really a specific case of looking at the world, apprehending the world, and interacting with the world at the level of its discursive formation. As Derrida puts it in his 1976–77 seminar, *Theory & Practice*, "modern theory is no longer a contemplation, or a passive or disinterested vision, but an active, intervening elaboration" (90). Literary theory examines textual effects in order to better address the real-life issues we encounter in and through these effects. In what is no doubt an overly schematic manner, one can therefore say that literary theory does not manifest itself as a method, as one set of interpretative tools that can be applied to texts (as we have seen, it is too heterogeneous for that); instead, literary theory constitutes a specific attitude regarding what the stakes in reading are. Putting things this way makes for an illuminating contrast to the idea that theory, fond of paradoxes, counterfactuals, and opaque jargon, is chiefly a solipsistic activity. Look at the work produced by theorists, and you will find it concerned with social, political, and ethical questions.

The positing of a political or ethical "turn" in Derrida's work, for example, misses the fact that his philosophy is politically pertinent from its early stages on. In his early work, Derrida critiques dominant ("phallogocentric," as he calls them) modes of thought – whose *ideological inflection* is precisely one of his main themes. Nicholas Royle proposes that we need "to get beyond the notion that his writing or his thinking, his language, if you will, takes on an increasingly political character, starting perhaps with 'The Force of Law' in 1989 or *Spectres of Marx* in 1993. It's political all the way down the line" (106). If *Of Grammatology* declares that there is nothing that escapes being text, then we should not read any of his subsequent works as deviations from, or corrections of, a deconstructive project originally undertaken in a more self-contained manner. Arguing that no interpretative activity and no linguistic practice is ever self-contained, Derrida's work in the 1960s and 1970s already engages in the critical analysis of frameworks that merely pose as natural, unpolitical, and self-evident. It counters this pose with a thinking of the situatedness of frameworks and the ideologically charged nature of claims to objectivity. As Derrida puts it in *Rogues*: "the thinking of différance [was] always a thinking *of* the political" (39).

The political, in this view, is not the social, economic, etc. reality we are left with once we strip away mere talk. As the negotiation of the world, the political is our implication in world–discourse interactions, of which we often may not even be intuitively aware since their very necessity teaches us to see them as how the world naturally appears. Theory's central precept is the belief that although we cannot escape our particular perspectives in order to obtain an objective view, we can render visible some of these world–discourse interactions and pay attention to their implications and effects. Let's return for a moment to gender studies. A theorist like Butler is not denying that our bodies present us with certain physical and biological characteristics. But remember that until quite recently, certain characteristics of bodies termed female were taken to mean that, naturally, women are apt to do certain types of work but not others, therefore, naturally, women belong in the domestic sphere, not the public one, and it follows that it is in the order of nature that women do not have the vote. It would be imprudent, to say the least, to assume that the present moment just happens to be the point in human history at which we have gotten rid of all such constructs. Looking back at how unquestioningly views were held whose denaturalization now seems painfully obvious to us, we should instead wonder just how many of today's "natural" categories remain to be revealed as political – discursive – categories in the future.

This agenda is not a relativist one; it is in many ways the opposite of relativism's implication that anything goes. In recent years, there have been occasional suggestions that the peddling of "alternative facts" and similar socio-political developments are theory seen through to its bitter end. The idea is that theorists, having abandoned caution in the past, will finally be forced to admit some things, by virtue of being facts, are not subject to debate. The problem with this view is that theory has always claimed that debate brings about important and all too real outcomes. Why else worry about the sexism or the transphobia enacted by certain uses of pronouns? There is thus a fundamental misunderstanding at work in the complaint that theory says the world is "merely" language. *Saying that our world is discursively constructed is the very opposite of saying that discourses can be taken lightly.* If discursive construction is formative of our experience, then discursive construction requires rigor, scepticism, and above all care for how we affect others. Theory is not exactly surprised by people's reliance on fantasies, but neither is it forced to accept any construct whatsoever. What is more, when asking why people buy into outrageous lies – and when analyzing how these lies really do end up changing reality in the process – beginning with the power of discourses packs more of a heuristic punch than describing human behavior as approximating the default principles of rationality and factuality. Theory, if I had to reduce it to one motto, reminds us: "It's not as simple as that."

And so the task of defining theory, too, is one that continually renews itself as contexts and applications change. Despite my attempt here to provide a general view, theory "as such" does not exist, except as an umbrella term that has its usefulness as long as it remains flexible and as long as we remember that far from designating the one magical discourse that transcends contexts and frameworks, "theory" covers over important debates internal to what the term purports to designate as a homogeneous field. In fact, the difficulties we encounter in describing theory can be seen as partaking in something like theory's essence, although "essence" is of course exactly the wrong word. Theory is programmatically difficult to pin down, and it is partly for this reason that it is programmatically controversial. Theory is the undoing of its own

Introduction 9

simplification, of its own solidification, of the belief that anything can be understood once and for all.

This investigative attitude is misrepresented by critiques that urge a return to the factual world as accessed through so-called objective or ideologically neutral modes of thought. Contrary to what these critiques often seem to assume, theory is neither a cynical and nihilistic exercise denying the possibility of meaning, nor a merely playful and inconsequential one denying the seriousness of our debates. Theory takes seriously the potential of what we have not yet thought. It revisits various practices and develops powerful articulations of new visions of inhabiting the world (as I suggest above, we can observe this power in the tell-tale responses of those particularly rattled by some vision). In so doing, theory does not issue itself a blank cheque to unleash any and all constructive activity. Yet in approaching its subject with care, it has to remain open to change. It cannot know in advance what new visions it will articulate (this is why the visions can be considered new), and so it cannot close down the question of how it should proceed.

This refusal to be pinned down is central to how *Joyce as Theory* connects unreadability, the claim that Joyce operated as a theorist, and an interpretation of *Finnegans Wake* as a deeply ethical work.

Responding to the Text: Derrida

I provide this review of theory in general and of Derrida's contribution in particular to indicate that theory's worrying of discursive standards is by no means an inconsequential activity, safely ignored by those whose interest is in the real world. Interrogating the normative and seemingly self-evident produces concrete effects. Yet this practical side of theory tends towards an instrumentalism that should have us ask another question. Is theoretical reading a form of literary criticism, or does it use the quite literal *pretext* of discussing literature in order to develop ideas that have little to do with the texts it pertains to study, although the ideas may be of importance to other fields, such as politics? (Note, by the way, that this is the exact opposite of the reproach that theory is solipsistic formalism. It always seems to me a bit of a case of damned if you do and damned if you don't.) The answer I would give is that it depends on how theory is employed. As in any other mode of interpretation, there is a risk of bringing preconceptions to the table and of tweaking the data so as to match the model. But this is not theory's intrinsic fate. It certainly is not its aim.

Subjecting the apparently self-evident to examination is not synonymous with a boundless mutability of meaning or with the irrelevance of a signifying gesture's unique intervention in the symbolic order. As Derek Attridge writes with regard to deconstructive reading: "The spectre of deconstruction is present – or perhaps somewhere between present and absent – whenever a wariness is expressed about too-simple appeals to

10 *Introduction*

categories such as truth, meaning and, indeed, presence" (*Reading* 37). Such undue simplicity, I propose, includes not only incautious assertions of objectivity, but also unbridled invention. To altogether abandon the question of what is present in a text is yet another unwary conceptualization of presence. Indeed, nothing could be further off track than the idea that Derrida's deconstructive project argues the irrelevance of authorial intention, and that literary theorists use this thought to make claims about texts that invert or ignore these texts' original meanings. To back up this claim, I will now provide a general outline of Derrida's hermeneutics that, like the above overview of theory, is designed to take on board readers not intimately conversant with Derrida's work (I will move on to an in-depth discussion of Derrida's views on signification in Chapter 1).

If, as we will see, Derrida insists that the lack of univocal clarity is what makes expression possible in the first place, it is always because the aberration, the misadventure, the effect we would *like* to be a mere secondary addition, can never be clearly identified or neatly separated from what we would prefer to be the purity of a self-evident, original, and central meaning. Deconstruction does not teach a toolkit for reading texts against the grain. It teaches that the grain behaves in a most curious manner: a manner that effectively frustrates the search for any such simple direction as "with" or "against" (instead, as I will discuss in Chapter 2, it grounds the notion of direction, of meaning's debt to specificity, in an oscillation that shuttles back and forth between the signifying gesture and the interpretative process). In Derrida's writings, however, this concern is often obscured by an annoying tendency to speak of possibilities when he analyzes irreducible risks. The "possibility of misunderstanding a signifier" should not be taken to indicate a choice, a decision to be made between the option of taking a speaker or writer at their word and the option of twisting their signifying gesture into creative new meanings. This reduction to clear-cut categories (including a clear-cut hierarchy between faithful readings and readings gone wild) misses that an interpretative shift is *always* possible, that its possibility consists in its *imperceptibility*, that the possibility of its occurring or its having occurred can thus *never* be excluded, that although this risk can be handled with caution and insight, it can never be *entirely* evaded, and that we can never reach a point where we can assert that the meaning we have now identified is *undoubtedly* the intended one.

We thus face an irreducible difficulty that calls, not for fanciful inventions, but for awareness and care. Derrida does not attest the reader a choice or an interpretative free pass. And he comments in no uncertain terms on how readings of deconstruction that ignore this point double back on themselves when they believe to have discovered in deconstruction a validation of carefree reading – a validation deconstruction yields only when it is itself read with insufficient care:

Since the deconstructionist (which is to say, isn't it, the skeptic-relativist-nihilist!) is supposed not to believe in truth, stability, or the unity of meaning, in intention or "meaning-to-say," how can he demand of us that we read *him* with pertinence, precision, rigor? [...] The answer is simple enough: this definition of the deconstructionist is *false* (that's right: false, not true) and feeble.

("Afterword" 146)

As I discuss in Chapters 1 and 2, Derrida's analyses show that certain commonsensical assumptions about baseline meanings and accessibility of others' intentions are undermined by how signification functions. Those who find fault with deconstruction typically take this argument as promoting a state of utter chaos, in which connections are random and thus meaningless. But this is not implied. Between these two extremes – incorruptibility of meaning and anarchic relativism – there is an entire scale on which signification plays out in complex ways. There is, in deconstruction, such a thing as a rigorous interpretation; but an interpretation's quality and apparent centrality can never completely assure us of the marginality of alternatives. The appearance of centrality is itself contingent on the conditions of its observation to an extent that we can and should problematize, but that is not exhaustively calculable. One might try to design some fail-safe interpretative procedure which carefully keeps biases in check, or relegates any possibility of error to some unimportant margin. But such a response remains blind to the fact that although uncertainty is *by no means total*, it is irreducible. As we will see, there is a minimal degree of uncertainty that remains insurmountable and that troubles our insight, indefinitely and never in the mode of exhaustively defined alternatives. The argument put forward by Derrida is that since no act of reading can fully overcome this uncertainty, *any* act of reading (indeed any production of meaning) is the result of decisions, made to the best of one's abilities, but not grounded in objectivity.

Deconstruction is an analysis of signification that focuses on how irreducible uncertainty structures signifying gestures. In doing so, deconstruction's aim is not to subvert or bypass the inherent meaning of such gestures; it is to show that the very notion of "inherent" meaning is problematic, since at the heart of meaning, we find not a solid core but a lack: a division of self from self. In this view, the ethical dimension of reading consists in acknowledging the complications caused by that lack. As Simon Critchley writes: "The ethical moment that motivates deconstruction is this Yes-saying to the unnameable, a moment of unconditional affirmation that is addressed to an alterity that can neither be excluded from nor included within logocentric conceptuality" (41). What Critchley here terms the unnameable is irreducible uncertainty: a signifying gesture's way of eluding calculation. It is something beyond signification's own capacity for pinning down – naming – and therefore also something beyond the conceptual realm of logocentrism (you cannot exhaustively describe how your situatedness will impact your reading: this is *why* there is an impact). Yet no act of interpretation can do without this element of openness, including, as Critchley notes, the logocentric constructions that disavow it. As I will argue throughout, the distortion, the unnameable or incalculable, the void or the secret, in short: the unreadable, is what drives signification. It is what has us relate to the excess of possibilities in a process that produces specific meanings based, in part, on our decisions.

The idea that reading involves active production is what, in *The Ethics of Reading*, J. Hillis Miller describes as "a necessary ethical moment in that act of reading as such" (1). As a reader, you are required to construct an interpretation, which has to be recognizable as an interpretation of the text you are reading. The ethical moment in the act of reading is thus a sense of being compelled, a demand for a reaction: not one in the unethical mode of total freedom, but one that "is a response to something, responsible to it, responsive to it, respectful of it" (4). The object of this responsibility is not a fixed attribute of the text; it is established as part of the relation between the text and the specific coordinates of a reading. True to Derrida's argument that any reading contains an irreducible dimension of acting on the text, for Miller, the responsibility of the reader is inseparable from "the real situation of a man or woman reading a book, teaching a class, writing a critical essay" (4). Yet this is not the only direction in which influence travels. Reading "faces in two directions" (4), which is to say that "The flow of power must not be all in one direction [from context to text]. There must be an influx of performative power from the linguistic transactions involved in the act of reading into the realms of knowledge, politics, and history" (5). If the interpretation you construct is recognizable as an interpretation of the text you are reading, it is because the act of construction, subtly influenced by your frameworks of knowledge, politics, and history, also allows the text to inform those frameworks.

On the one hand, reading thus enters into a specific situation within which a text can become the object of a certain responsibility. On the other hand, reading draws on the text to, as it were, *interrupt* this situation, to question and potentially change the frameworks that define it (including what Miller calls the realms of knowledge, politics, and history). *A reading is a situated encounter with a text, which draws on this text to inflect its own situation.* The important thing about decisions made in reading, then, is that they are demanded, but not spelled out, by the text, whilst being impacted, but not programmed, by our concrete situation. It is in this interaction between text and situation that a reader may construct a reading which is both a meaningful response to the text and at the same time shaped by decisions in Derrida's sense of the term: "A decision can only come into being in a space that exceeds the calculable program that would destroy all responsibility by transforming it into a programmable effect of determinate causes" ("Afterword" 116).

As Geoffrey Harpham comments, Derrida is "trying to determine the conditions under which a reading [becomes] truly responsible by identifying a phase of undecidability through which reading must pass, a phase in which conclusions that [have] been taken for granted become subject to disinterested questioning" (23). I would amend Harpham's description, however, insofar as I maintain that this questioning is not (and cannot be) disinterested; it is more accurately understood as being engaged in an interested reflection on interests.

The ethical dimension of reading is related to how texts exceed the programs in which, when reading, we are situated. It is related, in other words, to the text's *alterity*. Attridge suggests: "If I succeed in responding adequately to the otherness and singularity of the other, it is the other *in its relating to me* – always in a specific time and place – to which I am responding, in creatively changing myself and perhaps a little of the world as well" (*Singularity* 33). Otherness can lead us to reflect on, and potentially reinvent, the frameworks within which we read. This is the only adequate response to a text insofar as it manifests as other than these frameworks.

> There is thus an ethical dimension to any act of literary signification, and there is also a sense in which the formally innovative work, the one that most estranges itself from the reader, makes the most sharply challenging (which is not to say the most profound) ethical demand.
> (130–1)

Literary capriciousness need not equal profundity, but there is a sense in which a formal challenge entails a heightened demand at the ethical level.

Joyce as Theory investigates the question of this demand, and it should already be becoming clear that the demand made by a text as innovative as *Finnegans Wake* is likely to be a particularly challenging one. The questioning of frameworks that happens in moments of radical unreadability can be thought to call for new and altogether different types of meaning. Having said this, I am aware that my own reader may find the first two chapters of this book quite technical, more concerned with formal aspects of the reading process than with questions of ethics. It is important, then, to keep in mind the direct link theory establishes between analyzing signification and a critique of ideology that queries the notion of objectivity. Textual alterity, which I will discuss in Chapters 1 and 2, opposes itself to the neat unfolding of an exegetical program. It requires not only the application of interpretative frameworks, but also their constant rethinking. Yet if part of what places us in a particular position in the world are the discourses through which we conceptualize and articulate this position, then a change at the level of discourse is never innocent at the level of the self: it requires the sort of questioning of the self that may result in an ethical response.

This is why we can say that formal innovation entails an ethical challenge, why questions of ethics need not constitute a break with formal inquiry. The ethical implications I discuss in Chapters 3 and 4 – that the *Wake* advocates for plurality and for making responsible decisions – are linked to Joyce's examination of how uncertainty troubles signification. Finally, all of this is why, for my project, it comes as a considerable advantage of Derrida's philosophy (as opposed to other types of theory, concerned with more applied varieties of ethics) that he locates a question of responsibility at the formal level of language.

The Unreadability of the *Wake*

According to Derrida, a reader is required to *respond to the text*, which encompasses both active construction and meaningful reaction. In the opening pages of "Plato's Pharmacy," Derrida states:

> that person would have understood nothing of the game who, at this [*du coup*], would feel himself authorized merely to add on; that is, to add any old thing. He would add nothing: the seam wouldn't hold. Reciprocally, he who through "methodological prudence," "norms of objectivity," or "safe-guards of knowledge" would refrain from committing anything of himself, would not read at all.
>
> (64)

How, then, are we to read any text, let alone that famously unreadable text, *Finnegans Wake*, without either producing inexcusable additions or else total silence? The first and most crucial point to make here is that this question is neither mine nor Derrida's – it is Joyce's. Joyce is asking us how any interpretation can be produced in response to his writing. If my attempt at an answer in this book proceeds along theoretical lines, I thus want to be careful not to bring in theory by way of adding "any old thing." There is a risk, in a study titled *Joyce as Theory*, to effectively produce a reading of Joyce *through* theory. Some of my readers may feel that once theorists like Derrida or Lacan have put their spin on him, the "Joyce of theory" has become incomprehensible, unhelpful, divorced from his own themes and intentions, or simply off-putting. To my mind, speaking of Joyce *as* theory means, on the contrary, that there are elements of *Joyce's* text which are theoretical in their own right. My hope, then, is not to impose one of theory's preoccupations on Joyce, but to take seriously one of Joyce's own preoccupations: what Fritz Senn describes as "a recurrent, basic, Joycean motion," a motion guided by "an excessive bias, a tendency to overdo, to break out of norms, to go beyond" (35).

This Joycean motion is what raises the question of Joyce's understanding of understanding. His breaking out of norms is what suggests comparisons like the one made by Mitchell and Slote, who write that "the Derrida/Joyce relationship" concerns "a relentless pursuit for the limits of any and all [...] efforts at totalization (appropriation, establishment, comprehension)" (2). Joyce's writing is as active in this pursuit as Derrida's (or Lacan's). As Andrew Gibson has it:

> If anything is written all over Joyce's oeuvre, it is the refusal in principle of the "quick fix," whether artistic, political, intellectual, or ethical. It is in this respect, above all, that he resembles the great post-war French theorists – Derrida, Foucault, Lacan – with whom his name has so often been linked. Joyce's work draws its readers into a labour which knows no end.
>
> (18)

If I hope to avoid the danger of using Joyce's work only to exemplify theoretical considerations, it is because my starting point in now turning to Joyce is an observation about the text itself.

Finnegans Wake is difficult to read. This much most readers can agree on. Consider, for example, the following passage, which is the second paragraph on the book's first page:

> Sir Tristram, violer d'amores, fr'over the short sea, had passencore rearrived from North Armorica on this side the scraggy isthmus of Europe Minor to wielderfight his penisolate war: nor had topsawyer's rocks by the stream Oconee exaggerated themselse to Laurens County's gorgios while they went doublin their mumper all the time: nor avoice from afire bellowsed mishe mishe to tauftauf thuartpeatrick: not yet, though venissoon after, had a kidscad buttended a bland old isaac: not yet, though all's fair in vanessy, were sosie sesthers wroth with twone nathandjoe. Rot a peck of pa's malt had Jhem or Shen brewed by arclight and rory end to the regginbrow was to be seen ringsome on the aquaface.
>
> (3.4–14)

There is simultaneously too much meaning here and not enough. The material we are confronted with in this and almost every other passage from the *Wake* violates any number of conventions through which languages become what they are. As Seamus Deane writes, "The first thing to say about *Finnegans Wake* is that it is, in an important sense, unreadable" (vii). Yet in adopting this description, I would already raise the question of how we are to understand Deane's cautious qualifier, "in an important sense." There is unreadability here, but *Finnegans Wake* also poses the problem of what we are to do with unreadability as readers and as critics. Criticism may see it as its task to reduce difficulty, to elucidate the text and to present interpretations taken from the text but isolated and rendered more appreciable in their critical restatement. I find nothing inherently wrong with this approach, and partly follow it myself.

The problem is that the *Wake* invites these procedures and at the same time resists and problematizes them.

Here, I want to put my cards on the table from the start. If Joyce's text frustrates many of our critical protocols, I think the conclusion we should draw is that these protocols do not apply to *Finnegans Wake* in any straightforward manner. This, it has to be said, is not a position shared by all readers of the *Wake*. Approaching a passage like the one I have just cited, many will ask: how can we restate what we see and/or hear in this instance so as to appreciate its meaning? How, by a series of such restatements, can we gradually reduce the confusion so as to arrive at the formative logic which governs the selection of textual elements and the modes of their inscription? How, in short, can we solve the puzzle, and gain a foothold in this text such that our reading will no longer be desperate guesswork, but an informed account of what Joyce is doing?

I have to admit that these strike me as the wrong sort of question. As I will show, we have many indications that what Joyce is in fact doing is to rethink the usefulness of just such distinctions as "meaning" versus "confusion" or "informed" versus "desperate." The implications of this rethinking are the main argument to be developed in *Joyce as Theory*, but let me put the problem in a nutshell. If there were indeed a cleaned-up rendering of the text hidden behind Joyce's sound and fury, then why should Joyce have bothered to distort that text? Such an assumption reduces the complexity of Joyce's distortions to that of crossword-puzzle clues, which derive a certain entertainment value from doing things in a roundabout way, but expend their significance in that single act of translation. For reasons I will outline over the course of this book, I hold that this is a simplistic approach to *Finnegans Wake*. The *Wake*'s difficulty, I suggest, is irreducible, for if we fashion a readable text from its distortions, even if we do so with great rigor and only on the safest of grounds, we already pass over complications that put into question the very idea (and desirability) of readability.

The nature of these complications is such that theory can be helpful in addressing them (they have to do with the construction of interpretative frameworks, with discursive norms, etc.). But first and foremost, they are *Joyce's* subject. To employ a simplifying but helpful division, Joyce's text not only draws on these complications at the level of form, it also returns to them, again and again, at the level of content. On the one hand, the way *Finnegans Wake* is written obviously confronts us with some serious complications. On the dream of restoring readability, Attridge writes that the text "*enacts* this dream, by inducing its readers to carry out the same search, over and over" (*Joyce* 155). This, as I will discuss, is what theoretical readings of the *Wake* typically focus on. There is, however, a similar concern at the content level: "The *Wake thematizes* this dream again and again: it is full of searches for significance, origins, sources, truth, none of which reaches its goal" (155). Processes of reading, the workings of texts, difficulty, etc. are among *Finnegans Wake*'s themes. Hence my contention that the *Wake* contains a hermeneutics.

Here, the *Wake* can be seen to continue Joyce's hyper-awareness of the relation between what he writes about and the mode of its expression, something that has informed his work for a long time (think of the "scrupulous meanness" of *Dubliners*, the evolving languages of *A Portrait of the Artist as a Young Man*, the way in which narrative impacts narration and narration impacts narrative in *Ulysses*). These implementations of world–discourse interaction undermine any strict separation of Joyce's subject matter from his discursive strategies. Consider Karen Lawrence's reading of the multiple styles of *Ulysses*, about which she writes: "We see the styles as different but not definitive ways of filtering and ordering experience. This view of style obviates a 'spatial apprehension' of the book: one cannot see through the various styles to an ultimate Platonic pattern of meaning" (9). Form is not a veil we can remove to gain a clearer picture.

Similarly, the difficulty of the *Wake* is arguably neither an instance of purely self-serving aestheticism nor an auxiliary instrument of expression. It is not, in short, a superficial attribute beneath which we can postulate either an absence of meaning or a truer, perfectly straightforward writing. Rather, it is a meaningful implementation of alterity. Drawing our attention towards that which escapes comprehension, Joyce is driving a wedge between understanding and mastery, between linguistic capacity and linguistic purity. The underlying assumption that would associate these terms is that a matter is properly understood when it no longer raises any questions. Opposing this view, *Finnegans Wake* relies on an unassimilable alterity of writing in order to demonstrate the hermeneutic value of uncertainty: not in the mode of a lack of understanding, but in the mode of an appreciation of any understanding's being left with remainders it cannot integrate. It should be clear, then, why I begin this Introduction with a look at some of theory's reflections on discourse. Joyce's program in the *Wake*, as it appears through the lens of difficulty, is notably similar to the theoretical position. It works against the notion that the production of knowledge happens in the modes of presence and identity, and instead gives due consideration to the irreducible remainders that unsettle logocentric, univocal ideals.

Therefore, I will not so much apply theory to the *Wake* as draw parallels between the two. This means that next to theoretically inflected readings of Joyce, I will also undertake discussions of Derrida and Lacan by themselves. This will serve to clarify their often challenging concepts and terminology (and to offer correctives to misconceptions regarding their work, particularly their alleged incompatibility). If these discussion are not always carried out with a view to reading Joyce, it is because my aim is not to demonstrate Lacan's and Derrida's applicability to Joyce, but to identify elements in their thinking that, in a separate step, can illuminate concepts already operative in *Finnegans Wake*. As far as Derrida's work is concerned, it is worth pointing out that this procedure is not that different from any other deconstructive reading. Deconstructive fault-lines are at work in all writing, and deconstruction is therefore not a process that subjects texts to a logic alien to them. The quality that sets *Finnegans Wake* apart is not that it can be read with a view to these fault-lines (any text can), but that it is itself actively working with them. Joyce is in the precise sense of the word *self*-deconstructive. This is how, throughout this book, I will discuss the *Wake* as both a work exemplary of other texts (like them, it contains the inevitable fractures of meaning) and, at the same time, as a case of particular interest (it greatly amplifies these fractures and, in its meta-textual scenes, vividly explores their workings).

At this point, we run up against a paradox of reading *Finnegans Wake*. We struggle in vain to make any kind of sense of the *Wake* without immediately undoing some of its far-reaching interrogation of sense-making. The reception of *Finnegans Wake*, for all the ways in which it has singled out the book as the most unreadable in recent memory, is also proof of the assimilative powers of readers. Joyce may have spent an exorbitant amount of time and energy on tearing language to shreds; readers can still find ways to make sense of it. Since the present book, too, proposes readings that involve normalizations of Joyce's text, an important strand of my argument is that this is one of the points Joyce is making. Increasing his writing's difficulty, he confronts us with the strength of our desire for meaning – and with language's powers of producing meaning under extreme conditions. Yet there is also a risk of responding to Joyce's difficulty as if he were not raising any questions about intelligibility, but communicating in a manner whose intelligibility is merely eccentric.

Interacting with *Finnegans Wake*, we are at all points tempted to return to the exegetical model of removing the veil of form so as to perceive meaning in its ipseity. This is not just a manner of speaking: in *Wake* criticism, there is a long tradition of studies that aim for a return to intelligibility by isolating stable units of content. Nor do I want to suggest that this tradition is a history of misreading. Given the illegibility of *Finnegans Wake*, there is a sense in which *any* reading of it is a misreading, seeing how it is a deviation from the actual text. This complicates the distinction between reading and misreading without rendering the distinction any less significant or problematic. Conversely, the activity of making Joyce's text readable is in many ways an appropriate and necessary interpretative response. Throughout my argument, I employ generalizing notions of plot, situation, and character that derive precisely from this type of critical work. What I am taking issue with is the notion that such reduction to familiar categories can close the question of what *Finnegans Wake* is about. Which is to say I hold that the *Wake* does not deny meaning, but *pluralizes* it. Being a work of literary theory, *Finnegans Wake* maintains both that discursive constructions are serious business *and* the fact that they can never come to a definitive halt.

Backgrounds: Some Critical Responses

Attempts at defusing the *Wake*'s plurality date back to before its publication. The 1929 essay collection *Our Exagmination Round his Factification for Incamination of Work in Progress* already combines some pieces that prepare the reader for the radical novelty of Joyce's creation with other contributions that reintegrate the evolving book, serialized at the time as "Work in Progress," into familiar frameworks. In "Prolegomena to *Work in Progress*," Stuart Gilbert insists on the work's readability along the lines of a thorough but ultimately straightforward exegesis. As Patrick McCarthy notes in "Postlegomena to Stuart Gilbert's Prolegomena," Gilbert appears determined in his essay to emphasize "the coherence of what others regarded as an incoherent work" (34) and "to counter the charge that Joyce was a proponent of the literary avant-garde" (36).

If Gilbert may have started the trend, it is Joseph Campbell and Henry Morton Robinson's 1944 *A Skeleton Key to Finnegans Wake* that canonized it. Towards the end of their book, Campbell and Robinson assert that "In every passage there is a key word which sounds the essential theme" (357) as well as that "*there are no nonsense syllables in Joyce!*" (358). They thus assure us that although Joyce's literary extravaganza may look daunting, and although it demands some truly strenuous effort, there is nothing in it that requires us to think outside such habitual frameworks as central and peripheral meaning, or reading as explication. This has become the underlying assumption of many studies of the *Wake* that produce knowledge by boldly carrying conceptual light into textual and narrative darkness. Critical projects undertaken in this vein include William York Tindall's *A Reader's Guide to Finnegans Wake* (1969), Danis Rose and John O'Hanlon's *Understanding Finnegans Wake* (1982), John Gordon's *Finnegans Wake: A Plot Summary* (1986), John Bishop's *Joyce's Book of the Dark* (1986), Philip Kitcher's *Joyce's Kaleidoscope* (2007), and Edmund Lloyd Epstein's *A Guide Through Finnegans Wake* (2009), all of which retrieve from the *Wake*'s weave of materials something like a stable narrative world and/or a logic governing its presentation – although, it should be noted, with results that differ between these studies.

One significant departure from this style of reading is Margot Norris's 1974 *The Decentered Universe of Finnegans Wake*. In the book's final chapter, having analyzed what she calls the "lack of certainty in every aspect of the work" (120), Norris concludes that "The greatest critical mistake in approaching *Finnegans Wake* has been the assumption that we can be certain of who, where, and when everything is in the *Wake*, if only we do enough research" (120). The obscurity of the *Wake*, Norris proposes, is not a surface layer that can be penetrated so as to reach an underlying clarity; the text is obscure *through and through*. This idea of critically examining the very notion of certitude appears again in Colin MacCabe's 1978 *James Joyce and the Revolution of the Word*, which posits that "The difficulty of reading Joyce is a difficulty in our notion of reading" and that Joyce "presents literary criticism with its own impossibility" (2). A similar attitude informs several contributions to the 1984 collection *Post-Structuralist Joyce*, edited by Attridge and Ferrer. In Stephen Heath's essay, the post-structuralist program is stated in the following terms: "The text is never closed and the 'ideal reader' will be the one who accedes to the play of this incompletion, placed in 'a situation of writing', ready no longer to master the text but now to become its actor" (32).

The notion to be underlined here is that of refraining from attempts at mastering the text. Joyce's deliberate muddying of language requires us to develop critical responses which interact with the text without subjecting it to an exegetical mastery that forces Joyce's writing into the normative patterns it is trying to evade. Since this excludes the possibility of any stable solutions, the critical mode developed by Norris, MacCabe, Heath, and others perpetuates work on *Finnegans Wake* (though this does *not* entail that all interpretations are correct, as I will discuss in Chapter 3). Which is to say that criticism's goal is not a reduction yielding a final answer, nor an unleashing of random creativity, but an unending responsiveness to the strangeness of what Joyce is doing. As Slote puts it:

> Instead of trying to disambiguate the *Wake*, perhaps a more fundamental interpretive step would be to recognize why it has been *ambiguated*; that is, to recognize that reading the *Wake* is an exercise within the demesne of the equivocal apart and away from the demon imp hypostasis.
>
> (*Joyce's* 130)

In the introduction to a 2015 collection of essays, editors Kimberly J. Devlin and Christine Smedley suggest that what justifies grappling with an unreadable text more than seventy years after its original publication is not some distant prospect of cracking the code, but precisely Joyce's undoing of monovalence and his opening up of "semantic excesses – pluralities of possibilities, in terms of meanings – that veer off in multiple, nonexclusive directions" (2).

This line of inquiry is particularly interesting at the current moment, at which an important strand of *Finnegans Wake* criticism is again drawn towards an ideal of univocal lucidity: namely, the lucidity promised by the consultation of the *Wake*'s avant-textes. As I will examine at the end of Chapter 3, the genetic approach, although it holds readers accountable to a formidable standard of knowledge about the making of Joyce's text and – precisely by taking into account the range and variety of Joyce's sources – steers clear of the idea of a single, overarching narrative, also risks atomizing the text into manageable units. It thus emphasizes Joyce's creative process to an extent that potentially does away with much of what is remarkable, and disturbing, about that process's result.

To counteract the risk of neutralizing the obscurity of *Finnegans Wake*, it is necessary to give due consideration to the meaning of form, to the implications of Joyce's difficulty. John Lurz notes that in the *Wake*, writing resists the role of docile carrier of meaning. Since the form Joyce gives his writing often serves to *interrupt* codes of intelligibility, the "exteriority" of his writing "is not merely a part of the process of signification but is, rather, something to notice in its own right" (680). *Finnegans Wake* thus requires a reader "who is able to open his or her eyes to obscurity itself" (681), who is able to look *at* the page, not *through* the page. I would argue, for instance, that attempts at looking through the above-cited "Sir Tristram" passage – by transforming it into something meaningful – do violence to the fact that many of this passage's units, as they appear on the page, do not partake in any extant mode of meaning-production. However, I would also maintain that looking *at* this passage can show it to be evoking, manipulating, and even newly creating such modes, thus inviting us to read. What makes Joyce's experiment so compelling is that his manipulations demand not that we surrender meaning, but that we transform and pluralize the modes of its production.

I therefore only partly agree with Lurz's statement that "the printed letters and words in the *Wake* also function as a non-referential medium" (682), because I do not subscribe to the binary division this implies between lucid reference, on the one hand, and obscure materiality, on the other. Even where Joyce distorts the materiality of writing in order to disrupt procedures of reference, the disruption is itself productive of meaning. By contrast, Lurz's argument (though not his terminology) aligns itself with Allon White's proposition, in *The Uses of Obscurity*, that "it would be wrong to call 'Finnegans Wake' an obscure work" (20). In White's sense, obscurity continues the production of meaning, whereas he deems *Finnegans Wake* to be lacking "the desire for denotation" (20). Contrary to this verdict, I will argue that a sophisticated manipulation of desire is an important aspect of the *Wake*'s unreadability. I therefore believe that the *Wake* is a perfect example of White's notion that obscurity carries "distinct and distinctive kinds of meaning which are not secondary to an anterior obscured content. Obscurity signifies in the very act of obscuring" (18). Obscurity draws attention to itself, and this is precisely what takes place in *Finnegans Wake*. Lurz offers another formulation closer to this position when he writes that the task of Joyce's reader is that "of accessing (without dispelling) hiddenness as such – of looking at the *Wake*'s dark print itself" (683). Where the *Wake* is materially unreadable, it does not hide retrievable units of meaning. Its obscurity, at these moments, is more fundamental, since any light to be shed would touch only on things other than what is actually on the page. To look at the darkness of the page is not therefore to search for hidden meaning; but neither is it to cease looking. Rather, it is to look at hiddenness without a hidden, to appreciate the meaningfulness of an obscurity that challenges meaning itself.

What could be the meaning of such a challenge? Answering this question constitutes one of the main goals of *Joyce as Theory*, but I can illustrate the principle here by once more returning to Butler and drawing on their suggestion that to interrupt translatability (their term for the possibility of transporting information into familiar modes of understanding) is to adopt a position that can be as productive as it is "isolating, estranging, difficult, and demanding" ("Values" 203). The untranslatable or not fully translatable constitutes a painful breakdown of meaning, but it also contains "the possibility of meeting up with the limits of our own epistemological horizon, a limit that challenges what we know to be knowable" (206). It *challenges* this knowledge; it does not necessarily reconfirm it. Tracing the limits of our understanding, as Joyce's language does, need not newly confine us within them. Running up against the limits, we may find that the delineations of what is knowable are not absolute: we can change them, we can change the nature of knowing (articulating new visions, as I put it above). The untranslatable brings about disruptions that potentially break out of translatability and tautology, of repeating only what we already know we can repeat. The point is not, however, that such disruption will succeed in rendering *all* of Joyce's writing intelligible. The aim is not to expand a single, homogenous realm of intelligibility. It is to understand that breakdowns of intelligibility indicate the *partiality* of our discursive stances – and thus indicate a plurality of positions none of which need correspond to a discursive "master key."

The meaning produced by Joyce's particularly recalcitrant untranslatability can then be read along the lines of Sara Salih's suggestions about the ethics of difficulty. With regard to discourses that are not easily integrated into regimes of interpretative mastery (that are not easily translated), Salih writes: "it is possible to read 'difficulty' as an important ethical component of the radical democratic project" (42). Difficulty, in this view, is neither an element of elitist hermeticism nor of meaningless relativism; it is *democratic* because difficulty of this kind opposes itself to what Salih terms "the anti-democratic uses of 'clarity'" (42) – that is, "the exclusionary schemes of intelligibility which currently pass for the ontological norm" (43). The call for clarity all too often carries with it a prohibition of explorations and questions that are disconcerting because they break with existing modes of knowledge-production. Yet if, as theory argues, *all* modes of knowledge-production depend on discursive frameworks, such a prohibition can be seen to be exclusionary in a potentially problematic manner. It relies on an appearance of objectivity without examining the constructedness and mobility of this very appearance. Difficulty, which stops us from smoothly passing over construction's cracks, can be uncomfortable; it can also remind us of the possibility of questioning and, if necessary, renegotiating the frameworks we think and live by.

Taking seriously the alterity of Joyce's writing leads to precisely this kind of questioning of our frameworks – and of what a framework even is. If I say that the confrontation with the unreadability of *Finnegans Wake* allows for the construction of new types of meaning, I am not so much referring to this or that particular, innovative interpretation of *Finnegans Wake* as to the idea that Joyce invites us to question our understanding of interpretation and knowledge as mastery, and to rethink them instead as plurality. Yet this is not to say that the goal is to smash the very concepts of knowledge, its production, and its uses. Attridge clarifies this when he writes: "*Alterity* [...] is not a matter of simply *opposing* accepted norms, since opposition occurs within a shared horizon; rather, it's the introduction into the known of that which it excludes in constituting itself as the known" (*Work* 219). As far as the *Wake* is concerned, claiming that its unreadability is an example of alterity is thus again to say that the *Wake* does not deny meaning, but pluralizes it. Unreadability is not an inert element but a palpable effect (my reasons for this approach will become clear in Chapter 1). It marks not the impossibility, but the endless productivity of our response to that which exceeds our conceptualizations.

Reading *Finnegans Wake* without disregarding its strangeness thus leads, not to silences, but to the ethical problem of *encountering the other* (I discuss Derrida's analysis of hospitality in Chapter 4). At this point, we should recall Philippe Sollers's passionate defence, at the International James Joyce Symposium in Paris, 1975, of the political dimension of the *Wake*'s language. Speaking of what he calls Joyce's "trans-nationalism," Sollers ventures that "In what he writes, *nothing remains but differences*, and so he calls into question all and every community (this is referred to as his 'unreadability')" (4). And, famously, Sollers adds: "*Finnegans Wake* is the most formidably anti-fascist book produced between the two wars" (4). This is not to say that Joyce, writing in the 1920s and 1930s, is giving his readers a recipe how to beat Nazism – a patently absurd idea for any number of reasons. What is at stake here is rather an anti-fascist stance whose outlines Patrick McGee denotes when he writes: "if there is anything that the patriarch, the imperialist, the capitalist and the fascist fear, it is the desire for desire, which has another name: hope" ("Errors" 177). As we will see in Chapter 1, the *Wake* stages the logic of desire in such a way as to undermine the notion that any particular readability could serve as the answer to desire. If such desire in excess of desire can be put to service by some of the structures McGee names (Slavoj Žižek demonstrates how capitalism does this), it also opposes itself to the solidification of any given order. As Vincent Cheng argues in *Joyce, Race, and Empire*, "All attempts to assert the Self by denying the Other are problematized as unstable in the multipleness of *Finnegans Wake*" (269). Which is to say that the *Wake* opposes itself to monolithic, fascistoid thinking not by constructing a utopian, monolithic counter-narrative, but by destabilizing *all* forms of monolithic readability.

That this destabilization is to a considerable extent achieved through the *Wake*'s language is also argued by Len Platt. Writing about the *Wake*'s historical context with regard to racism, Platt ventures that "the *Wake* is the racist's [...] worst nightmare at a number of different levels" (33), partly because it "is designed as a monstrous failure – a failure to concoct 'pure', original language, to find racial origins and to construct the dimensions of racial identity" (21). In Joyce's text, the one pure utopia and/or dystopia is displaced by the challenge of an impure but lively chaos – especially linguistic chaos. Back to McGee:

> This is why *Finnegans Wake* is one of the most ethical books ever written [...], it does not present us with a spectre coming from the future but with the grace that demands that we live in the present, that we never surrender our desire (not even to utopia).
>
> ("Errors" 179)

In view of such readings, I would venture that as long as the comments made by Sollers remain but an anecdote to be retold (whether dismissively or approvingly), we have not yet developed a sufficiently serious answer to what he is describing as Joyce's challenge to meaning as legibility and to community as homogeneity.

Before leaving the subject of critical precursors, let me add some reflections on Joyce's presence in the work of Derrida and Lacan, in order to situate *Joyce as Theory* in relation to existing criticism concerned with these three authors. If to bring Derrida's and Lacan's thinking to *Finnegans Wake* is not necessarily to impose this thinking on Joyce, it is in part because "their abstract concepts have a concretely embodied textual precursor in Joyce's complex textuality. It was Joyce's text which made their ideas possible, so to speak, by providing textual-material collateral" (van Boheemen-Saaf 9). First of all, I would argue that this statement can do without the qualifying "so to speak," since Joyce's influence on Derrida and Lacan is something both of them document in their work. Lacan dedicates a year of his seminar to Joyce under the title *The Sinthome*. Derrida, who returns to Joyce time and again, remarks that "every time I write, and even in academic things, Joyce's ghost is always coming on board" ("Two Words for Joyce" 27). The fact that both Derrida and Lacan took inspiration from Joyce's work helps explain why the intersections between Joyce and Derrida and Joyce and Lacan, respectively, have been closely studied, while the perceived incompatibility of Lacan and Derrida explains why hardly any examinations draw on all three authors.

One type of criticism is concerned with how Joyce features in Derrida's and Lacan's work. A number of studies focus on Lacan's reading of Joyce in *The Sinthome*, and on the important changes Lacan's interpretation of Joyce inspired him to make to his system. Jean-Michel Rabaté's *Jacques Lacan: Psychoanalysis and the Subject of Literature* contains a chapter outlining these issues. Roberto Harari's *How James Joyce Made His Name* (a study in psychoanalysis, despite the title) gives a detailed account of Lacan's Joyce seminar over the course of more than 300 pages. More recently, Daniel Bristow has added his take on these matters in *Joyce and Lacan*, which is less concerned with reading Joyce than with understanding "post-Joycean psychoanalysis" (120). A similar focus is found in Colette Soler's *Lacan Reading Joyce*.

In Derrida's case, the encounter with Joyce is less concentrated in one key moment. Three short pieces ("Two Words for Joyce," "Ulysses Gramophone," and "The Night Watch") take Joyce's work as their subject. However, Derrida's reliance on Joyce is arguably more palpable in remarks scattered throughout his oeuvre (surfacing as early as *Edmund Husserl's "Origin of Geometry"* and notably in *The Post Card* and "This Strange Institution Called Literature"), since they indicate Derrida's sustained interest in Joyce. This interest has been documented in Alan Roughley's *Reading Derrida Reading Joyce* as well as, more recently, in a number of contributions to *Derrida and Joyce*, edited by Mitchell and Slote, and Slote's essay "Derrida's Joyce."

I will draw on *The Sinthome* in Chapter 1, on *The Post Card* in Chapter 2, and on "Two Words for Joyce" in Chapter 3. Apart from integrating these texts into my own interpretation of Lacan and Derrida, however, I will not attempt to assess Joyce's role in their respective oeuvres. My aim is not to trace Joyce's presence in Derrida and Lacan, as the above studies do, but to read Joyce, Derrida, and Lacan in conjunction. I propose to engage in the kind of intertextual conversation Peter Mahon describes when, with regard to Derrida, he speaks of "an expanded zone of Joycean-Derridean intertextuality" that extends beyond cases "where Derrida either explicitly writes on Joyce or mentions him by name" (353). Criticism situated in this expanded intertextuality not only scans theory with a view to Joyce, but also interprets Joyce with a view to theory.

I hasten to add, however, that the approach I follow does not *stop* with Joyce, either. Mahon, in *Imagining Joyce and Derrida*, takes into consideration many of the *Wake*'s meta-textual gestures and brings them into contact with Derrida's thinking. But Mahon somewhat arbitrarily limits the range of his results by assuming that Joyce's text is at these moments talking exclusively about itself. As I will discuss in Chapter 1, the theoretical insights that the Joyce–Derrida intertextuality has to offer are thus severed from other discourses. They are shown to hold true of the Joycean text and the Derridean text when it would arguably be more interesting to demonstrate their relevance elsewhere.

A structurally similar, though more intriguingly argued, limitation is employed by van Boheemen-Saaf, who in *Joyce, Derrida, Lacan, and the Trauma of History* relates the attitudes towards language expressed in Joyce's work to his Irish heritage and the historical trauma of colonialism.

26 Introduction

This leads to the fascinating suggestions that Joyce managed "to make his Irishness a model for modernity" (13–14) and that "theory owes a historical debt to the postcolonial experience," since "concepts which derive from the *experience* of the colonial situation as lived by Joyce are inserted into western writing as universal features of textuality and consciousness" (191). I believe that van Boheemen-Saaf is right in identifying Joyce as an early source of theory. However, to focus on the cultural specificity of his work is problematic insofar as an emphasis on the Irish writer's "loss of a natural relationship to language" implies those lucky enough not to be or have been colonial subjects *do* enjoy such a natural relationship, granting them "interiority of discourse and coherent selfhood" (2). Here, van Boheemen-Saaf's reading, like Mahon's, is not general enough. Beneath hegemonic (e.g. imperialist) discourses' carefully maintained pretence at being objective and stable, they too lack integral expression and coherent conceptualization of self. Which is to say that if Derrida and Lacan were able to interpret Joyce's insights as "universal features" of discourse, it is because these insights *are* universally applicable (though I agree with van Boheemen-Saaf that examining the historical origins of theory yields valuable insights, and that the colonial subaltern's situation is a particularly acute manifestation of these problems).

My suggestion is to have the writings of Joyce, Derrida, and Lacan illuminate each other in order to see what they can tell us about signification in general: about its inevitable complexity and fallibility. The existing studies that take this approach are some of the essays in the *Derrida and Joyce* collection edited by Mitchell and Slote as well as, for Lacan, the books by Thurston and Brivic. All of these combine reading an expanded intertextuality (Derrida/Lacan with a view to Joyce; Joyce with a view to Derrida/Lacan) with an interest in theoretical questions that point beyond these three writers. Mitchell and Slote suggest, in the phrase already cited, that the Joyce/Derrida intertextuality engages in "a relentless pursuit for the limits of any and all [...] efforts at totalization" (2), where totalization would signal mastery over meaning-production. The parallel to Lacanian approaches is seen in Thurston's proposition that "the literary act for Joyce will be shown to mark precisely the *breaking out of meaning*" (*James Joyce* 4), breaking out, that is, of meaning as totalized, given, already comprehended. Or, as Brivic puts it: "Joyce's inverted epistemology pursues not knowledge, but points where language and knowledge break down to reconstitute themselves for further comprehension" (*Explorations* 75).

If I subscribe to all this, why write another book on the subject? I suggest that the existing studies treat Joyce's writing, and *Finnegans Wake* in particular, as texts that cause or enact effects of unreadability, to the detriment of seeing them as texts that also *describe* these effects. Brivic writes that Joyce stages "confrontations with what cannot be understood" (4) and that his works "confront readers with an incomprehensible text that undermines their theoretical apparatus" (35). Although I agree, the focus on incomprehensibility and an agonistic relationship with the text places so much emphasis on shape, thingness, and overall effect (frustration) as to risk losing sight of content. This is a tendency that afflicts most efforts to read Joyce in a theoretical context. As far as I have been able to find, suggestions that "the pedagogical effect of Joyce's writing constitutes it as a theoretical discourse" (McGee, "Joyce's" 212) have always been paired with the idea that "The book's pedagogical effect derives from [its] stylistic emphasis" (211). A focus on style, form, object-like language, or a resistance to reading is frequently the stated program of theoretical approaches to Joyce: "we must pay attention not so much to *what* is said, but to its *how* and *to what effect*" (van Boheemen-Saaf 18). A lot of close scrutiny has thus been brought to bear on moments in Joyce that are fascinating in their unreadable, singular materiality. Yet studies have not systematically explored how this writing *speaks about* hermeneutic concepts in its own right. While the present volume builds on a vast textual corpus, it can thus innovate the existing approaches by foregrounding the theoretical thought articulated in *Finnegans Wake*. Or, as I put it at the beginning of this Introduction, *Joyce as Theory* reads Joyce as a literary theorist.

Doing so results in a number of timely interventions in current debates. For one thing, the hermeneutics put forward in *Finnegans Wake* leads from a technical analysis of meaning directly to ethical and political implications. My book's four chapters follow this modulation from hermeneutics to ethics, covering (1) problems intrinsic to signification; (2) how these problems complicate any given process of reading or writing; (3) the plurality of meanings these complications result in; and (4) that negotiating such pluralities is a matter of participating in a public realm. This seamless transition troubles the notion that contemporary modes of theory – such as gender studies, queer theory, critical race theory, or disability studies – have turned their attention to material, cultural, and political concerns which displace those of the linguistic turn. As I argue above, "linguistic" theory has never been about purely textual problems. It has always been concerned with how certain discourses produce effects of hegemony and marginalization *in social and political fields*. Detailing Joyce's understanding of these mechanisms and comparing it to the work of Lacan and Derrida can thus encourage us to think of present-day theory as more explicitly bringing out the politics that were always at work in theoretical thought, and not as a politicization of theory that breaks with how we used to do theory in the past.

My intervention also challenges academic trends which would tell us theory in general is a remnant of the past: that theory had its heyday and that revisiting the work of Derrida or Lacan now is to remain stuck in an approach which has been superseded (linguistic theory having been displaced by the contextual focus of historicism, genetic criticism, and cultural studies, whose dominance is presently being eroded by new formalism and an emphasis on reader response). I hold that this notion of finally "moving past" theory is misguided, for the simple reason that we have not moved past discourses that require theoretical analysis. We do not inhabit a post-ideological utopia. On the contrary, a vast number of people alive today are surrounded by a global neoliberal ideology that is trying to sell us the very idea of our being post-ideological. As Wendy Brown notes in her 2015 critique of neoliberalism, many discourses now present themselves as if they *cannot* be questioned on political grounds, masquerading as "best practices [which] stand for value-free technical knowledge" (139). I would draw a direct line here to Terry Eagleton's remark, in his 1983 *Literary Theory: An Introduction*, that "The claim that knowledge should be 'value-free' is itself a value-judgement" (12). If anything should convince us of the unabated relevance of theory, it is how badly we need a methodology right now that can break through a discourse's armour of purely technical expertise, to reveal the ideological stakes beneath. Joyce's hermeneutics can be instrumental in this task since he shows that the production of meaning is never a neutral appreciation of the facts, but a decision-making process steeped in readers' and writers' interests.

I do not, however, propose a theoretical reading, focused on applicability to today's politics, *as opposed to* an "empirico-historical" form of criticism or an attempt "to return to the work of art," to mention two of the chief alternatives identified by Attridge in *The Work of Reading* ("Introduction" 4, 3). If, as I claim, Joyce is himself a theorist, this means the kind of analytical focus I adopt is precisely one of the things to be found in reading for Joyce's *own* concerns as evinced by his text (or indeed as suggested by his historical context: for an examination of meaning-production and fascism, see my article "Building Metonymic Meaning with Joyce, Deleuze, and Guattari"). Here, as with many other aspects of my discussion, my goal is to demonstrate the continuity and mutual implication of forms of thought more often presented as methodologically or historically opposed to each other. This is the intention behind the final section of Chapter 3, in particular, which presents a critique of a critique of Derrida and which, I hope, shows that the approaches discussed are compatible once we move past the narrowest possible conception of what it means to follow these methodologies.

How to Speak of the Limits of Language: Lacan

At this point, I should clarify how Lacan will feature in these readings, and how I am planning on combining his work with that of Derrida. It is no doubt one of those coincidences we fetishize at our own peril that Derrida and Lacan had a memorable encounter in Baltimore (see Derrida, "For the Love" 49–51), once the home of Edgar Allan Poe, and the city where Poe died and is buried. It is nonetheless intriguing. The most tangible intersection of their work, after all, is their debate about Poe's short story "The Purloined Letter." Lacan uses his "Seminar on 'The Purloined

Letter'" to preface *Écrits*. "Le facteur de la vérité," included in *The Post Card*, provides Derrida's extensive critique of this seminar. Both authors would return to the subject (for instance, Derrida in "For the Love of Lacan," Lacan in "Lituraterre"), but the first two texts constitute the primary archive in which to read Lacan with Derrida or Derrida with Lacan. If, that is, you accept the idea of their incompatibility.

Joyce as Theory does not dwell on the Poe debate, although I briefly touch on it in Chapter 1. Despite this well-documented disagreement (comprehensively examined in *The Purloined Poe*, edited by Muller and Richardson), I suggest that Lacan's and Derrida's discussions of language are compatible in important respects. In "For the Love of Lacan," Derrida himself points out that his contribution is "unreadable for readers in a rush to decide between the 'pro and the con,' in short, for those minds who believed I was opposing Lacan or showing him to be wrong" (63). Derrida is making some restorative gestures in this lecture (which seems appropriate in a colloquium commemorating Lacan), but his statement is by no means reducible to retrospective teleology or apologetic adjustment. As I show in Chapter 1, Derrida's objections are aimed at Lacan's manipulation of such expressions as the letter, the phallus, or castration. I would therefore argue that it is chiefly Lacan's *rhetoric* that is at stake in Derrida's criticism.

If Derrida states that Lacan makes "the most strenuous, and powerfully spectacular, use of [...] the most deconstructible motifs of philosophy" (54), he also maintains that Lacan's work is "the closest" (55) to his own. By contrast, in those instance in which Derrida arrives at less generous conclusions, he also construes a version of Lacan that, as I will show, runs counter to important aspects of Lacan's thinking. This is not to say that deconstruction inverts Lacan's meaning in order to disagree with him. Derrida's reading of Lacan is arguably not deconstructive enough, odd as this admittedly may seem. Derrida readily adopts Lacan's often problematic manner of presenting his thought, without investigating how the rhetoric masks a more differentiated argument that can be shown to subvert many of the superficial problems. Consider, for instance, the relation between Lacan's interpretative order, the symbolic, and the distortive order, the real. (Here, I again give a brief rundown of Lacan's concepts, reserving a detailed discussion for Chapter 1.)

Lacan's symbolic encompasses the totality of interpretative codes, which is to say, all that assists us in *making sense*: the amassed knowledge passed down to us; the cultural and personal categories through which we filter experience; the worldviews, habits, rituals that help manage our activities and emotional states; as well as different forms of communication. This includes language, though not all of language – and this difference between language and the symbolic is one of the things that make Lacan relevant to an examination of Joyce's unreadability.

Symbolic codification imposes structures of identification and thus snatches experience from what Lacan terms the real. The main misreading

30 *Introduction*

to be avoided here is to imagine the real as objective reality before interpretation. The Lacanian real designates rather a *beyond of interpretation itself*, which it makes little sense to think in the absence of the symbolic. Žižek gives an interesting example when he writes that science touches on the real "in quantum physics, where we are dealing with the rules/laws that function, although they cannot ever be retranslated into our experience" (*Enjoy* 249). Objective reality before interpretation, which is what science claims to study, is still part of the symbolic as long as science's findings can be expressed in the categories of our experience. The real, by contrast, is the untranslatable, the scientific law which simply is what it is and whose mind-boggling strangeness messes with attempts to comprehend it. Which is to say that the real in Lacan is a *relational* category insofar as something belongs to the real as a result of being unthinkable. As Žižek puts it: "a certain fundamental ambiguity pertains to the notion of the Real in Lacan: the Real designates a substantial hard kernel that precedes and resists symbolization and, simultaneously, it designates the left-over, which is posited or 'produced' by symbolization itself" (*Tarrying* 36). Bruce Fink offers the following summary: "The real is perhaps best understood as *that which has not yet been symbolized*, remains to be symbolized, or even resists symbolization; and it may perfectly well exist 'alongside' and in spite of a speaker's considerable linguistic capabilities" (25).

This existence of the real and the symbolic side by side opens up the question – crucial both to Lacan's work and to my reading of *Finnegans Wake* – of expressing inexpressibility. As Fink writes, "we name and talk about the real and weave it into a theoretical discourse on language" (25). That is, we represent to ourselves the points at which symbolization breaks down; we describe effects of our inability to describe. In the middle phase of his teaching (the 1950s and early 1960s, roughly speaking), Lacan draws on some questionable strategies with regard to this relation. He posits an impossible, ideal signifier that would allow for symbolization without failure, and in a move I find more than a little strange, he terms this impossible ideal the symbolic phallus (more on this in Chapter 1). Since we lack the means to master the real, it is of course the absence of this signifier we in fact experience, an absence middle Lacan duly terms symbolic castration. The problem with these concepts is not only their awkward gesticulation in the direction of sex or gender. By assigning to the irruption of the undomesticated real a specific location on the (imaginary) body, castration would seem to categorize the real in a manner that then allows for further (symbolic) processing. As Michael Lewis writes in *Derrida and Lacan*, "through this fantastic image, the real presents itself to the signifier in a manageable form" (167). It is this specificity, in the description of what is by definition inexpressible, that Derrida attacks.

This is not, however, the whole story. In Chapter 1, we will see that in contrast to the imaginary phallus, which is related to corporeality, the symbolic phallus and symbolic castration can only be interpreted as arbitrary nomenclature. This makes their reliance on a gendered framework distinctly unhelpful, but it also means that as names for a beyond of symbolization, they are as undescriptive (or descriptive) as the term "real" itself. Furthermore, in the late phase of his teaching (the 1960s and 1970s, through to his final seminar in 1980), Lacan re-evaluates the relation between the symbolic and the real. As a label for the real, symbolic castration is a kind of "suture" (Lewis 162) which both separates the symbolic from the real and holds them in place relative to each other. As a result, the symbolic achieves a strange sovereignty over the real, describing it while remaining disconnected from it, operating from a safe distance. By contrast, late Lacan conceptualizes the border between symbolic and real as "porous" (165). In late Lacan's thinking, the real is seen to act upon the symbolic; the symbolic order, no longer at a safe distance, is now "full of holes. And it is in these holes that the real exists" (165).

If the real is the unthinkable and inexpressible, then the real intersects the symbolic order at all the various points at which our conceptualizations fail. These intersections work on the symbolic, changing it. As I discuss in the following chapters, late Lacan comes to conceive of the real as an order of experience that impacts the formation and function of discourses in absolutely crucial ways. The real is where meaning is not, but the real and the symbolic invade each other, creating impasses and palpable gaps and producing meaning in the process. One upshot of this late Lacanian approach is that unreadability can be interpreted as a manifestation of such porousness. The unreadability of *Finnegans Wake*, for example, is not a break with the normal topology of language. It is an instance in this topology of the real slicing into the symbolic, creating effects in language that are not of the symbolic. This view of unreadability as something at work in language itself which, far from remaining mute, produces effects there, helps gain some purchase on the deeply paradoxical problem of symbolizing the limits of symbolization. A possibility emerges of the real being experienced almost directly: where it tears palpable gaps into the fabric of symbolic codification. This does not mean that the real becomes more identifiable. On the contrary, whereas middle Lacan reserves the right to designate the real in a strangely descriptive manner, late Lacan states categorically: "The real can only be inscribed on the basis of an impasse of formalization" (*S XX* 93).

The interaction and mutual invasion of symbolic and real is in fact the single most important idea late Lacan derives from his reading of Joyce. Middle Lacan tends to conceptualize a predicament imposed on the subject from the outside: society initiates the subject into the codes and norms that make up the symbolic order, and where the initiation doesn't quite work, or where the symbolic itself is incomplete or contradictory, glimpses of the real will crop up in the form of symptoms. Accordingly, Lacanian therapy traces the subject's history of meaning-formation in order to enable a truthful perception of the mismatch that led to the formation of a symptom. This radically changes in the 1975–6 seminar *The Sinthome*. Joyce's ability to actively *manipulate* the real in his texts – to purposely work with a register of impasse and distortion – opens up a new perspective for late Lacan. Joyce becomes Lacan's example of the emancipation of the subject. The goal of Lacanian analysis is recast as an imitation of Joyce's artistic achievement. Meaning, truth, indeed any interpretation of the symptom or its history are left behind, and instead therapy aims to guide the subject to a moment of radical agency in which they become able to actively reshape the knot that braids together their imaginary, symbolic, and real, thus completely redefining the framework of their experience. The boundaries of the three orders is porous, its delineation something the subject can be seen to change (I am reminded here of Butler's suggestion that we can "[challenge] what we know to be knowable").

Since this constellation is not unique to Joyce, but precisely late Lacan's model of the three orders in general, this is to say that *Finnegans Wake*, in the late Lacanian view, is not categorically different from other forms of linguistic expression. The difference is one of intensity and explicitness (what I call the self-deconstructive characteristics of the *Wake*). Through radicalization, Joyce draws attention to the fact that *any* symbolic codification (bar the mythological ones we attribute to prelapsarian beings and societies) is haunted by imperfection. Any codification encounters remainders it cannot assimilate: the real is always already at work in the symbolic. Where sense-making and the formation of a subject's position keep functioning, this functionality is thus seen to necessarily involve a response to the presence of the real. This, I want to argue, is one of the core ideas connecting late Lacan, Joyce, and Derrida. The *absence* of symbolic codification without gaps, of total readability, of pre-programmed and univocal signification, is the very thing that enables our response and responsibility.

I thus agree with van Boheemen-Saaf, who writes that "If Lacan's 'real' is that 'which prevents one from saying the *whole* truth about it,' there is more truth in combining Derrida and Lacan than in privileging one perspective to the other" (28). If an out-and-out conflation of Lacan's and Derrida's work would risk suppressing differences, an integrative approach can draw on their correspondences while also allowing each theory to remain distinct, providing a variety of perspectives to bring to Joyce's problematizing of unreadability.

Outlines: The *Wake* in This Study

Before I end this Introduction with abstracts of my chapters, let me briefly situate the scenes these chapters focus on in a summary of some of the *Wake*'s stories and *dramatis personae*. In this summary, I will not problematize any scenes or any aspect of their telling, but aim to provide a narrative backdrop for my interpretation. To give a sense of setting and character relations, I draw on essentializing strategies, yet I understand my account here to be well short of completion. It does not cover the entire text and it is partial with regard to the sections covered.

Chapter I.1. of *Finnegans Wake* introduces us to the idea that this is in many ways a book about crises, downfalls, and resurrections. There are allusions to various historical and mythological events, particularly conflicts, that relate this theme to a cyclical pattern of rise and fall repeating itself throughout human memory. The chapter also introduces Humphrey Chimpden Earwicker (HCE). He could be considered an individual embodiment of human fallibility, although the nuclear family that is the *Wake*'s nearest approximation of main characters (HCE, ALP, and their children Issy, Shem, and Shaun) also undermines notions of individuality by blending with any number of historical and fictional figures and archetypes. I.2 closes in on HCE and his history. We learn about a mysterious crime he may or may not have committed, and witness how this alleged transgression becomes public knowledge. I.3 and I.4 are largely concerned with HCE's trial. The motif of an investigation is then carried over into I.5, which features the examination of a missing piece of evidence, a letter. It also introduces in more detail the figure of Anna Livia Plurabelle (ALP), who either wrote or dictated the letter. I.6 stages a quiz that is also a parade of the book's main characters and motifs, following which I.7 returns to ALP's letter by giving us a different account of its creator. In the mode of derogatory comments made by Shaun (the Postman), we learn about the literary output of his twin brother Shem (the Penman), who throughout the *Wake* is hinted to have had a hand in the letter's production. This chapter also firmly establishes the rivalry between the two twins, already featured in some of the histories of I.1. Finally, I.8 closes Book I by returning to ALP, this time in her manifestation as Dublin's river Liffey.

Book II gives us a sense of what could be called the family life of these characters. II.1 shows Issy at play with her friends and her brothers Shem and Shaun. At the end of the chapter, they are called home by their parents, and II.2 centres on the children doing their homework. II.3 tells us about the events taking place in the bar downstairs, where HCE the publican falls out with his customers over what appears to be yet another manifestation of his possible guilt. II.4 is a boat journey (reminiscent of Tristan and Isolde) that may or may not be a dream dreamt by HCE, who has downed all the alcohol left by his guests and subsequently collapsed.

The first three chapters of Book III hinge on Shaun, the first and third chapter once more being organized as investigations. Shaun is questioned by four old men in III.1. Then, in III.2, he gives a sermon to an audience that includes Issy. In III.3, he again becomes the subject of an interrogation by the four, this time while he is asleep or in a trance, a state in which he responds to questions by channeling the voices of other characters. One of the people given the floor in this manner is HCE, who talks about his achievements as a builder of cities. The enquiry, however, is again cut short when III.4 takes us back to the family home, with Shaun, Shem, and Issy now in bed in their childlike roles.

The single chapter of Book IV is in many ways a mirroring of I.1. It conjures up more scenes from history and matches up the many disgraces and falls that take place throughout the book with the possibility of a new beginning. This possibility is represented by ALP in her river form, flowing into Dublin Bay to merge with the sea and eventually return as a cloud of rain (one of Issy's manifestations), while also returning us to the beginning of the text by way of the loop that famously connects the book's last (partial) sentence with its first.

Out of this jumble of narratives, with its protean mutability of characters, the following chapters focus on those moments in which Joyce's writing becomes meta-textual: the creation and examination of ALP's letter, Shaun's comments on Shem's literary workshop, Shaun's ventriloquism illustrating how one discourse inhabits another, various appearances of the myth of the perfect language, and city-building as the creation of a public space that harbours public discourse.

In Chapter 1, "Reading What Is Not There," I turn to ALP's letter, whose location and content mystify characters throughout the book. As readers of the *Wake*, we share this predicament. Regarding the version of the letter that actually appears in I.5 (see 111.10–20), Tindall confidently asserts that here is "The letter, before us at last" (102). By contrast, Bernard Benstock introduces an element of caution when he writes that "It is difficult to resist the temptation to assume that the variation of the letter that appears here is *the* letter" (35). ALP's letter is not presented to us in a straightforward way; to treat its text as known is effectively a temptation. And even though Benstock seems willing to give in to this temptation to some extent, he notes: "Although this can safely be said to be *the* letter chapter, the actual text of that letter within chapter five does not give us either the first or the most complete version available in the *Wake*" (34). Capable of being authentic without being complete, and vice versa, ALP's all-important letter comes before us decentred and pluralized, with aspects of its reliability scattered throughout several competing versions. In Chapter 1, I argue that this raises the question of the essence or core of a signifying gesture. I discuss Derrida's and Lacan's views on signification, including Lacan's description of the Joycean sinthome as an untranslatable idiosyncrasy. Finally, I show how I.5 ridicules a Shaun-type figure's futile attempt to bring ALP's letter into agreement with his phallogocentric ideal of essential meaning.

In Chapter 2, "The Penman and the Critic," I focus on Shaun's rant about his brother in I.7. The usual approach to this section is to cast it as a parody of attacks on Joyce. There are certainly allusions of this kind; the problem is that this reading assumes what stands at the center of the chapter is not linguistic production as Joyce sees it, but a detraction from his views, in the form of Shaun. I would venture that this idea passes over fascinating opportunities offered by "Shem the Penman" to see

Joyce presenting his ideas on processes of reading and writing. Shaun's response to his brother's writing incorporates both his understanding of that writing and his expression of that understanding: it is a production based on an interpretation of another production. In reading this intricate construct, I want to take Shaun's aggression seriously as part of the point Joyce is making. The vehemence with which Shaun puts forward his position can tell us a lot about what is at stake in reading and writing as Joyce understands it. Shaun's irritation (which I analyse as his *anxiety*) resonates with *Finnegans Wake*'s insistence that language operates without taking recourse to the stabilizing concepts of centrality and essence. When we also take into consideration the multiple filtering of one voice through another (Joyce's through Shem's, Shem's through Shaun's, Shaun's through Joyce's), I.7 emerges as a complex statement on what it means to read or write. Shem and Shaun depict the interconnected roles of reader and writer, including a writer's lack of control and a reader's responsibility. I furthermore bring to bear on these considerations Shaun's role in III.3, which in its own way takes up the motif of one voice reproducing another.

Chapter 3, "Tower of Babel," continues to examine the plurality of voices in the absence of essence, reading a short passage from I.1 about the loss of univocal clarity, and relating this section to several others that describe how such a loss opens on a potential plurality of meanings. The argument here is that Joyce casts this plurality as one of the positive upshots of imperfect language. The passages in question include some of Joyce's implementations of the philosophy of Giambattista Vico as well as of the biblical tales of the flood, Babel, and Pentecost. By linking his own linguistic chaos to these mythological registers, Joyce enters into a dialogue with a long-standing tradition of thinking about language's lack of perfection. Vico writes about how our ancestors invented language in their helpless attempt to imitate the sound of thunder. The various lineages of Noah, separated after the flood, all develop their own linguistic varieties. The unifying project of the Tower of Babel is fragmented, by God's intervention, into linguistic confusion. And at Pentecost, the interlocutors who are given the miraculous ability to understand one another create a wild but productive disarray of voices. I argue that in each of these narratives, a frightful event or a state of chaos (a destructive tendency) goes hand in hand with some form of linguistic and cultural development (a creative tendency). At the end of this chapter, I explain why I am not convinced that we can reduce the meanings of *Finnegans Wake* to such elements as we can trace to their avant-texte sources.

Chapter 4, "Making Do," explores the *Wake*'s staging of plurality with a view to social life. The chapter returns to III.3 and examines this section's description of HCE's city-building as an example of public and discursive space. The issue here is that by rendering plurality productive, we are by no means assured of generating only positive results. As the challenge of organizing an urban community demonstrates, high levels of instability and change also mean high risks and therefore necessitate careful decisions. Like the narratives discussed in Chapter 3, moreover, HCE's account of his building activities is frequently poised between creation and violence. I relate this ambiguity to Derrida's understanding of hospitality, which similarly locates the idea of co-habitation between the beneficial and the problematic. Yet I also suggest that, from a Lacanian perspective, we should not mourn the fall from a once perfect condition, but embrace such a fall's emancipatory potential together with its challenges.

In *Finnegans Wake*, questioning the (linguistic) grounds on which we construct meaning entails thinking about (social) frameworks of interaction and about our (ethical) response to the other. The response to an opening: this is the concept that turns unreadability from a formal problem into an ethical one. And it is indeed a *problem*: the constructive possibilities that Lacan, Derrida, and Joyce all associate with this opening should not be taken to mean that all responses are equally valid. Such arbitrariness would abolish ethics. Instead, a common question informing Derrida's, Lacan's, and Joyce's work is how we construct and evaluate responses in the absence of certainty.

1 Reading What Is Not There

The Desire for Meaning

An absence of certainty calls for a response. In this chapter, I argue that if *Finnegans Wake*, unreadable as it may be, is the object of interpretative activities, this is because an absence of certainty, far from stopping such efforts, inspires them. This dynamic is depicted within the *Wake* as the problem of reading ALP's letter. Many of the *Wake*'s narratives attribute importance to the letter, casting it as a missing piece of evidence, as an object meriting close scrutiny, or as the one truthful account of something as yet unknown. Take the trial scenes that make up most of I.3 and I.4. There, the presiding judges hope that the evidence of a written document will illuminate the case: "Will whatever will be written in lappish language [...] bright upon us, nightle, and we plunging to our plight? Well, it might now, mircle, so it light" (66.18–23). The trial ends, however, before any consultation of the letter can be undertaken. This elusiveness of the vital piece of information is a motif that returns time and again in *Finnegans Wake*. Accordingly, an examination of the authority bestowed on the letter should pay attention to the ways in which this authority is tied to the letter's absence.

If ALP's absent letter is called upon to do away with uncertainty, it connects the notions of certainty and desire in such a way that desire is the desire for a certainty that *absents* itself. The core of what a message is truly about – essential meaning – far from giving minimal stability to interpretation, constitutes a destabilizing and catalytic notion. As is made clear by the letter's palpable effect on characters who do *not* possess it, and as I will show with regard to Derrida and Lacan, essence is an interpretative ideal we can never quite do justice to, but which gives rise to a persistent desire that drives the interpretative process.

The efficacy of this desire also plays an important role in what I will call Joyce's *non-words*. Under this heading, I subsume the coinages in *Finnegans Wake* that are not actual words but are different from any word in any given language. The category is thus unavoidably provisional (a non-word may turn out to be an unfamiliar expression or an expression in a language not previously considered), as well as deliberately makeshift (given the vagueness of its terms "word" and "language"). Yet for reasons I hope to make clear over the course of *Joyce as Theory*, the category of the non-word is of some use in an examination of signification in the *Wake* precisely because it is less specific than those of, say, the pun or the portmanteau. The sole defining feature of a non-word is the difference between Joyce's creation and any conventional form, which is also to say that the somewhat binary distinction between words and non-words I will implement throughout leaves room for many different varieties and degrees of distortion, fusion, punning, multilingualism, nonsense, and other effects. In particular, I propose to include in the category of the non-word those expressions in *Finnegans Wake* that differ only slightly from a standard word (especially in English) and that taunt us with their apparent recognizability. I will not undertake an examination of the complex notion of the "standard form." What interests me here, what is most curious and momentous about non-words, is the readiness with which we *disregard* the differences that separate them from actual words.

I.5, the chapter dedicated to ALP's letter, begins with the phrase: "In the name of Annah the Allmaziful" (104.1). There is at least one non-word here, but – and this I take to be Joyce's point – we can come up with ways of making the phrase readable. In the non-word "Allmaziful," echoes may be found of "almighty" and "amazing," perhaps also of "maze," and of Latin "alma" as in "alma mater": "nourishing mother." Other non-English transformations include German "Almosen": "alms," "charity." Open Roland McHugh's *Annotations to Finnegans Wake* on page 104 and you find the Turkish word "mazi" given as another suggestion, translated as "olden times." Further interpretations offer themselves when we consider the non-word in its context. McHugh adds "Allah the Merciful" (104) as another reading – or rather as another resource for the process, in McHugh's apt phrase, of "mentally superimposing" (xiii) glosses over Joyce's text. Yet all these superimpositions are spawned by a string of letters that (to the best of my knowledge) forms no word at all, be it in Turkish, English, German, Arabic, or Latin. The interpretations we derive from Joyce's text can thus be seen to involve a material transformation of the text, which is to say, an active manipulation that goes beyond what is actually given in the text, but which at the same time desires to reveal something offered, implied, or indeed hidden in the text. If we actively interfere with the text, producing meaning from it and in it, I propose that this is an expression of our *desire for meaning*. We could take one glance at the first page of *Finnegans Wake*, shrug our shoulders at its weirdness, and give up. In fact, many of Joyce's readers do have more or less that reaction. Still, many others feel the urge to press on. It is this urge I am interested in, as well as the way in which ALP's letter serves as a meta-textual symbol of this urge.

In keeping with my argument that *Finnegans Wake* can tell us a lot about signification in general, it is important to underline from the start that desire for meaning is also operative in the absence of non-words. It is related to the definition of a signifier as something that refers to something else. This capacity for referring, which I will call *referentiality*, can be distinguished from all constellations that give rise to a specific *reference*. In principle, we can imagine a situation that does not allow for any assumption about content, but that leaves in place signification itself, in the sense of sheer sign-ness (think of an ancient inscription that has become untranslatable, but which we recognize as some form of text). Referentiality is this text-ness or sign-ness. It does not require the availability of reference, only (the assumption of) its past or future possibility. Even where there is no hope of an actual reading process, we remain aware of a signifier's power to gesture towards something that remains hidden as long as the signifier is not deciphered. Signifiers that cannot be read remain *significant* in the sense that they point to a mystery beyond their own presence. Of course, this mystery is ultimately a result of the decision to consider something a signifier at all. It is not an intrinsic quality of that thing. Yet the idea of this mystery prevailing even in the absence of a concrete reference points us towards a crucial gap between reading as a relation to something (potentially) to be read, and reading as the production of *a* reading. This is the gap between referentiality and reference. In competent reading, this gap remains hidden, as recognizing something as a signifier coincides with forming an idea of its meaning. Yet once we examine the gap, we see that what in these cases appears to be an automatic, unidirectional process is in fact a precarious undertaking.

The non-words of *Finnegans Wake*, which introduce the obstacle of a material distortion between referentiality and reference, render this precariousness palpable. As soon as we decide that, in a reading of the *Wake*, its non-words cannot be ignored, we have also decided on the presence of a certain referentiality (i.e. the non-words cannot be ignored because, presumably, they mean something). Yet as soon as we try to grasp this meaning, we are confronted with the fact that a non-word is strictly illegible. Reducing it to one or several words that it resembles, evokes, translates as, etc. will always ignore the material differences that separate it from any and all of these normalizations. The non-word's *true* reference thus indefinitely absents itself; we are left with a referentiality without reference. Joyce's text invites us to read its non-words, but the only way of reading a non-word is to produce a reference ourselves, by hazarding a normalization of whose distance from the non-word we ourselves must be the judge.

Derrida's analysis of what he terms *iterability* shows that this pattern – producing meaning by actively crossing over from referentiality to reference – also applies to signifiers whose references may appear unproblematic. In "Signature Event Context," Derrida argues that in order for a signifier to be meaningful at all, it must remain meaningful in various contexts; it must carry its meaning into situations that will not be the same every time the signifier is used. Yet in this very capacity to be used, to appear *again*, not here but elsewhere, to "break with every given context, engendering an infinity of new contexts in a manner which is absolutely illimitable" (12), there is a drift away from stability towards transformation and heterogeneity. In order for the signifier to function in contexts that cannot be exhaustively anticipated, it cannot remain inert. If there were perfect inertness, utter indifference to all specific activation, then a signifier would remain mute – always. Therefore, Derrida argues, the signifier's iterability is the "logic that ties repetition to alterity" (7), where alterity is not a force operating on the signifier from the outside, but a constitutive part of its legibility, and thus of its function and identity. As every context draws on the signifier in a potentially different manner, the very notion of a signifier remaining usable incorporates alterity. Not only is each iteration potentially different; if transmission itself already involves alterity, this also entails an imperfect comparability of iterations (we cannot exhaustively know or control how different each iteration is, which is precisely why we cannot prevent there being differences). Iterability opens up the gap between referentiality and reference, between the signifier's functioning as a signifier and the variable meanings produced by its actual iterations.

In this view, Joyce's non-words exemplify a logic underpinning the very possibility of signification in general. Our material interference with non-words is a radicalization of the production of meaning through iterations that always involve alterity (here, we see the twofold nature of the *Wake* as both exceptional and exemplary). This impact of alterity, however, raises the question of what guides a reading. How can the gap between referentiality and reference be negotiated in such a manner that a reference is not randomly imposed on the signifier, but attempts to do justice to the signifier? In *Of Grammatology*, Derrida argues that although such an attempt at doing justice should be a part of reading, it can never rely on a stable core in the sense of a signifier's meaning prior to the disruptions of various contexts. Instead, our thinking of original or essential meaning has to come to terms with the idea "that the origin did not even disappear, that it was never constituted except reciprocally by a nonorigin, *the trace*, which thus becomes the origin of the origin" (61, my emphasis).

The trace brings us from Derrida's thinking on signification to his thinking on being. Or rather, Derrida holds that being and signification are based on the same underlying principle: differentiation. The trace activates a referral or identification; it makes signification possible by providing a notion of origin and identity. The operation by which the trace provides this notion is inseparable from differentiation as "a structure of reference where difference appears *as such*" (46–7), which is to say, appears as the most fundamental difference: the difference between that which is itself and that which is different. For Derrida, that is, an entity takes on existence and form by virtue of how it is differentiated and differentiates itself from what it is not. *It is differential relations that give rise to units and identities, not the other way around.* If "The trace must be thought before the entity" (47), it is thus because any entity or origin to which signification could point already relies on, as Geoffrey Bennington puts it, "the 'first' distinction between anything and anything," which is precisely "the minimal referral (not yet a reference in the normal sense of the term) that the trace involves" (94). The trace-structure is Derrida's name for a differentiation which is not semantic (*pace* readings that admonish Derrida for reducing the world to signification) but ontological. Again Bennington: "Language and world have, if you will allow me, the same general *texture*" (95). The very possibility of anything being identical to itself – or being distinguished, referred to, or signified via its identity – is antedated by the originary relational framework in which referral is not a secondary effect but constitutes the primary differentiation by which any entity establishes itself as the entity it is.

The trace thus partakes in what is perhaps Derrida's most famous (non-)concept: "*The trace is the differance* which opens appearance [*l'apparaître*] and signification" (65). The workings of *différance* mean that a signifier cannot point to an already self-identical origin, an identity capable of asserting itself as a presence independently of any structure of reference. Nor is identity defined in a once-and-for-all differentiation, resulting in a henceforth stable self-sameness. As différance, the trace is both difference and deferral, that is, spacing and temporalization, that is, inscription in a differential system and inscription in a history of relations that subjects the system to change. The trace is the impossibility of separating the system from the history, the spatial from the temporal, différance from différance; it marks the impossibility of accessing an entity as an unchanging presence. Again Derrida: "The outside, 'spatial' and 'objective' exteriority which we believe we know as the most familiar thing in the world, as familiarity itself, would not appear without the grammè, without differance as temporalization" (70–1). Which is to say that both identity in being and reference in signification are a matter of continual negotiation. It is against this background that we should think the trace as *the origin* of the origin of signification. The play of differences across spacing and temporalization means that there are no unchanging presences, no stable cores that ensure identity. If we can nevertheless conceptualize individual entities and specific references, Derrida holds, it is because the trace also appears as a placeholder for something that has never existed: it represents the *fiction* of a signifier's discrete and stable origin.

In this function, the trace "replaces a presence which has never been present" (*Writing and Difference* 295). It gives rise to a notion of reference which dissimulates that there exists no predetermined presence to which to refer. Or, as *Of Grammatology* has it: "the movement of the trace is necessarily occulted, it produces itself as self-occultation" (47). I take this to mean that precisely because signification cannot rely on a self-identical presence, but works by negotiating meaning within the differential trace-structure, we proceed by occulting this process. To get a grasp on the problems posed by signification's non-origin in différance, we posit an origin that is an essence outside différance. The very purpose of this essence is to remain a somewhat vague assumption. It is not to be accessed (that attempt would ineluctably return us to differential conceptualization); it is to be hypothesized as a plenitude we hope to have at least partly captured in our reading. And although any such hope is itself nothing but a specific constellation of differential relations, it marks the point at which we, as it were, stop following the network from relation to relation, and instead look on their gathering as indicative of an overall direction or thrust.

Whereas the trace-structure is the totality of relations, each individual trace is therefore also a vanishing point orienting these relations around its very movement of slipping away. This is the origin or essence that the trace evokes and whose impossibility it obfuscates. More than representing an interpretative outcome that we imagine as being given somewhere (and that we may or may not aim to access), essence is thus chiefly a name for the *absent ideality* against which we implicitly measure interpretations when we ask whether they are coherent, relevant, and so on. Such ideality can only be a hypothesis or projection, since it is what no signification can ever access or produce. Yet it is also what guides the play of signification, enabling the move from referentiality to reference by providing this move with a direction and an aim. Which is why it makes sense to say that even readings that dispense with the simplistic idea of a single correct answer incorporate essential meaning as a *palpable absence* towards which reading directs itself.

This understanding of the Derridean trace-structure helps illuminate the desire for meaning. Analogous to the way in which desire can be thought as desire for what is *not* given, interpretation can be understood as sustaining itself by projecting an element it never encounters. It is easy to see that where the process of reading attempts to close the gap between referentiality and reference, it directs itself towards something that cannot be obtained because it does not exist: essential, unchanging meaning (I would only have needed to discuss iterability to argue this). Yet a consideration of the trace-structure shows that although essential meaning – of course! – does not exist, we let ourselves be taken in by the ideal of essential meaning insofar as for this ideal to remain imaginable is the minimal condition of identification and differentiation in general. I therefore propose that the trace not only refers to the past (the signifier's imaginary origin); it also points to the future. Contained in the trace is the effort, both extended into the future and continually cut short, to unearth essence. This effort does not succumb to the impossibility of its success. It structures our readings by both driving them and denying them closure. It renders them points on a trajectory towards a solution that is forever arriving, never to arrive. That is to say, if my interpretation appears to do violence to Derrida's deconstruction of the transcendental signifier as signification's stable center, consider that in the form of an unstable mirage or phantom, this center is declared to be one of language's undeconstructible elements. *Writing and Difference* asks: "But is not the desire for a center, as a function of play itself, the indestructible itself? And in the repetition or return of play, how could the phantom of the center not call to us?" (297).

Here, I disagree with Martin Hägglund, who in *Radical Atheism* puts forward an important exegesis of the impossibility of stability in Derrida. Hägglund notes that any presence beyond différance amounts to self-destruction, indeed to an absolute *impossibility*. Citing Derrida's remark that "life without différance" is "another name for death" (*Of Grammatology* 71, qtd. in Hägglund 28), Hägglund ventures that différance is "the condition for everything that can be thought and desired" (28). Clearly, then, essential meaning beyond différance cannot, as I propose, be an object of our desire. Any unchanging meaning would by its very lack of change (i.e. of iterability) mark the death of meaning, which is to say that the possibility and – according to Hägglund – the desire for meaning always operate within différance. The problem with Hägglund's argument is that he moves from demonstrating that permanence beyond différance can never be actualized to claiming that such a beyond *cannot be desired*: "that *one cannot want* absolute immunity and that it has never been the aim of desire" (119). By putting things this way, Hägglund casts us as intuitive logic-machines who desire only that which is possible: only that which can actually be attained and which, if attained, would be good for us. Such neat adherence to the possibilities of being makes for an impoverished concept of desire. While I agree with Hägglund that, according to Derrida, all being is subject to différance, this changes nothing about the fact that we quite frequently desire permanence, certainty, immunity, etc. Desire cares nothing for the logical contradictions involved.

Desire, I would suggest, is precisely the name we give to the fact that the operation of différance, the formation of the trace-structure, *can* gesture beyond its own possibilities, to an origin whose imaginary nature it occults. That everything I desire always turns out to be finite, imperfect, changeable (and thus not *quite* desire's fulfillment), that indeed the very act of desiring relies on conceptualizations that are trace-structures which cannot give rise to a permanent entity, does not mean desire has to be non-contradictory and limit itself to aiming at the finite. Here, Hägglund's take is at best a patchy reading of Derrida, who makes his position quite clear. "The approach to these limits is at once feared as a threat of death, and desired as access to a life without différance" (*Of Grammatology* 244). We desire life without différance – even though life without différance is another name for death. This is Derrida at his most paradoxical, yet least ambiguous. He states outright that we do *not* only desire the thinkable and desirable. By contrast, the limitation Hägglund imposes on Derrida's thought (no effects above and beyond the differential relations between entities that *are* or at least *are thinkable*) parallels the reductive reading of Derrida by those Lacanians who admonish Derrida for neglecting the paradoxical causality of lack (a causality Hägglund expressly rejects, see 192–5).

The assumption that Derrida offers no tools for conceptualizing effects beyond differential relations informs Žižek's reading of Derrida, which I will have occasion to discuss. It also underpins Michael Lewis's book *Derrida and Lacan*. Consider the question of how a (finite) individual who wishes to make sense of a signifying gesture can deal with the infinity of differential relations that make up the trace-structure. Lewis explains that we do this by dissimulating the infinity:

> If the infinite references of the signifier constitute a material mesh, then what occurs in consciousness is the *idealisation* of this mesh. [...] Due to its finite nature, consciousness represses the dependence of meaning upon an infinity of material signifiers, and so it represses the signifier itself, in favour of the conscious signified.
>
> (24–5)

Which is precisely how I would read Derrida's analysis of the origin/ trace. Whereas the network of relations never comes to rest, thus infinitely postponing the identification of original/essential meaning, we produce actual (conscious) meaning by no longer following the thread of differential relations but looking at how they coil around the vanishing point that is the trace. Actual meaning is thus a kind of gestalt image of essence that covers over (or represses or, in Derrida's phrase, occults) the workings of the signifier.

Under its Lacanian name, *objet petit a*, this gestalt image is frequently presented as the key insight of Lacan's not paralleled by anything deconstruction offers. As Lewis puts it: "the object *a*, the cause of desire, depicted in the fantasy, [...] makes the absolutely unreachable infinity seem like something that could one day be attained, and that is *desirable*" (167). In other words: "The symbolic order needs the fantasy, the fantasy that the object *a* can in fact be attained" (190), for in this way, "Lacan can account for the way in which differentiality is limited, and a meaningful totality instituted, even if this is grounded on a notion of oneness that is itself a fantasy" (238). But this is precisely what Derrida argues when he says, as Lewis writes, that "The system of textuality extends infinitely and thus any belief in a moment of presence that would remain outside, precedent to, and governing this text is illusory" (1). Lewis does not realize it, but his terms "illusory" and "fantasy" are different ways of expressing the same idea. Essence outside différance is illusory, yes, but it is a necessary and productive illusion.

Essence beyond différance does not exist, it cannot even be thought (in the sense of conceptualized), yet Derrida maintains that this changes nothing about our being impacted by desires that are contradictory both in the sense of self-destructive and in the sense of imperfectly thinkable. He speaks of the impossible desire for an essential meaning as a "desire of a purely idiomatic voice that would be what it is and would be in some way indivisible" ("Dialanguages" 136). And even though "this dream is forever destined to disappointment; this unity remains inaccessible," it is clear that "this 'dream' institutes speech, writing, the voice, its timbre. There cannot not be this dream" (136). This is confirmed once more in Derrida's final seminar, where he states: "What I called 'phantasm' [in previous sessions] is indeed the inconceivable, the contradictory, the unthinkable, the impossible. But I insisted on the zone in which the impossible is named, desired, apprehended. Where it affects us" (*Beast II* 148). The unthinkable is desired. This poses a serious challenge to Hägglund's reading of Derrida, which frequently uses formulas like "everything that can be thought and desired" (10, 19, 28, 48, 111, 115, 157) to designate a set of entities within différance. It is worth noting that Hägglund actually cites Derrida's remark about the voice that would remain indivisible, but in a tell-tale breakdown of exegesis dismisses Derrida's description of desire in this passage as "untenable" (156).

Derrida's various references to our desire for the impossible undo much Lacanian critique of his work in one fell swoop, since they point towards the paradoxical causality that informs Derrida's thought just as much as it does Lacan's. In Derrida, too, as Michael Naas comments, "that the phantasm *is not* does not mean that it has no power" (*End* 74). We should not make the mistake of assuming that what remains inexistent is bound not to have any impact. I take Derrida's point to be that we are not as rational as that. By projecting (more precisely: hypothesizing without conceptualizing) something that cannot be, the trace introduces into signification certain effects of absence, even loss. Yet the trace also enables us to step over the gap separating referentiality from reference. It gives to this step a trajectory, but not a definitive outcome, by inscribing it into a specific network of differences that is also an imaginary course towards an essence. Insofar as reading structures itself in response to this course, it thus lets itself be affected by an absence. Interpretation produces meaning by turning an absence (essential meaning) into a presence (actual meaning, reference, interpretation).

The Missing Missive

Returning to *Finnegans Wake*, we can now say that Joyce's non-words are concerned with precisely this dynamic. On the one hand, it is impossible to find the true reference of a non-word. Since non-words are not words, any reference we can come up with is always going to be the reference belonging to a word that is not quite what Joyce wrote. In this view, non-words illustrate that actual meaning is something we produce in the absence of essential meaning. On the other hand, this is not to deny that in this production, we may (and arguably should) do our best to be rigorous, to approach something like the true meaning of what Joyce wrote – which is to say that essential meaning is left in place as an absent ideality. It is important to note that in putting things this way, I allow myself a slight imprecision in using the phrase "reference belonging to a word." What I have argued up to this point is precisely that when we examine how regular words generate references, we come up against the same active production that non-words also illustrate. If non-words provide us with an opportunity to examine such production, it is thus not because Joyce's distortion of words adds a new step to the process of interpretation. Rather, non-words magnify a step typically below the threshold of our attention.

This is where ALP's letter comes in – or fails to come in. For ALP's letter, too, illustrates the effects of an essence that absents itself. As indicated above, ALP's letter is often associated with the missing and vital bit of information that would resolve some conundrum within the *Wake*'s narrative. The mysterious document is hinted at, talked about, studied, and searched for throughout the *Wake*. But most of all, it is simply not there. It is conspicuous by its absence from many of the passages that discuss it and examine it. One of these is found in the trial scenes of Book I, chapters 3 and 4. There, the letter is referred to by the four judges as the lost piece of evidence that might clear up the case of HCE's misdemeanor and "bring the true truth to light" (96.27). Unsurprisingly, however, the scenes end without the letter ever having surfaced, or any truth having been pronounced. This marks the starting point of the motif of characters looking to the letter for answers, but finding themselves disappointed one way or another.

The document next appears in chapter I.5. The whole of this chapter is comprised of an analysis of the letter by "a grave Brofèsor" (124.9); yet in all of the roughly 21 pages taken up by his account, little transpires about the letter's contents. Instead, there is a focus on the outward appearance of the letter that, as I will argue in the final section of this chapter, parallels the way in which the trace provides an overall gestalt of meaning that duly covers over the more unsettling mechanics of meaning's production. Since too close an inspection of the letter could only lose itself among the dangers of signification, the professor very sensibly opts to examine the letter's "outer husk" or envelope (see 109.1–36), discussing for instance the damage done to it by its "residence in the heart of the orangeflavoured mudmound" (111.33–4). It is interesting that Joyce originally drafted the version of the letter we now find in Book IV as a part of I.5, but eventually decided not to include it in that chapter (see Fuse 98–9). The deliberate nature of this omission adds to the elusiveness of the object that the professor discusses.

The letter resurfaces in a similar capacity in book III, where it features in the two scenes of the four old men questioning Shaun. In chapter III.1, the four press Shaun to "read the strangewrote anaglyptics of those shemletters" (419.19–20). Shaun, however, evades the question. Instead of revealing anything about the letter's content, he comments on the letter's address and its author, Shem (see 420.17–421.14 and 421.21–425.3). Similarly, when in chapter III.3 the "senators four" (474.21) encounter Shaun in his incarnation as "Yawn" (474.11), they return to the letter several times without eliciting any clear answers (see 478.1–2; 483.1–6; 489.33–4). Throughout their quizzing of Shaun the postman, a personified carrier of meaning, the four are frustrated in their endeavor. Interestingly, the narrative structure balances this frustration with unflagging insistence, possibly even growing obsession: having failed in III.1, the four are back in III.3 to try again. I find it hard not to see in this a depiction of Joyce's readers, in our stubborn insistence on reading *Finnegans Wake*.

The actual text of ALP's letter appears to feature in *Finnegans Wake* several times, for instance as the "Boston" Letter in I.5 (111.10–20), as ALP's "cushingloo" in I.8 (201.5–20), and, most prominently, as the "Reverend" letter in book IV (615.12–619.19; for a list that includes minor manifestations of the letter, see Hart 232–3). Initially, this would seem to contradict the idea of the inaccessibility of the missive. However, these various manifestations of the letter are not exactly authentic renderings. Patrick McCarthy points out that "No two version of the document are identical" ("Last Epistle" 725). I would argue that Joyce is thus presenting us with an idea close to what Derrida calls repetition tied to alterity. It is not possible to activate the same unchanging letter at different moments. The only presence we can turn to is actual meaning, which is produced in subtly different ways each time we call on it.

McCarthy ventures that "no single account of the letter is more accurate than any other" (726). The letter can be present without therefore putting an end to the search for its true message. I would read this mingling of presence and absence in conjunction with the fact that the presence of a signifier in the *Wake*, far from constituting an antidote to the absence of essence, is what makes this absence painfully palpable (especially where the signifier in question is a non-word). Absence is part of the signifier and of the letter. McCarthy pays particular attention to the version in Book IV, which plays with the narrative expectation that the text will end with the reveal of the authentic message. This incarnation of the letter not only differs from other versions contained in the *Wake* – say, in "the omission of the four X's that represent kisses" (727). It actually responds to previous discussions of the missive. The seemingly final version, McCarthy explains, "appears to have been altered by commentary on it" (730). For instance, this letter's phrase "About that coerogenal hun" (616.20) echoes "About that original hen" (110.22), which is part of the description given by the professor in I.5. Instead of providing a definitive rendering, the "final" version of ALP's letter thus demonstrates the porousness of the boundary between the text and such belated manipulations as should be distinct from it. If the letter is the

Wake's symbol of the looked-for answer, it is clear that readers like the professor are very much involved in the production of any actual answer on offer.

McCarthy concludes that ALP's letter, despite seemingly being included within the text we are reading, "is free – that is, irreducible to a consistent level of meaning, or even to a definitive text. In this, as in other respects, it is a model of the mysterious, compelling, kaleidoscopic work of which it is a microcosm" (732). The idea that ALP's present yet absent missive constitutes a microcosm, synecdoche, or model of *Finnegans Wake* has proven a highly successful avenue for interpretation. Examples of it can be found in *Wake* criticism ranging from attempts to isolate stable meaning (Tindall, with regard to the professor's comments in I.5, writes that here, "for several pages, the letter and the *Wake* are plainly one," 107), to examinations of the *Wake*'s unstable multitude of meanings and styles (Slote posits that "statements apropos this mysterious 'Letter' have a self-conscious aspect and could be said to characterize the conundrums of the *Wake* itself," *Joyce's* 128). Whereas the letter is thus frequently described as a *mise en abyme*, a metonymy for *Finnegans Wake* itself, I would foreground a different aspect. The letter's conspicuous motion of absenting itself also ties in with the concepts of essence and the desire for meaning. It thus allows for a metaphorical reading that relates ALP's missive to the signifier in general.

Consider the palpable yet unfailingly frustrated interest in this document demonstrated by both the *Wake*'s characters and its narratives. The impatient awaiting of this continually hoped-for, continually overdue, continually elusive letter, I would suggest, corresponds to nothing if not the desire in interpretation caused by the very thing that can never be present: essential meaning. One critic who takes a similar view is Mikio Fuse, who argues that

> While [the letter] is a synecdoche of the *Wake* in that it exemplifies the ineluctable betrayal of the Word by both readers and writers, the Letter is equally *any* document that was, is, and will be articulated in any language, inasmuch as any iteration inevitably falls short of the Word Itself. While "that ideal reader" can read the Word without stumbling over "paralyzed" language, we (the real) readers must sin when reading. This is typified in our readings of the *Wake* because to make *any* particular sense out of it we inevitably betray the Word-Letter by focusing on only one or at most some of the many available senses it opens up.
>
> (114)

In the terminology introduced above, this is to say that the distorted language of *Finnegans Wake* bars us from making the transition from referentiality to reference without noticing it. It confronts us more explicitly than most texts with the desire that is necessary for the process of interpretation. It is desire that has us step into a text and produce meaning there. In the case of the *Wake*, this desire expresses itself in our insistence on "sinning," on continually subjecting to interpretation a text whose non-words are strictly speaking illegible. ALP's letter extends this dynamic from the non-language of *Finnegans Wake* into signification more generally speaking. It implicates, as Fuse puts it, any document at all. If a non-word presents us with the prospect of a legibility that is never given, the *Wake* suggests that a letter/text likewise promises an answer it continually withholds. And if a non-word's illegibility will not put an end to our attempts to decipher it, the letter's/text's failure to fulfill its promise, similarly, is far from destroying interest in it. I subscribe to the reading Fuse proposes, and I would add that the symbolic dimension of ALP's letter registers not only our inevitable stumbling over language, but also the desire that *teases* us with this stumbling and that still has us interpret, against our better knowledge. What makes both non-words and ALP's letter so interesting is that they keep asserting their presence, provoking the enduring suspicion that a signifying gesture may in fact be taking place, while leaving us without the possibility of isolating and fathoming that gesture. And in this, crucially, they constitute not an exemption from the typical relation between referentiality and reference, but this relation's exemplification.

Here, my interpretation differs from an otherwise similar Derridean reading of the *Wake*. In *Imagining Joyce and Derrida*, Peter Mahon highlights the role played by desire, but he does not go beyond casting ALP's letter as a synecdoche for the elusiveness of the *Wake* itself. He links the figures of Finnegan and HCE (see 20, 81) as well as the image of letter (see 84–5) to a "structural principle of ever-receding withdrawal and pursuit that shapes not only book I but also the paradigm for the pursuit of truth as presence across the entire text of the *Wake*" (21). In the case of the letter, this pursuit manifests itself as the fact that "There is no pristine Platonic *eidos* in the letter; there is only distortion" (85), meaning that a "pursuit of truth as presence" can only demonstrate that no such presence exists. Up to this point, I find myself in agreement with Mahon's approach. However, he treats the desire-inducing distortion as an attribute particular to the *Wake*. Mahon proposes that "the text of the *Wake* functions as a theatre of mimicry" (138), where the reader of this text is invited to imitate exegetical procedures depicted in the text, and he says that "In this theatre the object that the reader imitates withdraws" (138). But he does not explore the possibility of taking these dynamics of pursuit and withdrawal as a general description of reading. Instead, he singles out Joyce's text as sharing these mechanisms with a select few, giving rise to "the situation of the reader-writer in Vico, Joyce, or Derrida" (179). The result is a detailed but restrictive examination of how a number of Joyce's motifs can be read as self-reflexive commentary. By contrast, I maintain that Joyce's meta-textual images hold true of other texts as well. Far from belonging to specific modes of philosophy, myth, or fiction, the act of reading-writing – reading as an active production – is one under which all reading can be subsumed.

To argue for such a general scope is not to say that *Finnegans Wake* is anything less than unreadable. Read the non-word I discuss at the beginning of this chapter, "Allmaziful," and you have not read Joyce's text; you have transformed the text to make it say something you can read. My point is that such transformations are the very thing that sheds light on the transition from referentiality to reference in other, more conventional and readable forms of writing. As the tripartite structure I borrow from Fuse – Letter, *Wake*, word – suggests, these transformations are relevant to how readings of standard texts necessarily fall short of capturing essence. The unreadability of *Finnegans Wake* exemplifies something about all reading. This is what I call Joyce's self-deconstruction: if a non-word raises in a very particular way the question of essential meaning (when transforming a non-word into a word, which word do we go for?), it reflects a conundrum that, due to iterability, all signifiers confront us with. In the absence of essence, readers are the producers of meaning.

Yet for all that, the process of production is not random. In ALP's letter, Joyce gives us an image of the focal points that both drive production and give it direction. The *Wake* thus draws our attention to the role of desire in signification; it reveals, as Norris puts it, "the desirous or libidinal aspect […] of intellectual activity" ("Joyce's Heliotrope" 4). In doing so, it drives home "the painful truth of desire, that it is constituted of a gap, a space, a lack, an absence, a distance at the heart of desire" (14). This lack, far from being abstract and merely inferred, is palpable in the very presence of words, in their refusal to yield anything like essence. Amplifying this refusal, whilst also demonstrating our undiminished desire to overcome it, the non-words of *Finnegans Wake* illustrate the extent to which reading consists in "hoping against hope all the while that, by the light of philosophy, (and may she never folsage us!) things will begin to clear up a bit one way or another" (119.4–6). Read as a metaphor for this dynamic, ALP's letter illustrates both that the ultimate answer escapes us *and* that we are capable of idealizations that compensate for that fact.

The Shape of Lack

Joyce can thus be seen to share with both Derrida and Lacan the idea of an impossible desire's impact on signification. I now want to turn to the fact that he also shares with them the image of a letter standing for the signifier. Indeed, both Derrida and Lacan relate their own discussions of letters to *Finnegans Wake*. Lacan alludes to the *Wake* in the "Seminar on 'The Purloined Letter'," where he refers to Joyce and where, in the French original, we read: "*A Letter, a litter*" ("Le séminaire" 25), misquoting the *Wake*'s "The letter! The litter!" (93.24). Emphasizing distortion (the crucial piece of evidence that looks like a piece of scrap paper), this shows that in Lacan's discussion of the signifier as a cause of desire and interpretative activity, the *Wake* is already kept in mind. It is likewise kept in mind in Derrida's discussion of letter-sending in *The Post Card* which, as we will see in Chapter 2, makes explicit reference to Shaun the Postman. And, of course, the letter/signifier is also the intersection of Lacan's and Derrida's work that spawned their well-known debate about Poe's "The Purloined Letter." What I want to show in the present subsection is that their positions on this matter can be aligned. Their confrontational exchange about Poe would then constitute an instance of expressions having gone awry – which in the context of the arguments I will now review is a highly appropriate event to have taken place.

In *The Post Card*, Derrida uses the image of postal delivery to discuss signification. He argues that "a letter can always – and therefore must – never arrive at its destination" (121). To salvage this formulation from a non sequitur, he specifies: "in order *to be able* not to arrive, it must bear within itself a force and a structure, a straying of the destination, such that, in any case, it *must* also not arrive" (123, translation modified). Or, as he has it in another section of *The Post Card*: "a letter does *not always* arrive at its destination, and from the moment that this possibility belongs to its structure one can say that it never truly arrives, that when it does arrive its capacity not to arrive torments it with an internal drifting" (489). With regard to the signifier, this is to say that there is always the *possibility* of its not arriving (not achieving the result intended by the sender), and due to this possibility, it can never *fully* arrive (in the sense of fully assuring sender and receiver that the risk has, on this occasion, been evaded). The straying of the letter, then, is another image Derrida uses to describe what happens to a signifier between sender and receiver due to the logic of iterability.

Initially, there seems to be a diametric opposition between this line of thought and the sentence that concludes Lacan's "Seminar on 'The Purloined Letter:'" "a letter always arrives at its destination" (30). If the incompatibility of this statement with Derrida's view of signification seems blatant, however, we should ask how Lacan is using this expression. For Derrida as for Lacan, the letter symbolizes the signifier. Yet we cannot take Lacan's use of "destination" to mean what it would stand for in Derrida: the successful transmission of meaning as intended by the sender. To interpret Lacan's "a letter always arrives at its destination" in this manner is to disregard the argument that this sentence concludes.

It is helpful to briefly sum up the plot of Poe's short story. In Paris, a Minister steals a compromising letter that enables him to blackmail the Queen. Though it can be inferred that he keeps the letter on his premises, the police, secretly employed by the Queen, in multiple searches prove unable to retrieve the document. Only Poe's detective Dupin succeeds in exposing the Minister's ruse: he has made no effort at all to conceal the letter, openly displaying it in a card rack where it escaped the attention of the policemen who were looking for a hidden object. Note that like

ALP's absent letter, which inspires several of the *Wake*'s investigations and interrogations, the Queen's letter propels the narrative forward by absenting itself and making this absence present. It is most productive of hypotheses, schemes, and actions when it is inaccessible but when, at the same time, this inaccessibility is sharply *felt* by the characters. Lacan's reading, which casts this letter as the signifier in general, uses that productiveness to illustrate the extent to which, as he puts it, "the signifier's displacement determines subjects' acts" (21). If Lacan speaks of the letter reaching its destination, we should read this as a signifier *unfailingly producing its effect* on the writing or speaking subject.

Lacan describes this effect as being above all a manipulation of desire: "Such is the signifier's answer, beyond all significations: 'You believe you are taking action when I am the one making you stir at the bidding of the bonds with which I weave your desires'" (29). This weaving is decidedly *not* based on an ideal of lucid communication, with letters obeying our intentions and always showing up where we want them to be. At this stage of his teaching, Lacan sees the symbolic as a locus of alienation, and therefore as a force that renders the subject enigmatic to herself or himself (a view that will only become more pronounced as Lacan's thinking begins to posit intrusions of the real into the symbolic). The "Seminar on 'The Purloined Letter'" takes recourse to the classic Lacanian formula "the unconscious is the fact that man is inhabited by the signifier" (25) – the unconscious is structured like a language – which is virtually synonymous with the statement: "*the unconscious is the Other's discourse*" (10). To middle Lacan, signification is something that imposes itself without ever properly belonging to us. As he puts it elsewhere in *Écrits*, it is the Other that can be conceived of as "the locus of speech" ("Direction" 524).

Understood as the realm of the Other, signification is all about desire. According to middle Lacan, we engage with texts and other signifying gestures in no small part because of a need to be told by the Other what the name of the game really is. We scour the symbolic in the vague hope that some signifier will finally stop sending us to yet another one (and, again, it seems to me that despite the futility of the project, one can do worse than citing this hope as an explanation for reading *Finnegans Wake*). But like the chase for an origin beyond différance or the chase for ALP's letter, this search is frustrated, indefinitely. As Lacan has it: "we can say that it is in the chain of the signifier that meaning *insists*, but that none of the chain's elements *consists* in the signification it can provide at that very moment" ("The Instance" 419). Lacan's chain of the signifier is notably similar to Derrida's system of relations from which meaning emerges not as a discrete element but as a state of the system itself: the elusive shape or trace left in the system by a movement of absenting. This elusiveness perpetuates the desire for meaning. The signifier, as Lacan puts it, weaves our desires. Or, as he has it in *Seminar V*: "desire is a by-product, as it were, of the act of signification" (316). This is as close as Lacan comes to a definition of the human condition. We are unfortunate creatures indeed, for having invented language, we are doomed to desire. I therefore agree with Žižek's assessment that Derrida's critique "misreads the Lacanian thesis, reducing it to the traditional teleological circular movement, i.e., to what is precisely called in question and subverted by Lacan" (*Enjoy* 11). If Derrida speaks of the letter's loss of destination, and Lacan of its trajectory, we should read this as a loss that constitutes a trajectory, insofar as the trajectory consists in nothing else than the *uncertainty* that the straying of the signifier necessarily causes.

We thus arrive at a significant overlap between the images created by Derrida, Lacan, and Joyce. Like the recipient of Derrida's straying letter, the readers of ALP's ever-changing missive are menaced by a subtle but irreducible uncertainty, which means that even where they hold the letter in their hands, they still cannot know whether they have obtained it in its original, authentic form. There is a part of its message that escapes us. Like the Queen's purloined letter in Lacan, moreover, ALP's absent/present missive makes it clear that this uncertainty is not an inert attribute. The letter's absenting itself has a specific trajectory: it gives rise to a desire that is productive of meaning.

The notion of an effect resulting from an absence, however, raises a question I have so far avoided in the interest of reading Derrida and Lacan in parallel. Before considering the encounter with absence in late Lacan, and then returning to ALP's letter in the last subsection, I here need to address *symbolic castration* in middle Lacan. Although the term "castration" does not appear in the "Seminar on 'The Purloined Letter,'" Lacan makes it clear that the chief example of signifiers' transformative power over subjects – the example of the Minister – is a case of symbolic castration. Here is how Lacan describes the scene that greets Dupin when he enters the Minister's room: "Between the jambs of the fireplace, there is the object already in reach of the hand the ravisher has but to extend" (26). In the original, this reads: "entre les jambages de la cheminée, voici l'objet à portée de la main que le ravisseur n'a plus qu'à tendre" ("Le séminaire" 36). By punning on the fireplace's posts ("jambages") as legs (French: "jambes"), between which the card rack containing the letter is spotted, Lacan likens to castration the appropriation of said letter by Dupin, which turns the Minister from robber into robbed, including a number of castrating effects this entails. Tracing the signifier's manipulation of desire, Lacan's discussion insists that one key effect is the powerlessness – the castration – to which we are reduced as a result of not truly possessing the signifier. In Derrida's view, this approach evades the lack that compromises language, since it offers the place of castration on the imaginary body as the locus of this lack, paradoxically implying that the lack is identifiable and expressible. As Derrida puts it in *The Post Card*: "that which is missing from its place has in castration a fixed, central place, freed from all substitution. Something is missing from its place, but the lack is never missing from it" (441).

The phallus is indeed Lacan's name for the hypothesized, impossible signifier that would render the symbolic transparent to us. In "The Signification of the Phallus," he offers a number of observations from clinical practice on which his choice of this term is based. I will not discuss these reasons, however, because the most pertinent criticism of Lacan's terminology is that precisely insofar as the phallus is said to *signify* (as opposed to coincide with or correspond to) power, essence, authority, etc., it is not an index but an arbitrary name. As Butler puts it, the phallus must be open to "signifying in ways and in places that exceed its proper structural place within the Lacanian symbolic and contest the necessity of that place" (*Bodies* 55). The gendered framework which prompts Lacan's nomenclature raises serious issues, for the term risks reasserting a phallocentrism it claims to be merely *observing* in a specific cultural setting. At the same time, the universal applicability of "phallus" means that it is possible, by Lacan's own admission, to dissociate the term from that original framework, and use it as the name of the missing signifier in virtually any constellation. In the evaluation of the resulting mismatch between the term's derivation and its application, I cannot agree with Derrida's argument that the specificity of a name entails an undue specificity of meaning. Derrida maintains that the concept of castration introduces two consequences into the thinking about language, to which he refers as logocentrism (signifiers as providers of essence) and phallocentrism (the phallus as a marker of power and knowledge). He states that when it comes to phallocentrism and logocentrism, "the stresses can lie more here or there according to the case"; yet, "in the last instance, a radical dissociation between the two motifs cannot be made in all rigor" ("This Strange" 59–60).

My contention is that the synthesis of these aspects into *phallogocentrism* underestimates the extent to which the Lacanian phallus is meant to evoke not a presence but an absence: not an implementation of logocentric reasoning, but its rejection. Gilbert Chaitin makes this point when he writes that the phallus "represents completeness, but only by virtue of symbolizing the process by which that completeness is irrevocably lost" (61). The term "phallus," then, is not the means by which Lacanian thought claims to regain power over the breakdowns of the symbolic, over the intrusions (the castrating cuts) of the real. The phallus represents the impossible signifier to which we ascribe such power. For even though "there can be no such signifier [...] you can name the absence of this signifier" (94). The phallus, then, is not a name that can master the symbolic and the real: it is the name of the fictional name that could. In Seminar VIII, Lacan says that the phallus constitutes "a symbol [...] in the place where *the lack of a signifier* occurs" (235, my emphasis). Referring to this absent, impossible signifier as an object of desire is the equivalent of Derrida's insistence that desire can extend to what cannot even be conceptualized. I would thus compare the Lacanian phallus to what Derrida calls the phantom of the center or the dream of an indivisible voice – expressions that give us no reason to believe that providing these names interferes with the spectrality of what is being named. Providing a name is not the same as providing a conceptualization.

Lacan explicitly states in Seminar VIII that "the phallus as a signifier" is the phallus "as given over to an entirely different function than its organic function" (231). This is to say that the *imaginary* dimension of the phallus (written "φ"), where lack remains tied to a corporeal image, cannot impose a conceptualization on its *symbolic* dimension (written "Φ"). If we wish to avoid self-contradiction, the dissociation of these two dimensions is necessarily absolute. At the point where the phallus is a signifier indicating "the lack of a signifier" – no longer a known lack but precisely a lack of signification, knowledge, and control – it is, by the same token, no longer motivated by any *known* correspondences between the organic phallus and what is lacking. It is instead motivated by a tendency to presume that the phallus might just be a fitting symbol of a thing that would grant knowledge and control. This tendency is phallocentric, laughably so, but not logocentric, for the characterization this naming undertakes cannot extend to what it names, but only to certain effects of its lack. Taking this particular view on those effects is highly arbitrary. Given how many other images of lack could provide a fitting symbol here, there is no compelling reason why the symbolic phallus and the imaginary phallus should share a name. Yet this very arbitrariness of the name means that the name does not grant any undue control. If anything, the disconnection of the "phallus" from its bodily root confirms iterability and castration. Butler cites Jane Gallop's apt remark that the "inability to control the meaning of the word *phallus* is evidence of what Lacan calls symbolic castration" (126, qtd in Butler, *Bodies* 28).

This absence of what would be paradoxical control is central to my project of examining unreadability. There is no self-contradiction in conceptualizing the *limits* of conceptualization and in pointing to – even naming – a beyond that cannot be conceptualized. I should address a possible Lacanian objection, though. By refusing to characterize this beyond (by relating it to certain psychosexual imagery), am I refusing to investigate how this beyond works? And in doing so, am I not reducing the Lacanian approach to the shortcomings of a Derridean perspective, whose focus on differential relations draws our attention away from the efficacy of what is beyond them: the castrating real?

In the Introduction, I cite this description of the Lacanian real: "a certain fundamental ambiguity pertains to the notion of the Real in Lacan: the Real designates a substantial hard kernel that precedes and resists symbolisation, and, simultaneously, it designates the left-over, which is posited or 'produced' by symbolisation itself" (Žižek, *Tarrying* 36). In other words, the real is the impossibility of symbolic completion (there are always leftovers the symbolic order cannot master), but that is not all. Lacan's thinking does not stop at recognizing that codification is bound to go awry. It explains *how* codification goes awry. For the real is also the "substantial kernel" that precedes and indeed *forms* the symbolic order, which is why Lacan speaks of "the very thing that forms a discourse, namely the real that passes through it" (*S XIX* 6). The beyond, the uncodifiable kernel, organizes codification around itself. Take Lacan's *objet petit a* in its role as the object of desire. This object is a manifestation of the real. Lacan holds that what ultimately makes it desirable is not any characteristic that can be identified and analyzed, but some aspect beyond the expressible. The object of desire captivates you. Precisely because you cannot quite think it through, it occupies your thought and shapes your actions. Much the same goes for the *objet petit a* as an object of anxiety or phobia. In these cases, it is again the thing you cannot quite process that exerts a formative influence on your behavior (hence Lacan's subsuming of these qualitatively very different experiences under the same heading).

The substantial kernel of the real, then, is another name for this formative, intrusive power, for an agency that does not originate with the symbolic. With regard to the first question posed above, I would now argue that we should not conflate an investigation of this abstract topology (the real impacts the symbolic) with a characterization of the real as a specific object or event (for instance castration). Consider that the object of my phobia – my *objet petit a* – can be a thing of marvelous indifference to you, an ordinary element of your symbolic. This illustrates the ultimately contingent manner in which we elevate actual objects to the status of *objet petit a* (a mismatch that also reveals itself every time you attain an object of your desire – and inevitably realize it is not *quite* the *objet petit a*, not quite the satisfaction of all your desire). Saying that there is no getting rid of the real, that it invariably affects the symbolic, is thus not the same as saying that the same object or event invariably acts in this role. Colette Soler argues along these lines when she writes "Lacan realised that those who speak suffer less from the Other's norms that vary across cultures than from the real restrictions proper to the logic of language" and that "his Oedipal metaphor was itself the formula for a symptom, one among others, nothing more" (118–19). I believe we can hold on to the Lacanian insight that the *objet petit a* impacts the symbolic, while rejecting the link Lacan tries to establish, at a certain point in his teaching, between this general topology and the specific manifestation of it that is castration. As Butler notes: "if we concur that every discursive formation proceeds through constituting an 'outside,' we are not thereby committed to the *invariant* production of that outside as the trauma of castration" (*Bodies* 154).

The notion of the outside of discourse brings me to the second of the above objections: the idea that deconstruction reduces everything to the symbolic, to effects of differential codification, thus losing sight of the formative power of the real. This would miss the point of the Lacanian topology, for as we have just seen, the real is not just a leftover, an *effect* produced by symbolization's failure; it is also a *cause* acting on symbolization. What makes Lacan's take on signification interesting is just this paradoxical simultaneity and circularity. To return to the so-called "object-cause" of desire: how does the *objet petit a*, the object which causes desire, come to be? Žižek's answer is that desire "produces its own object-cause" in the sense that "the process of searching itself *produces* the object which *causes* [the process]" ("Why Lacan" 39). That is, desire itself projects the *objet petit a* that then acts as desire's aim and focal point – and thus as its cause. This structure holds true of the real's effect on the symbolic in general. Manifestations of the real vary; the real is basically the blind spot produced by any given symbolic constellation. If nevertheless we should not regard the real as a mere product of the symbolic, it is because we can say much more than that symbolic codification is bound to go awry. The symbolic is in fact organized around the real. The structure of our desires, obsessions, anxieties, phobias, etc. is defined by how the symbolic *incessantly circulates around its blind spots*, which thus constitute important topological points, shaping codification and experience.

This is the paradoxical causality Derrida supposedly ignores when he insists on the impossibility of anything beyond différance – yet it should be becoming clear that this same causality is discussed by Derrida as the trace. The trace is the *objet petit a* by another name. Both are focal points emerging from the very process on which they in turn bestow direction and coherence. Like the *objet petit a*, moreover, the trace coincides with its own absence. Desire may organize itself around an object, but no object you attain is ever the true *objet petit a*, which is always somewhere else, withdrawing from your activities, which it also structures. Signification may organize itself around the sense of an origin, but no meaning you produce is ever the true origin, which is always somewhere else, withdrawing from your interpretation, which it also structures. The trace is thus Derrida's version of the very concept that Žižek holds up as the Lacanian antidote to deconstructive relativism: to the "interplay of symbolic overdetermination" (*Sublime* 78). To this understanding of what Derrida argues, Žižek opposes the *objet petit a* as "the real kernel around which this signifying interplay is structured" (78), lending specificity to the field of meaning.

> The self-referential movement of the signifier is not that of a closed circle, but an elliptical movement around a certain void. And the *objet petit a*, as the original lost object which in a way coincides with its own loss, is precisely the embodiment of this void.
>
> (178)

Which is what Derrida says of the trace. The *objet petit a*/trace *is not*; it marks the blind spot evading and menacing any codification and differentiation, yet, at the same time, it operates as the vanishing point that organizes codification and differentiation around its own withdrawal.

Both Derrida and Lacan thus provide us with the conceptual tools to describe a paradoxical folding whereby the outside of codification appears as a catalyst of codification itself. We can now add ALP's letter to this list as a third element that resembles both the trace and the *objet petit a*. ALP's letter draws attention to itself by withdrawing from our grasp; it creates effects by absenting itself. If we are to take this seriously as one of Joyce's images for what happens in signification, we should conclude that the obtainability of answers is put into question in *Finnegans Wake*. Like Lacan and Derrida, however, Joyce does not stop at this point, simply diagnosing that signification is ultimately not grounded in anything. For ALP's letter also mirrors the circular formative process that characterizes the trace and the object-cause of desire. In the interaction between I.5 and book IV that I outline above, one manifestation of the letter is impacted by the discussion of another manifestation. The letter is thus not only the subject of a search; it contains itself certain elements of this search, *a search that can therefore be seen to shape the very thing it is looking for*. We form an idea of the letter because we desire the letter, and we desire it because of that idea. The circularity here is analogous to how desire and the trace/*objet petit a* reciprocally give rise to each other. As Shari Benstock writes, "desire" constitutes both "[t]he missing 'content' of the dreamletter," that is, the thing we hope to receive from it, and "the urge to its own production (to dream, to write)," that is, the process through which we create it ("Letter" 169). Drawing on the Lacanian object-cause of desire, van Boheemen-Saaf applies this notion to the whole of *Finnegans Wake*: "Joyce's text [...] involves us in searching for, and eventually creating its desired object" (68).

Meaning is actively created, not passively received. In the process of this creation, the *search* for that which is dreamed or desired, but never given – that which cannot be given because it does not exist – is immensely productive. On this, Derrida, Lacan, and Joyce agree. This search is how the trace-structure produces meaning in Derrida. It is how the signifier weaves the subject's desires in Lacan. And it is what is at stake in ALP's letter, whose effect on the *Wake*'s narratives and characters illustrates the efficacy of that which withdraws from our understanding.

Joyce's Creative Void

I now want to discuss in more detail Lacan's view of this efficacy, in particular a crucial transformation his view underwent. This transformation concerns the question of how a subject comes to terms with the imperfection of the symbolic order, and it constitutes the single most important change to Lacan's system brought about by the encounter with Joyce's work in the 1975–6 seminar, *The Sinthome*.

We have seen that, according to Lacan, it is signification that gives rise to desire, and that this is because signification incessantly circulates around its blind spots: moments of breakdown that mar conceptualization. Lacan agrees with Joyce and with Derrida that there is no essential meaning and that, nonetheless, symbolization is haunted by an idea of essence: an idea which structures and disturbs the symbolic. As Harari puts it: "in Lacan's eyes, every enunciation is in pursuit of an enunciated it will never find" (133). One of the elements that remain constant throughout Lacan's work is his insistence that this inability to perfectly grasp the world through symbolic appropriation is constitutive of our existence. It is, as I put it above, the human condition according to Lacan (and Lacan really does reserve this description for *human* subjects). "How to say it? That is the question. One cannot speak any old which way, and that is the problem of whoever inhabits language, namely, all of us" (*S XX* 100).

Something that changes over time, by contrast, is Lacan's view of what exactly it means to inhabit language – and what psychoanalysis has to offer by way of help. At the height of his structuralism, middle Lacan declares that "the unconscious is structured like a language" (*S XI* 20). At this stage, "language" is still basically synonymous with "symbolic," as becomes clear when we compare Lacan's famous dictum to the following version: "the unconscious is structured as a function of the symbolic" (*S VII* 12). If we are linguistically constituted subjects, middle Lacan means by this that we are inhabited by the symbolic, that our unconscious is a function of the symbolic order that surrounds us. In a 1957 article, Lacan can still say that the subject is "the slave of a discourse in the universal movement of which his place is already inscribed at his birth" ("Instance" 414). Accordingly, when Lacan states in 1958 that we are "at the mercy of language" ("Direction" 525), this is not yet about the fundamental flaws inherent in all language, but said chiefly with a view to the idea that, as Lacan puts it in a paper from 1960, "the subject constitutes himself on the basis of the message, such that he receives from the Other even the message he himself sends" ("Subversion" 683). Far from granting the subject a capacity of self-expression, language is held to impose the discourse of the Other, which middle Lacan conceives of as the social and linguistic settings into which the subject is born. Again from the 1957 text: "the experience of the community [...] takes on its essential dimension in the tradition established by this discourse" ("Instance" 414).

Against this backdrop, middle Lacan conceptualizes *symptoms* as the inevitable by-products of this imposition. The symbolic order is never fully at our disposal. It is the locus of the Other and that which we receive from others – which makes using it to bestow sense on our experiences a task fraught with difficulties. Accordingly, Lacan's view of analysis around this time centers on the goal of making the analysand realize all this. For instance, in 1953: "Analysis can have as its goal only the advent of true speech and the subject's realization of his history" ("Function" 249). True speech here means that the analysand is finally no longer kidding themselves as to the powers of speech. They let go of the idea that the symbolic order provides transcendental truths, and come to recognize it as a flawed, contingent system. As long as they hold on to the notion that the symbolic *could* provide wholeness, they will feel that their symptom is indicative of a lack in themselves. This is the efficacy of the symbolic order's withdrawal from us. We keep producing meanings that always fall short of desire's fulfillment; we keep looking for some missing piece of knowledge or ability which would make us whole. During analysis, the analysand learns to speak the truth about their history and the history of their symptom formation: that the lack is not in them, but in the symbolic order they inherited. They can stop looking for the missing piece, because the social reality into which they were born does not contain it. Middle Lacan defines this insight as the end-point of analysis, seeing how with this realization – no one can give you the thing you lack – the analyst, too, no longer has a function. "It is from this idealization that the analyst has to fall" (*S XI* 273).

This solution, which I only sketch here in condensed form, is emotionally intelligent. It seems to me that proceeding along these lines might relieve some deeply entrenched guilt and liberate the analysand from an impossible project of having to know. Symptoms dissipate as the subject lets go of the oppressive belief in the Other as the so-called "subject supposed to know," and comes into their own as a subject allowed to live and act. In this conceptualization of analysis, however, middle Lacan also pessimistically thinks the subject as a passive recipient of processes of sense-making from which they can, at best, liberate themselves so as to embrace *not knowing*. Here, the change introduced in *The Sinthome* "marks a radical shift from the firmly held position about language holding us" (Harari 301).

Having moved away from the structuralist emphasis on the symbolic, "by the mid-1970s Lacan has come to conceive of the human subject as precisely a knot or chain in which real, symbolic and imaginary are linked together" (Thurston, *James Joyce* 94). The fundamental level is no longer one of these three orders, but instead the idiosyncratic braiding of the knot itself. This is where Lacan introduces his fourth order, which we should read as the unique solution a particular subject finds to the problem of making symbolic, imaginary, and real combine in this subject's experience. As Lacan has it, "this fourth term [...] completes the knot of the imaginary, the symbolic, and the real" (*S XXIII* 27). The fourth order, moreover, is the titular sinthome: "you have the possibility of binding them together. With what? With the sinthome, the fourth ring" (*S XXIII* 12). If my subjectivity is the way in which I knot together the orders of my experience, and if it is the sinthome that ties this knot, then what this new term, *sinthome*, means is that my symptom *is* my subjectivity, that my subjectivity is necessarily symptomatic.

This offers the subject an interesting avenue out of being "held" by the symbolic. The starting point is the same: "the neurotic *believes* in his symptom, considers it to be meaningful. And he thinks that if this 'meaning' is unveiled, his suffering will cease" (Harari 81). The process of analysis, as in middle Lacan, consists in stripping away the formations which invest a symptom with meaning and thus effectively perpetuate the symptom's place in the analysand's thought and experience. It is here that Lacan introduces a new idea. Where the disinvestment in old forms of meaning truly succeeds, it opens on a different organization of experience: a braiding of the knot that is of the subject's own making. This *making*, however, is radically meaningless. Where the subject tries to create new meaning for themselves, they will fall back on the lures of the symbolic, on the seductive call of such questions as: Why am I suffering? What does my symptom mean? What course of action might bring it under control? They will then continue to stake their sense of self on a completeness which the symbolic never actually delivers. By contrast, a new braiding comes about where the subject manages to make use of "the *sinthome*, which can come about through the *assumption* of a symptom – that is connecting to the symptom's *real*" (Bristow, 2001 65). The decisive change happens when the subject taps into the utter meaninglessness of their symptom and thus discovers a dimension of their subjectivity beneath and beyond symbolic sense-making.

It is the possibility of creativity and agency at this level that Lacan learns from Joyce. Joyce, says Lacan, succeeded at freeing himself from the imperative of meaning. "In his efforts dating back to his first critical essays, then in *A Portrait of the Artist*, and ultimately in *Ulysses* and ending in *Finnegans Wake*, in what is in some sense the continuous progress that his art constituted, it is hard not to see how a certain relationship with speech is increasingly imposed upon him – namely, this speech that comes to be written while being broken apart, pulled to pieces" (*S XXIII* 79). What really makes an impression on Lacan is that Joyce's achievement does not end there, resulting in meaninglessness pure and simple. Instead, Joyce's writing discovers a different know-how. As Thurston puts it, "Lacan sees in Joyce a subject who sees through [...] the laws and conventions of discursive reality" and who reveals "the void of creative jouissance-in-language" (*James Joyce* 197). This void is not part of the symbolic or the imaginary, yet neither can it be identified as the real. It constitutes an active response to the meaninglessness of the real which results in a *different* meaning-production. Again Thurston: "the writing of the knot cannot be situated in symbolic structure, psychological meaning or the mute insistence of the drive; in other words, the knot itself is irreducible to the registers it inscribes" (195). Still, Lacan tells us that "Through this artifice of writing, I would say that the Borromean knot is restored" (*S XXIII* 131). There is a binding of the three orders that is irreducible to them, and that constitutes the subject's ability to shape, reshape, or restore the orders' intertwining in a creative act – in Joyce's case, the act of writing. This is what Lacan calls the sinthome, and as far as language is concerned, the example of Joyce makes clear that the sinthome marks "a degree of freedom in the way that each speaker organizes the marks of the Other" (Harari 300). The symbolic is constitutively flawed, so it is in vain that we chase along its signifying chains the mirage of some final answer. Yet what late Lacan comes to emphasize through Joyce is the possibility of this flaw being turned into a creative opening.

Based on these comments, I now want to point out two things Lacan is *not* doing when he brings Joyce into his discourse. First of all, Lacan is not glossing or unpacking Joyce's texts. In fact, he hardly reads Joyce at all. It is easy to point to basic mistakes Lacan commits, such as getting plot details wrong. For instance, Lacan thinks that Stephen teaches "in Trinity College" (*S XXIII* 53). On these grounds, Joyceans are occasionally unwilling to consider Lacan might have anything of interest to say when it comes to Joyce. It is important, then, to stress that Lacan never claims to be producing literary criticism. As Colette Soler puts it quite bluntly: "in *The Sinthome*, there is no fascination whatsoever with the text of the author who is his object; nor will one find anything that resembles a proper literary analysis" (4). Although Lacan's engagement with Joyce lacks the qualities of commentary, explication, and occasionally even of basic familiarity, as a critique of Lacan, this is disingenuous, because Lacan is quite simply not interested in reading Joyce in this way. He is intrigued by the oddity of Joyce's writing, and his intervention remains mostly at the level of working with this sense of bafflement.

Lacan produces the kind of take on Joyce that focuses on the thingness and materiality of the writing. Lacan hardly seems to care whether the *content* of Joyce's writing corresponds to anything in his own thought (and since his seminar is not a literary one, and is not trying to be a literary one, Lacan is under no obligation to show any such thing – a point not always granted in evaluations of Lacan's work by Joyceans). As Thurston observes,

> turning to those texts offered [Lacan] a way to show forth, not a confirmation of some preestablished doctrine or interpretative method, but an exemplary *resistance* to interpretation. And Lacan saw this resistance not as merely a baffling theoretical dead-end, but rather as a provocation to reconceive, to reinvent his psychoanalytic thinking.
>
> ("Introduction" xvi–xvii)

In Joyce's texts, Lacan encountered elements he could not interpret. If these texts afforded him an opportunity to reinvent his teaching, it is because Lacan reads them as being part of the formation of Joyce's subjectivity. The various ways in which these texts interrupt codification are taken as examples of how subject formation makes use of unreadable, absolutely idiosyncratic elements. According to Lacan, at certain points in Joyce's artistic fashioning of his self, nothing but a brazen interruption of legibility would do. Eventually, Joyce "was only able to find the solution of writing *Finnegans Wake*" (*S XXIII* 106).

However, the other thing Lacan is not doing in *The Sinthome* is to treat Joyce as a case study. Harari writes: "He does not seek to discover the relation between the life and the work in a kind of guaranteed specular game" (25), identifying in the work traits known from the biography. If anything, Lacan is interested in the opposite: tracing the impact the work made on the life. That is to say, again, that *The Sinthome* reads Joyce's texts as illustrations of the role a certain type of creativity plays in subject formation. One thing that undoubtedly irritates many readers of the seminar is that, as the title of session five, Lacan asks: "Was Joyce Mad?" (*S XXIII* 62). The question is misleading, however, without the answer Lacan provides: "why shouldn't Joyce have been mad? [...] being mad is no privilege" (*S XXIII* 71). The question of Joyce's "madness" is not about Lacan wishing to diagnose Joyce. It refers to a process of breaking out of the symbolic order: a process in which we are all implicated to a greater or lesser extent. Remember that this is the same seminar in which Lacan equates subjectivity with the sinthome. Subjectivity is the idiosyncratic, meaningless, unreadable core of who we are, which is to say that it constitutes "an irreducible 'psychotic' kernel in every individual" (Harari 145). This psychotic element is what bestows true agency – true creativity and individuality – on the subject's tying of their knot: precisely what Lacan says Joyce succeeded in doing. Therefore, as Brivic explains, "Joyce should not be seen as, say, psychotic in the bizarre distortions of the *Wake*, but as someone working with the exploration of psychotic patterns for a liberating purpose" (*Joyce Through* 13). What is more, this is what Lacan recommends we should *all* do. To put it in sensationalist terms, Joyce is not the problem – a clinical case to be presented – he is the solution. Joyce's work is Lacan's example of what analysis should bring about: the emancipation that comes with fully fledged subjecthood.

The potential problem with Lacan's reading (or non-reading) of Joyce is a different one. Lacan sees the radical creative gesture, which escapes and reshapes the symbolic, as *the way out of* the subject's endless search for an answer. He envisions an emancipatory act that cuts through hesitation and deferral and braids a new knot of subjectivity which, if the act was indeed successful, we are to imagine as relatively stable. A successfully completed analysis should probably bring about some lasting change in the subject's experience. In this context, connecting with the sinthome means that you are finally no longer looking for an answer. Joyce, by contrast, seems invested in unending creativity. His non-words' referentiality without reference perpetuates the task of interpretation. The vicissitudes of ALP's letter are similarly caught up in a productivity that knows no end. And the fact that all of *Finnegans Wake* forms a textual loop is another indication that these processes inside the text and around the text are designed to continue ad infinitum. We could say, then, that reading the *Wake* locks us into an interpretative activity that is structurally similar to neurosis. Indeed, many readers of the *Wake*, including some Joyceans, do find their relationship with this text highly frustrating.

I would venture, however, that *Finnegans Wake* is sinthome-atic insofar as it abolishes the neurotic mirage of the distant possibility of an ultimate solution. Joyce wants us to keep searching, but not by believing in the prospect of the end of the search.

In *The Sinthome*'s session of 16 March 1976, Lacan says of Joyce that "what he puts forth [in *Finnegans Wake*] is the sinthome, and a sinthome such that there is nothing to be done to analyse it" (106). A Lacanian reading of the *Wake* is not a diagnosis; it is precisely the realization that no diagnosis – no ultimate answer of any kind – is forthcoming. Still, this does not put a stop to reading. In his address to the 1975 James Joyce Symposium, Lacan states: "Read a few pages of *Finnegans Wake* without striving to understand it. It's quite readable" (144). I don't think that Lacan is contradicting himself here or changing his opinion. The point is precisely that even though nothing can be done to analyse the *Wake*, it remains readable, it compels us to read. Testing the motivating force that drives our reading activities, Joyce shows us that this force manifests quite independently of the availability of any answer.

The *Wake* is dedicated to nothing if not a demonstration of the desire spawned by unreadability – as well as the possibility of turning a breakdown of meaning into an opportunity for the production of meaning. Faced with a symbolic order perforated by intrusions of the real (i.e. by moments of breakdown), we find that these intrusions constitute what, with Thurston, I would term the creative void at the heart of language. In the presentation to the Symposium, Lacan goes on to state that Joyce is "the pure symptom of what is involved in the relationship to language" (146). Affirming the absence of essence, Joyce finds a presence of the real to which we respond with a sinthome-atic invention. If Lacan concludes that psychoanalysis should enable the subject to abandon their belief in the end-point of symbolic sense-making, the Joyce of *Finnegans Wake* forces us to adopt a similar stance: production in the absence of a final answer.

A reading of the *Wake* in this Lacanian style leads to two suggestions. Firstly, we can once again say that *Finnegans Wake* is not operating outside "normal" modes of signification. Much like Derrida, who sees the abyss of the trace as the reference point without which language could not function, Lacan casts the encounter with the meaningless as the kernel around which meaning forms. This is how *all* meaning is produced, including meaning we feel we access intuitively, as evinced by the fact that where we try to actually pin down some intuitively received meaning, it slips away along the signifying chain. We should not try, then, to distinguish invention from a "standard" mode of receiving meaning, for doing so can only obscure that actual meaning is *always* derived from a slipping away. Amplifying this process, Joyce presents us with moments that truly encapsulate the breakdown of codification; yet he also demonstrates the possibility of inhabiting this breakdown.

Secondly, this understanding of meaning necessitates a reconsideration of the reader's agency. Joyce confronts us with the fact that meaning is not given, but produced. Here, the theme of ethics announces itself. On the one hand, the active production of meaning contains an interesting emancipatory potential – which is what Lacan latches on to in his (non-) reading of Joyce. On the other hand, such production raises questions about a reader's responsibility towards the writer and the written. It is important, then, that one aspect of sinthome-atic invention is the subject's responsibility for how they braid the knot of their experience. By encouraging us no longer to be beholden to the symbolic order (to figures of authority, traditions we imagine hold all the answers, obsessive private rituals, etc.), Lacan is not suggesting that anything goes. On the contrary, Lacan argues that the subject who breaks out of inherited meaning finally *stops* avoiding responsibility, that taking responsibility is part and parcel of taking charge of one's own being. As Harari explains, "Knowing oneself to be responsible entails occupying a position diametrically opposed to that of 'blaming' the unconscious" (83), of considering the unconscious purely a depository of the symbolic, i.e. the realm of the Other. Instead, laying claim to the sinthome goes through an encounter with the unconscious "as something to be assumed by the subject" (83). For readers, analogously, stepping up to the active production of meaning entails assuming the meanings they produce.

I should emphasize that none of this is to argue against the possibility of reading – against our experience that we do indeed read. Joyce's text ropes us into a search for meaning that is evidently productive (I myself am presenting a reading here that I believe to be a response to what Joyce wrote). The point is to read while stopping short of actually buying into *essential meaning as obtainable*, as an answer that is given and need merely be found. This brings me back to the argument I make in the Introduction that discourse is mobile – contingent on historical, cultural, and other contextual particulars – and that part of theory's project is to reveal this mobility. If theory criticizes claims to objectivity, it is because in such claims, a dominant discursive position is construed as the neutral outlook of occupying no position at all. Here, Joyce's approach is a theoretical one: it is not that we cannot or should not engage in discourse, but that we should do so without chasing a sense of neutrality that would protect us from ever taking a stand.

Van Boheemen-Saaf diagnoses this when she speaks of "the reader's implication" in Joyce's texts and concludes: "We can no longer maintain our illusion of transcendent objectivity; we must either engage the crack in the looking-glass or repress and ignore it" (46). Either we choose to produce meaning while confronting the crack of language's constitutive imperfection: that it does not provide meanings that are simply there. As I discuss in Chapter 2, this confrontation causes anxiety. Our second option is to *repress* the crack, to act like meaning is simply given – but this strategy returns us to anxiety just the same, via the detour of a cover-up desperate to hide the absence of essence. I will now show that in the professor's examination of ALP's letter in chapter I.5, Joyce does indeed link the absence of essence to the failure of an interpretative project that would hide behind notions of neutrality and hermeneutic decency.

Revealing Absence

ALP's letter resembles the *objet petit a* not only as the object of desire, but also as the object of anxiety. As I will elaborate in the next chapter, anxiety is a response to the proximity of the object of desire, insofar as such proximity threatens to reveal that the object of desire is the object-cause *produced* by desire: not a retrievable essence that got desire underway by absenting itself, but a *projection* which dissimulates that there is no essence to begin with. It is this dissimulation that risks being found out on closer inspection, hence the discomfort accompanying proximity to the object. This ambivalence of *objet petit a*, which generates desire by its absence and anxiety by its presence, is at work in I.5. In a passage describing the letter's envelope, the professor comments on his own method:

> Admittedly it is an outer husk: [...] Yet to concentrate solely on the literal sense or even the psychological content of any document to the sore neglect of the enveloping facts themselves circumstantiating it is just as hurtful to sound sense [...] as were some fellow in the act of perhaps getting an intro [...] to a lady [...] straightaway to run off and vision her plump and plain in her natural altogether.
> (109.8–20)

If ALP's letter is an image for the signifier in its relation to the signified (involving both absent ideality and actual meaning), the "enveloping facts" can be taken to mean anything from the signifier's material inscription to the context of its setting down. At one level, the professor is thus voicing a reminder not to proceed too hastily, but to base reading on material evidence, on contextualization, etc. This attitude, however, is complicated by his use of an image linking meaning (the letter's "literal sense" or "psychological content") to female nudity ("her natural altogether"). The link is a classic philosophical topos, and one to which *Finnegans Wake* frequently alludes. Another instance is found in a description of ALP in I.8: "Anna was, Livia is, Plurabelle's to be" (215.24; echoed in 226.14–15). This echoes Plutarch's account (or one of its many reiterations in philosophy, literature, and esotericism) of the Isis-cult in Ancient Egypt. Plutarch states that the shrines of this religion carried reminders of the hidden nature of truth: "In Saïs the statue of Athena, whom they believe to be Isis, bore the inscription: '*I am all that has been, and is, and shall be,* and my robe no mortal has yet uncovered'" (25, my emphasis). The allusion places ALP in a figure of thought that equates truth with the naked woman: the disrobing of the goddess. Another example is the geometry problem in II.2, the correct answer to which is a diagram of ALP's genitalia (I will discuss this scene at the beginning of the next chapter). And when I.5 lists the possible titles of ALP's letter, ALP is referred to as "*a Woman of the World who only can Tell Naked Truths*" (107.3–4).

Due to the professor's participation in this topos, his explanation takes on some problematic aspects. Why indeed compare a letter to a nude woman in the first place? The instruction not to picture her that way can only half make up for the leering nature of the metaphor itself. What is more, the admonition to avert one's eyes, the gesture of clothing nudity in a robe which hides truth from the impudent gaze of mortals, introduces another strange element into this account of reading: the failure to actually confront truth. If truth is female, but femininity should be tastefully hidden, this can only result in the hiding of truth itself. On this basis, I now want to argue that in limiting himself to "decent" reflections, the professor is not following a modest approach; he is engaging in a *phallogocentric* project of exegetical mastery that is as immodest as it is restrictive. In the professor's account, that is, we have a case in which the strategies of phallocentrism really are combined with those of logocentrism. Superficially respectful, the description he gives, in a phallocentric reduction of femininity, appropriates the lady as a figure of truth. Through this figure, logocentrism promises that truth is given – though elsewhere, hidden from our gaze, which means that phallogocentrism displaces truth, interdicting any examination of it.

The question, then, is why truth so urgently needs to be hidden away. We can begin by considering what the "outer husk" suggests. In another Lacanian reading of ALP's letter, Hanjo Berressem proposes that "Lacan's reading of Poe suggests that the letter in *Finnegans Wake* might be read as a similar 'allegory of the signifier'" (145). To produce this allegorical correlation, however, Berressem accentuates not the letter's absence (with the letter consequently exemplifying desire), but its ragged appearance (representing the many imperfections of the symbolic order). The thing expressed by language "becomes a victim to the inevitable distortions and anamorphoses of language, which the outer appearance of the letter symbolizes" (146). The many partial destructions and defilements that the envelope of ALP's letter has undergone show how language never quite does justice to what it expresses. Language always falls short of perfectly natural expression, in the sense of an expression that captures essences without interfering with them. Here, another parallel suggests itself between nudity and truth: the *indecency* of the naked body resembles a certain indecency of meaning – hence the need to avert our eyes. Commenting on the "outer husk" passage, Berressem writes that "Joyce stresses, within a complex modulation from questions of language (signifier/signified) to questions of sexuality (nudity/clothing), the impossibility of an ideal signified or meaning as well as naturality" (149). In other words: no expression of ideas without a loss of naturality in both language *and* sexuality. In culture, the naked body cannot truly function as the last vestige of naturality. As Lacan has it: "Is nudity purely and simply a natural phenomenon? The whole of psychoanalytic thought is designed to prove it isn't" (*S VII* 227). It is this reversal that troubles the professor's alignment of nudity and meaning. Just as clothes hide not nature (there is no need for clothing in nature), but the absence of nature, the presence of the letter hides the absence of ideal meaning: hides the fact that meaning is not "natural," but constructed.

The opposition between nature and culture Berressem invokes corresponds to the classic Judeo-Christian account which relates both clothing and imperfect language to original sin. If Adam and Eve's existence in Eden is associated both with nudity and with transparency in expression (I will discuss the ideal nature of Adamic language in Chapter 3), the postlapsarian condition is characterized by clothing and by a linguistic experience in which ideas are obstructed by the signifiers that try to express them. The wearing of clothes after the fall implies an understanding of nudity that cannot be thought at the same time as the absolutely spontaneous character of nudity before the fall, which is uncontaminated by shame. As we will see in Chapter 3, Joyce is indeed in dialogue with a tradition that connects cultural advance to a decrease in spontaneity and purity. This tradition is what Derrida calls an "insistence upon nudity, fault, and default at the origin of human history" (*Animal* 44). In the perspective opened up by this insistence, "There is no nudity 'in nature'" (5), instead, we are called upon to think nudity as historical and cultural. We "have to think shame and technicity together" (5). Historical, postlapsarian, non-utopian culture, with its indecent knowledge and its imperfect technics of signification, taints both language and the body. It does not cover up a nudity/meaning that beneath the cover provided by clothing/signification continues to exist in its prelapsarian state. Rather, it *replaces* that which it hides: with nudity ashamed of itself and with meaning that shamefully fails to capture essence.

We can now see how phallogocentrism projects both of these effects on femininity (it is femininity that has to be covered up; femininity is meaning). Phallogocentrism follows the procedures of a fetishism that, having equated truth and presence with the phallus, with impeccable logic settles upon femininity as the image of mystery and absence, only to immediately take this mystery as an indicator of a *hidden* presence and truth, thus carrying out the curious reversal that is fetishist disavowal. Disavowal, writes Evans, "is the failure to accept that lack causes desire, the belief that desire is caused by a presence" (44). If women are mysterious and desirable, the phallogocentrist reasons, it must be because they have a secret. Holding on to this belief, he then wavers between two equally misogynist attitudes. Either he appeals to a hidden essence still to be revealed. This is the topos of denuding, of mastering, of getting femininity under control. Or he stipulates that essence should *not* be approached (anxious, of course, that this ultimate reference point should reveal itself not to be a presence at all, but a projection). This is the topos of femininity as simultaneously divine and abject: whatever you do, do not go near woman.

Since phallogocentrism cannot make up its mind between these options, it gets caught up in a discordant series of terms: "truth-unveiled-woman-castration-shame" (Derrida, *Post Card* 416). Woman is revered as the symbol of truth, yet the shame that results from the actual impossibility of obtaining an uncastrated or prelapsarian essence is likewise attributed to her. Biblically, the fall that leads from Eden to postlapsarian history is primarily associated with Eve, not Adam. This shaming forms part of a stigmatization of the feminine that traverses phallogocentrism for all its declared idealization of femininity; it is part of an obsessive scolding and praising, veiling and unveiling. What all of these modes have in common is that they exclude the woman's point of view. They are modes of looking at woman as a mystery, a goddess, or an impurity – in short, as an *other* – on which the (male) observer needs to impose interpretations and/or measures of control. As Laura Mulvey puts it in her famous essay on the male gaze in cinema, "the woman as icon, displayed for the gaze and enjoyment of men, the active controllers of the look, always threatens to evoke the anxiety it originally signified" (22). In describing the male response to this threat, Mulvey identifies the same ambivalence I am concerned with here. "The male unconscious has two avenues of escape from this castration anxiety" (22).

Its first option is to keep the fearful mystery at a distance, choosing "complete disavowal of castration by the substitution of a fetish object" (22). Derrida examines this strategy in *Spurs*, where he writes about the image of truth as female nudity veiled that "only through such a veil which thus falls over it could 'truth' become truth, profound, indecent, desirable. But should that veil be suspended, or even fall a bit differently, there would no longer be any truth, only 'truth' – written in quotation marks" (59). This is how I would read the professor's metaphor of the nude lady, which links meaning to nakedness while stipulating that an envelope should screen meaning from too direct an examination. The professor is covering up the unbearable absence of essence by means of a fetish. Like the wearing of "definite articles of evolutionary clothing" (109.23), the covering up of imperfect, actual meaning is "suggestive, too, of so very much more and capable of being stretched, filled out, if need or wish were" (109.26–8). It is suggestive of the fetishist idealizations appealed to by a phallogocentrism which is as impatient with actual meaning as it is with real-life nudity. And it is capable of stretching so as to accommodate the fiction of essence: an essence which is not in fact there but which phallogocentrism preserves by displacing it.

One might ask, at this point, how this is any different from our implicit belief in essence as an absent ideality, which I argue above is an underlying feature of all signification. Isn't the substitution of a fetish more or less what happens in the formation of the gestalt image that is the trace/*objet petit a*, which covers over the workings of the symbolic? If I would classify the professor's procedure as more problematic than that, it is because he also makes use of phallogocentrism's second avenue of escape. This is the hope to still lift the veil, to resolve the mystery, to pin down essence after all – "investigating the woman, demystifying her mystery" (22), as Mulvey has it. This, I would suggest, is what we see in I.5 when the professor indulges in a fantasy of violence and male domination: "who thus at all this marvelling but will press on hotly to see the vaulting feminine libido of those interbranching ogham sex upandinsweeps sternly controlled and easily repersuaded by the uniform matteroffactness of a meandering male fist?" (123.7–10). Referred back to the letter, the promise of control is one of finally making sense, of cracking the code and delivering one uniform, matter-of-fact reading. The professor's question makes it clear that such reduction and demystification is achieved through violence, specifically the "male fist." In short, this is phallogocentrism bearing down on femininity, subjugating it.

In this view, the professor can hardly be said to partake in the standard mode of fetishism I analyze above, in which a certain occultation protects us from the ever-changing network of the symbolic becoming too distractingly transparent. The professor's predilection for stern control and uniform matter-of-factness aligns him with a project of misogynist and phallogocentric mastery that is fascinated by transparency – while shying away from the complexities that transparency ends up revealing. Very little separates the professor's approach from how all meaning-production directs itself towards something that is not there. As we will see in Chapter 2, anxiety in signification is all about the double nature of the *objet petit a*: causing both the impulse to control and the impulse to idealize from a distance. Following this pattern, however, we need not cast the image or idea of the woman as the manifestation of *objet petit a* (here, I distance myself from middle Lacan, who does just that). Nor do we have to adopt the professor's logocentrism, which never veers from taking the desired essence as *given*, if only as a distant prospect of stern control or as a suggestion of so very much more. I.5 makes clear what the cost of this belief is. The professor is so busy listing factoids that he never really confronts what he encounters in the letter: distortion, uncertainty, omission, mobility, absence.

There is one telling moment, however, in which he lets slip that he is aware this is what he *would* encounter if he were to really look. "Closer inspection of the *bordereau* would reveal a multiplicity of personalities inflicted on the documents or document" (107.23–5). If one were to look closely, that is, the letter would complicate its authorship as well as its very unity as one document. This would raise questions as to its origin and as to the univocality of its meaning. But that is as may be. "In fact, under the closed eyes of the inspectors the traits featuring the *chiaroscuro* coalesce [...] in one stable somebody" (107.28–30). At this point, where transparency would reveal the absence of essence, the professor, rather than complicating matters, chooses to produce an impression of stable identity by recommending those inspecting the letter close their eyes. We therefore need to consider the likely possibility that the professor's exegesis is far from doing justice to its subject matter, that it runs counter to the significance of ALP's letter, trying to pin down something whose productivity lies in absenting and pluralizing itself, and that Joyce is not asking us to imitate this examination or align ourselves with its assumptions, but to understand its shortcomings.

Joyce signals the failure of the professor's strategy. The materiality of Joyce's text undercuts the professor's discussion, demonstrating how the very aspect he urges us to focus on can subvert his project of keeping the enigma of language at a safe distance. Consider the following passage, from the chapter's closing section, which describes the origin of several holes that perforate the letter: "they ad bîn "provoked" ay Λ fork, of a grave Brofèsor; àth é's Brèak – fast – table;; acùtely profèššionally *piquéd*, to = introdùce a notion of time [ùpon à plane (?) sù' 'fàc'e'] by pùnct! ingh oles (sic) in iSpace?!" (124.8–12). Here, as with non-words in general, Joyce stages the instability of the signifier by distorting it at the level of its material carrier: precisely the level that, in the professor's view, should protect us from any disturbance to sound sense. Where the self-identity of words should be most evident – in the factuality of their material inscription – both the surface of the letter and the typography of Joyce's text have been distorted by violent lashes of the fork/pen that give us only the enigmatic materiality of a ruined inscription, of non-words.

Even as we try to grasp it by means of only the soundest method, focusing on the facts of materiality, ALP's letter slips away. Its materiality itself is shaped in such a way as to suggest that what is hidden beneath is not – and never has been – the pure essence of meaning. The letter thus potentially provokes our frustration; yet its elusiveness becomes important precisely at the point at which we give in to the desire to read nonetheless. Insofar as ALP's letter can be seen as standing for *Finnegans Wake* as well as for the signifier in general, both the letter's perforation described in this passage and the distorted inscription of the passage itself point towards the perilous nature of the act of reading, alerting us to how this act proceeds by filling in the gaps and holes that threaten to derail it. As van Boheemen-Saaf puts it, *Finnegans Wake*

> "litters" the letter of representation, smearing the signifier with the darkness of non-meaning, non-differentiation and obscenity (an intention staged *in* the text as the pricking of holes in the letter, burying it in a dungheap, staining it with tea, etc.), as if to give a *location* and presence to the non-figurability of discursive trauma. But Joyce's text also *possesses* and *owns* this location. The text not only attempts to stage the impasse from which it originates, it claims to inhabit its point of trauma; and it is marked by a jubilant self-consciousness.
>
> (158)

Barring us from traveling smoothly over silences and breakdowns of meaning – from intuitively proceeding from referentiality to reference without paying heed to that process's abyssal undecidability – Joyce's text undermines signification, yet also preserves it, subjects it to scrutiny, and makes it into a temptation. These operations are irreconcilable with the professor's project of covering up language's shameful impurity.

The professor's pedantry and condescension, moreover, make him a likely candidate for an incarnation of Shaun, who seems to reprise this role when, in I.6, he lectures on "The Mookse and The Gripes" (152.15). There, a speaker designated as "Jones" (149.10) – which in the pairing of the twins suggests John/Shaun, as opposed to James/Seamus/Shem – ventures that "my explanations here are probably above your understandings" (152.4–5). Upon delivering the tale of the Mookse and the Gripes, he then delights in the fact "that I am a mouth's more deserving case by genius" (159.26). In the next chapter, I discuss the problems posed by Shaun's rhetoric, by his taste for superiority and control, and by his disdain for his brother Shem. On the basis of these attributes, I propose to read Shaun as implicated in phallogocentrism. If Shaun's/the professor's investigation in I.5 associates him with the phallocentric view of femininity as truth, we will see that his discourse on Shem's writing betrays a logocentric belief in the availability of essential meaning.

The challenge of *Finnegans Wake* is to a significant extent based on its rejection of the phallogocentric striving for decency and clarity. Whereas the Shaun-type professor would cover up the indecent way in which essence absents itself, the text in which the professor's account is presented draws attention to the void at the heart of language. More radically than most texts, the *Wake* challenges us to confront and affirm this void: to keep in mind that actual meaning is not the given, self-evident alternative to what is not there. The latter line of thought would return us to belief in essential meaning, reappearing in the guise of sensible pragmatism. Actual meaning, instead, is produced in the act of interpretation. And in the case of the *Wake*, actual meaning includes the meaning of a signification that should not even be taking place: the signification of non-words.

This impossible yet persistent signification invites us to accept actual meaning *as* non-essential – a demand that can be associated with Shem the Penman. Joyce opposes Shem's role as the writer-figure to Shaun's fetishizing of clarity, visibility, and the materiality of the signifier's surface. In the following chapter, I show that in his artistic production, Shem readily embraces the source of uncertainty and failure. In Shem the Penman and the chapter known as "Shem the Penman," the *Wake* can be seen to illustrate an anti-logocentric attitude: to tolerate that in language which exceeds control, indeed to inhabit it.

2 The Penman and the Critic

Excessive Denial of Excess

I now want to turn to Shaun's counterpart, Shem. Shem is the penman to Shaun's professor and postman, thus arguably representing the position of the writer. He also persistently subverts Shaun's phallogocentric perspective. Since I argue in Chapter 1 that the *Wake* demonstrates the shortcomings of Shaun's hermeneutics, I should add that Shem's strategies do not contrast Shaun's position with a "correct" agenda – an endeavor that could only reduplicate logocentrism. Rather, Joyce allows the same perils and anxieties to encroach on the role of reader *and* writer, in a manner that complicates their distinction.

In the first part of this chapter, I discuss section I.7. of *Finnegans Wake*, known as "Shem the Penman." I.7 is a curious entry in the corpus of Joyce's writing about literary creation and his own task as an author. The entirety of "Shem the Penman," bar a brief dialogue at the end, is a marathon tirade in which a Shaun-type narrator vilifies Shem. There is a transgressive quality to the fierceness of this rant. It is suspiciously relentless and markedly repellent. From the start, Shaun's attack raises questions about its own validity and purpose. From the first paragraph on, the narrator admits to what may well be libel, openly stating that he is "Putting truth and untruth together" (169.8–9). He flaunts a self-congratulatory attitude, sneering at Shem's cheap diet, which is largely based on canned goods ("So low was he that he preferred Gibsen's tea-time salmon tinned, as inexpensive as pleasing," 170.26–7), and poking fun at Shem's status as a social pariah ("he had been toed out of all the schicker families," 181.3–4). Disapproving remarks about Shem's appearance, manners, and views are thrown in everywhere for good measure. All of this raises the question why Shaun's attack on Shem is given such prominence in the text – that is, what this chapter conveys other than the twins' enmity, which is presented in more intricate fashion in other parts of the book.

My suggestion is that I.7 is in part about clashing models of signification. To explore this aspect of Shaun's outburst, it does not suffice to gloss his various insults. A different approach is needed if we are to understand the chapter's inquiry into the positions of reader and writer. We need to take into consideration the *distress* that manifests itself in the vehemence with which Shaun is making, or indeed not making, his point. Through his forcefulness, Shaun, despite himself, is drawn into a mode of expression that is governed by irrationality and chaos. I will read Shaun's distress with a view to what I have introduced as the *anxiety of language* – though we will presently see that I am taking some liberties in my usage of "anxiety" when I apply it to the indecent structure of meaning. The heuristic gain for which I include this term in my argument is not psychoanalytic description but hermeneutic mapping. The defining contrast between Shem and Shaun that emerges in this respect is not a conflict between such categories as Shem's madness or weakness and Shaun's rationality or severity. Instead, the chasm that divides them is Shem's acceptance and Shaun's denial of an anxiety-inducing process neither of them can evade.

Take the scene in chapter II.2 in which the brothers solve a geometry problem as part of their homework. If Joyce's punning on Shem's name throughout the *Wake* indicates that he can be identified with shame and with non-essential (sham) meaning, this section demonstrates Shem's own acceptance of that which he cannot understand and which therefore constitutes a shameful distortion of phallogocentric certainty. Here is the task the twins have to solve: "Problem ye ferst, construct ann aquilittoral dryankle Probe loom!" (286.19–20). Given that the equilateral triangle is the *Wake*'s siglum for Anna Livia ("ann"), this geometrical construction is yet another instance of the phallogocentric logic that equates ALP's nudity with truth. Shaun, who here appears as Kev, is unable to solve the problem: "Oikkont, ken you, ninny? asks Kev" (286.26–7). He subsequently appeals to Shem: "Oc, tell it to oui, do, Sem!" (286.30). In the process of explaining the solution to his brother (the diagram on page 293), Shem, appearing as Dolph, also draws ALP's genitalia, or illustrates how Shaun could get a look at ALP naked: "we carefully, if she pleats, lift by her seam [...] the maidsapron of our A.L.P. [...] And this is what you'll say. [...] plain for you now, [...] the no niggard spot of her safety vulve, first of all usquiluteral threeingles" (297.7–27). When Shem unveils ALP's nudity, what he reveals is the site of symbolic castration. It is a locus of Shaun's lack of knowledge (of anatomical knowledge/ of the answer to the geometry problem), and thus a locus that even as it formalizes and apparently controls Shaun's defeat also confirms this defeat.

The situation is analogous to how ALP's letter confronts the professor with the presence of the unknown. And like the Shaun-type professor, Shaun in the homework scene responds to the real thing with abjection. As the upholder of the phallogocentric view, he promptly displays the appropriate castration anxiety, which he enacts in the form of aggressiveness against Shem. In a phrase that echoes the scene of Cain's murder of Abel in Genesis – "And Cain was very wroth" (Gen. 4.5; all references to the Bible are to the Authorized King James Version) – we read: "And Kev was wreathed with his pother" (303.15). Shem, by contrast, does not appear to be agitated by ALP's otherness. This does not change the fact that the scene is conveyed from a male perspective that conceives of femininity as difference and mystery. But within this phallocentric framework, Shem's reaction does not follow the lines of logocentric reasoning. What is unveiled to the twins is, to them, otherness; yet Shem shows no desire to censure the presence of the unknown, to deny it, or cover it up with a fetish. Hence his untypical role in this scene as both Abel and the more able of the two brothers (Shem typically being identified with the wrongdoing of Cain): the one who can do the task at hand and suffers his brother's wrath for it.

I propose to read Shem's success with the geometry problem as an example of his ability to endorse alterity: an ability that sharply separates him from Shaun's anxious need for certainty and control. In I.7, that need reveals itself to be connected to language. The accusations Shaun levels against his brother tell us something about Shaun's own ideas about what language should do. If Shem's discourse does not meet Shaun's standards, then from the content of Shaun's criticism, we can surmise that these standards revolve around decency, discipline, purity, and hard-edged clarity. By contrast, Shem's output is disparaged as being intrusive ("unsolicited testimony," 173.30), full of mistakes ("all the different foreign parts of speech he misused," 173.35–6), unintelligible ("his usylessly unreadable Blue Book of Eccles," 179.26–7), sloppy ("every splurge on the vellum he blundered," 179.30–1), offensive ("nameless shamelessness," 182.14), chaotic ("messes of mottage," 183.22–3), or plain repellent ("obscene matter," 185.30).

Throughout, this lowness of discourse is linked to the circumstances of Shem's life – the position of the outsider who lives in a ruined house, eats poor food, works surrounded by litter, and writes on his own skin for lack of paper. Littering is fused to impure writing in Shaun's description of Shem's house, "known as the haunted inkbottle" (182.30–1). In Shem's workshop, "The warped flooring of the lair and soundconducting walls thereof, to say nothing of the uprights and imposts, were persianly literatured" (183.8–10). The very surfaces of the house are littered with literature: written all over in patterns reminiscent of a Persian carpet. Here, we also encounter the chapter's most infamous image, that of Shem's own body serving as "the only foolscap available" (185.35–6), on which he writes with ink made from his own excrement. To Shaun, Shem's habits thus ultimately betray a disorder: a "pseudostylic shamiana" (181.36–182.1). There is some psychological realism to this conflation of exteriority and interiority. Patrick Moran points out that "Shem's living area, which has become unlivable because of his failure to discard seemingly valueless objects, closely resembles the spaces created by compulsive hoarders" (285). That Shaun's narration aligns this behavior with Shem's writing suggests a permeability at multiple levels: an interaction between

Shem's mental space, his embodied social and material situation, and his literary output. With regard to Shaun's statement that Shem is "writing the mystery of himsel in furniture" (184.9–10) – that Shem's surroundings are formed or altered by his writing of his self – Moran comments that, in turn, "Shem's selfhood is inscribed in or understood through the associative networks of the hoarded objects that surround him" (299). Shem not only expresses himself through his creative process, he is also defined by this process – indeed the writing Shem produces *leaves its mark on him*, psychologically and physically.

Yet if Shaun wishes to dismiss Shem's practice on the basis of its transgressive characteristics, Shaun's discourse gets caught up in its own form of manic behavior. There is a self-defeating side to his performance, which begins by stating, in the very first paragraph, that its target's "back life will not stand being written about in black and white" (169.7–8), and which then proceeds to engage with that life for what adds up to the better part of twenty pages. Shaun appears to repeatedly postpone the moment when his point will finally have been made. He propels himself forward with exclamations such as "Aint that swell, hey?" (171.29), "Be that as it may" (182.4), and "O, by the way, yes, another thing occurs to me" (190.10). Although he wishes to defend a discursive ideal based on clarity and reason, his own outburst thus has him pile up accusations in a frantic manner that betrays nothing if not his own lack of control. The more this excessiveness fashions Shaun's condemnation of Shem for not being the polite, coherent, and comprehensible writer Shaun implicitly posits as the model of that role, the more it becomes apparent that Shaun's own narrative falls massively short of these attributes. My proposition is that this contradiction is not incidental, but should be read as part of Joyce's portrayal of what I refer to as the anxiety of language. Before continuing my reading of "Shem the Penman," I will therefore clarify how I use this term.

The Anxiety of Language

"Anxiety" is an expression borrowed from Lacan, but intended to tap into Lacan's topology of intelligibility and distortion more than to convey any particular affective state – without abandoning the thought that Lacan's approach can tell us something about why a confrontation with certain texts (including Joyce's and, at a different level, Shem's) can be an unnerving experience. Anxiety is the experience of an impasse and an increase in intensity: an incessant back-and-forth or a frantic circling around something the subject can neither grasp nor turn their back on, something they have as little power to resolve as to abandon.

The notion of a lack of power is already part of how Freud defines the term. In *Inhibitions, Symptoms and Anxiety*, he revises his earlier analysis of anxiety as pent-up libido and suggests instead that anxiety is an expectation of helplessness. What brings about the shift from realistic anxiety to neurotic anxiety (the latter being what psychoanalysis concerns itself with) is a "displacement of the anxiety-reaction from its origin in the situation of helplessness to an expectation of that situation" (167). That is, anxiety is less a confrontation with something that renders the subject helpless than it is an unspecified but intense *dreading* of such a confrontation: neurotic anxiety, writes Freud "is anxiety about an unknown danger" (165). In other words, anxiety "has a quality of *indefiniteness and lack of object*" (165).

Lacan's account of anxiety is a reworking of this theory that inverts its main point. Emphasizing the failure to control the object through codification, Lacan links anxiety to "the essential object which isn't an object any longer, but this something faced with which all words cease and all categories fail, the object of anxiety *par excellence*" (*S II* 164). The non-object of anxiety makes its presence felt all too strongly. This heralds a difference between Freud and Lacan that is more fully developed in Lacan's seminar on anxiety. Whereas Freud stipulates that fear has an object but anxiety does not, Lacan asserts that "*anxiety is not without an object*" (*S X* 131). Anxiety, in Lacan, is the experience of the real's imperviousness not as an inertia, but as a force that makes itself known, that intrudes into our codifications and confronts us with "the function of lack" (131). Anxiety's non-object, then, is the lacking object: the *objet petit a*, and thus the same as the object of desire. After all, the desired symbolic core is also an absence that *eludes* symbolic negotiation and appropriation. Anxiety is the result of one's becoming aware that the core is absent. It is a sudden confrontation with the incompleteness of one's means of codification. As Lacan puts it, the "sudden emergence of lack in a positive form is the source of anxiety" (*S X* 61). This is to say that anxiety results when the *objet petit a* actually asserts itself, when, as Evans writes, "something appears in the place of this object" (12), so that *objet petit a* is no longer a desirable absence but an intrusive presence.

I will clarify in a moment how this paradoxical transformation comes about. First, I want to add that the gap in signification, which switches from formative attractor to distortive interruption, affects not only reading (and listening) but also writing (and speaking). In *Writing and Difference*, Derrida describes "the anguish of writing" (9), which in the original reads: "l'angoisse de l'écriture" (*L'écriture* 18), employing the very term that English translations of Lacan render as "anxiety." Though Derrida is not using "angoisse" in the psychoanalytic sense given to it by Lacan, this is more than a mere similarity of terminology. There is a congruence here of arguments about codification and its failure. Derrida proceeds to link the "anguish of writing" both to the limited powers of speech and to the corporeal narrowness of its apparatus: "the necessarily restricted passageway of speech against which all possible meanings push each other, preventing each other's emergence" (9). That is, once we *realize* that our powers of speech cannot control the throng multitude of meanings, this realization can become the Lacanian "lack in a positive form," which interferes with speaking (or writing), preventing the emergence of words confidently spoken.

Indeed, Derrida's image of a narrow passageway in which anxious speech chokes on itself resembles Lacan's suggestion that a silent scream, a scream that gets stuck in your throat, is a corporeal manifestation of the *objet petit a* (Lacan makes this comparison in the unpublished Seminar XII, *Problèmes cruciaux pour la psychanalyse*). A silent scream marks a point at which the breakdown of the symbolic order is so complete that you cannot express this breakdown, not even by way of an inarticulate exclamation. Your pre-emptive awareness that no expression will capture your meaning is too strong – and so is your awareness that no expression will capture that failure. You are locked into silence as a result of the realization, as Lacan puts it, that "Saying it all is literally impossible: words fail" ("Television" 3). This failure does not constitute an outer limit of what can be said: the real as opposed to such truth as can be calmly and safely spoken. Lacan immediately adds that "it's through this very impossibility that the truth *holds onto* the real" (3, my emphasis). The impossibility of safe emergence structures language as an inner limit, marking, as it were, the innermost truth of what we speak. Hence our hesitation, our correcting ourselves, our over-compensation. Compare this to Shaun's language in I.7, which endlessly adds to itself in an effort to be over and done with its subject. Shaun's frantic rush for control and the suffocating silence described by Lacan and Derrida, I venture, are the same thing: the attempt to say *only* what you want to say, but say that *fully*. For whether you use many words or few, you will come up against the impossibility of saying precisely what you meant to say. Again Derrida: "Speaking frightens me because, by never saying enough, I also say too much" (*Writing* 9).

What I term the anxiety of language is thus a nagging awareness that something about language is interfering with our control. We can look at this interference from the Lacanian point of view and call it an irruption of the real. We can equally well describe it from the Derridean point of view as signification's all too limited power over the changeability of its effects. Here, it is worth reiterating a point I make in Chapter 1, since it concerns an element in my reading of Derrida diametrically opposed to an idea which has gained wide acceptance. The received opinion has it that Derrida's work can be summed up in a statement he never made: that there is nothing outside of the text. It is all up for grabs, it is all interpretation and instability, therefore Derrida's thought remains blissfully untroubled by anything that might actually center interpretation. Žižek is an example of the considerable platform that has been given to this reading; in the Introduction, I have already cited his verdict that deconstruction "[dissolves] the substantial identity into a network of non-substantial, differential relations" (*Sublime* 78). Such an emphasis on relational and contextual (i.e. spatial) networks, however, pays insufficient attention to the temporal aspect of différance: the negotiation of origins.

The problem posed by differentiation is not one of absolutely free play, but of the organization of play around a gestalt image of stability. This is why Derrida speaks of a "hesitation between writing as decentering and writing as an affirmation of play" (*Writing* 297). If there is hesitation here between two things, it is because play and decentering are not the same. In fact, the play of language relies on effects of *centering*. For Derrida, there would be no anxiety of language if one could simply "affirm the nonreferral to the center" (297) – such a nonreferral, of course, being exactly what Derrida is frequently taken to be advocating. Nor would there be any anxiety if there was a center outside play, a center that "closes off the play which it opens up and makes possible" (279): an origin outside différance. What causes anxiety is the necessity of negotiating some stability *within* play: "anxiety [the French text again has "l'angoisse," 410] is invariably the result of a certain mode of being implicated in the game, of being caught by the game, of being as it were at stake in the game from the outset" (279).

This implication takes place by way of the trace, which as I show in Chapter 1 resembles nothing so much as Lacan's *objet petit a*. Žižek writes that the *objet petit a* "stands simultaneously for the imaginary fantasmatic lure/screen and for that which this lure is obfuscating, for the Void behind the lure" (*Parallax* 304). The trace combines the same properties: it is the fictional origin that orients ("lures") the play of language, providing signification with a trajectory towards a phantasmatic goal. Being phantasmatic, however, the trace also withdraws from signification's play; it thus constitutes the point at which signification comes up against its own breakdown. I would furthermore suggest that in both Derrida and Lacan, anxiety is the result of a shift from considering the former aspect to considering the latter: from essence absenting itself to the confrontation with the absence, from *objet petit a* as an absence to *objet petit a* as a presence, from the trace as the projection of essence to a contemplation of the trace-structure revealing that essence does not exist.

The anxiety of language, then, is the flipside of the desire for meaning. That signification is hardly a matter of pinpointing essences is a problem precisely insofar as we desire essence. This is not to suppose we conceptualize essential meaning as given or obtainable. Rather, it is to make sense of a strange oscillation whereby, even though the desire for essence is of course continually frustrated, we reintroduce the phantasmatic point of this desire's fulfillment as soon as we set out to construct another reading that is on topic, relevant, rigorous, or otherwise *approaching* the notion of correctness. In the topology of desire and anxiety, "essence" is precariously suspended between providing a reference point for interpretation and revealing this reference point as illusory. In Lacan, the *objet petit a* is the object of desire, the promise of a desirable but absent essence; yet from a different point of view, *objet petit a* is the object of anxiety, the making-present of essence's impossibility (lack in a positive form). In Derrida, the trace is a projection, both in the sense of a reference point that is being projected and in the sense of a process of projecting that, when examined, reveals the reference point's fictional nature.

Either of these effects can catalyze the other. When desire takes us too close to the source, threatening to reveal its imperfect nature, anxiety may kick in. And when anxiety threatens to become dominant, it may have us withdraw to a distance from which desire is once again possible. Lacan asks: "But what does experience teach us here about anxiety in its relation to the object of desire, if not simply that prohibition is temptation?" (*S X* 54). That which must be avoided is also that which continues to hold our attention in thrall. The model of anxiety thus helps us understand why Shaun's reactions to Shem's writing (discussed above) and to ALP's letter (discussed in Chapter 1), as well as our own reaction to Joyce's non-words, are potentially caught up in an oscillation in which desire and distortion are not so much opposed to one another as edging each other on. Since the object of anxiety and the object of desire are the same thing, the result is a double movement that wavers between, on the one hand, dissociating itself from language's shameful impurities, covering them up or simply passing over them, and on the other hand, toiling to keep these impurities in check, studying their fault-lines ever more closely in the hope to still find them surmountable obstacles on a path to essence. In short, the movement of anxiety resembles that of the moth which, in the "Circe" chapter of *Ulysses*, circles the chandelier, "colliding, escaping" (15.2042), repulsed at one moment, drawn back at the next. The *Wake* combines these motions into a "collideorscape" (143.28), linking the kaleidoscopic production of images to an uneasy fusion of opposed forces.

The topology of the Janus-faced object even writes the script of signifying processes that remain untouched by anxiety in the sense of an affect. Consider the following four cases: (1) Some writers and readers will refuse to interrogate their own approach, happy to assume they got every detail right. I would suggest that even in these cases of desire seemingly satisfied, meaning functions as an object of anxiety. Precisely where this approach seems furthest from any anxious back-and-forth, it most trusts its results and is therefore most threatened by their constructedness. This is the no-nonsense reader curtly telling you that his reading, after all, is objective – a position which anxiously patches over the threat of signification's imperfection. (2) A related but more extreme case are indifferent or cynical participants in a debate who genuinely do not care whether they have made sense of a signifying gesture or whether their signifying gesture makes sense. Their untroubled attitude is the direct result of their not caring about an answer. If meaning fails to be an object of desire, it is by the same token not an object of anxiety. (3) Some processes of reading or writing advance with great scrupulousness so as to be done with wavering. Even where methodical and patient (as opposed to obsessive and obviously anxious), such processes can be mapped onto the topology of anxiety, since their precision gives rise to an ever-more refined understanding of the absence of essence, and thus of the necessity to keep going. In their very attempt to overcome uncertainty, these processes lock themselves into a potentially endless addition and/or retraction of meanings. (4) There are, finally, forms of writing and reading that are neither overly bold nor overly cautious, but competent and productive. They yield neither to haste nor to unending differentiation, but respond to the text in careful and meaningful ways. Are these, then, the forms of reading and writing that do away with anxiety?

I suggest that we may instead describe these cases as proceeding right *through* anxiety. As the above instances indicate, any strategy that would resolve anxiety ends up reproducing anxiety. Lacan comments: "Anxiety is not doubt, anxiety is the cause of doubt" (S X 76). That is, our agitation in proximity to the *objet petit a* is not an uncertainty or doubt, it rather constitutes the certainty we most want to avoid: that the working of the symbolic order has been upset, that some element of the real is messing with symbolic appropriation. It is when we try to turn *away* from this certainty (when we try to resolve anxiety) that we give rise to any number of doubts: whether and how the symbolic might be reconstituted after all, what interpretation or course of action would achieve this, whether an envisioned way of phrasing or doing things is useful, and so on. Any such consideration will have us dwell further on the real's interference, which is how anxiety reproduces itself, locking us in its characteristic hyperactive paralysis. By contrast, Lacan continues, "To act is to snatch from anxiety its certainty" (77). We escape the deadlock of anxiety through a *decision*, which partakes in the certainty of the real precisely insofar as a decision interrupts symbolic deliberation. "The truly original creative act for Lacan is an event outside discourse: it cannot be rehearsed or repeated, accounted for or translated" (Thurston, *James Joyce* 83). Lacan's reasoning here closely corresponds to Derrida's argument that any true decision proceeds through the aporia of an undecidability (see Derrida, "Force of Law"). This does not mean that decisions are random, but that reading or writing involve a kind of *leap of faith* which decides on a meaning that, though rendered possible by the signifying gestures in question, is not – cannot be! – uniquely and perfectly identified by these gestures.

In other words, your decisions are not creative acts free from all concern (there would be no anxiety if they were); instead, they make you responsible for identifying a possibility that is never completely self-evident (because essence does not exist). Going through anxiety means that you find yourself in the presence of a gesture you cannot completely fathom, and that you then nevertheless articulate a response to this presence. This, I hold, is true even of readings that make these decisions without registering them (including the instances listed above of trying to abstain from decision-making). They, too, produce meaning in response to a signifying gesture. As I argue in Chapter 1, actual meaning is always produced in the act of interpretation – and *Finnegans Wake* makes us confront that fact. As Jeremy Colangelo argues, "*Finnegans Wake* forces us to face a source of great anxiety. This anxiety lies in the reader's inescapable responsibility for their own interpretations" (75). We can now add that any such interpretation announces itself in defiance of self-perpetuating calculation. It does not wait to be granted permission. Rather, as I will now show, in taking a leap of faith, the production of meaning tries to retrospectively establish its own legitimacy, showing itself to be based on what the writer did. Yet if I have argued so far that a reader cannot secure univocal clarity, describing signification in the register of desire and anxiety will suggest that neither can a writer.

The Peril of Writing

As a starting point, consider that a writer's search for ever more precise formulations performs the potentially unending back-and-forth of an anxious deadlock, which cannot escape the fact that the more we say, the more we open ourselves up to runaway meanings and to possibilities of being misunderstood. Nor can this effect be evaded by means of writing less or writing more boldly. Any simplification, where it reserves the right to retain some core meaning seemingly stripped of misleading complexity, already constitutes a return to the anxious striving for minimal precision. Whether through rigor or haste, *denying* uncertainty precipitates anxiety in a self-defeating manner. This, as we have seen, is Shaun's problem.

Shaun's attack on Shem is a desperate struggle for control over an unreadable presence. To Shaun, Shem's writing is an unbearable distortion, it is the "positive form" of everything about language that Shaun's phallogocentric position holds in abjection. In other words, Shem's literary output fulfills for Shaun the function of something appearing in the place of the *objet petit a*. By circling around this object with morbid fascination, Shaun's attack stages the logic of an anxiety that, in reacting to the point where the symbolic breaks down, proves unable to quite undo or get over this breakdown. As we have seen, a reaction may instead succeed in tapping into that breakdown itself (the real at the core of signification). But in Shaun's case, the response is an increasingly violent reproduction of anxiety. If Shaun demands control, clarity, precision, and so on, his struggle comes to demonstrate the impossibility of these demands. Which is also to say that Shaun serves not simply as the creative figure's passive counterpart. In generating a discourse about Shem, Shaun, too, takes on the role of an author. The loss of control to which he falls prey in this role contributes to I.7's investigation into the creative process.

We should therefore pay more attention to Shaun's rage than is usually the case in interpretations of I.7. Perhaps the most commonly found strategy in approaching this chapter is to read it as a prolonged instance of irony in which Joyce, although he speaks through Shaun, also speaks against Shaun and remains at a distance from him (to be identified instead with Shem). Interpretations thus dissociate Joyce from Shaun's flawed discourse, with the result that we do not take seriously that discourse or its flaws. This problem is especially tangible in examinations of I.7's sources, since among these, hostile reactions to Joyce's work (with which the initiated reader of Joyce can be expected to disagree) figure large. With regard to such material, there is a tradition of biographical contextualization which can be subsumed under Tindall's verdict that "Shaun embodies all disapproval of Joyce" (132). The fascinating notion of Joyce speaking through Shaun – that Shaun's voice is how Joyce chooses to present his account of the writer at work – is thus narrowed to an approach that only hears Joyce speaking against Shaun. For instance, having shown that many of Shaun's points are parodies of negative remarks made about Joyce's writing by contemporary critics, Ingeborg Landuyt proposes that "The result of Joyce's accumulations is a quite recognizable description and condemnation of his person and his methods as seen through the eyes of his critics that simultaneously should be read as his defense" (159). I fully subscribe to the proposition that "Shem the Penman" is a portrayal of Joyce, and that it constitutes a defense of his art. Yet the phrase "as seen through the eyes of his critics" puts a problematic spin on things. It posits that in defending Joyce's take on writing, "Shem the Penman" portrays that take from what amounts to a second-hand and second-rate perspective. A focus on Joyce's irony in I.7 thus draws our attention away from what Joyce himself is saying about writing, since a reading of I.7 as ironic defines the chapter's scope in terms of the opinions that are the targets of Joyce's irony.

By exclusively identifying Joyce with Shem, and Shaun with Joyce's critics, we end up assuming that Shaun's outburst has little to offer beyond a confrontation between Joyce and his detractors. Dismissing Shaun's aggressiveness, we get ahead of ourselves. We keep Shaun's excess at a distance, and thus we effectively reproduce his anxious mode of reading which bars him (and us) from perceiving that Shem's (and Shaun's) writing may enact something about the *inevitability* of writing's excess. At the level of this enactment, Shaun's viciousness and eagerness are no longer opposed to Joyce's own position; they can be seen to put this position into practice.

I will now turn to what provokes Shaun's anger in the first place: Shem's writing. This writing appears to be a manifestation of complete introversion. In its very materiality, it remains with Shem and around him, surrounding him as an inscription on the walls of his house, on his furniture, and on his own body. It thus forms what would appear to be the private archive of a private mania. Given that this literary output does not reach the public sphere – does not, in fact, reach a single reader other than Shem himself – we may again ask why Shem's writing provokes

Shaun's venom as much as it does. Part of the answer may be found in a self-contradiction Shaun produces when he accuses Shem of harboring the intention to "study with stolen fruit how cutely to copy all their various styles of signature so as one day to utter an epical forged cheque on the public for his own private profit" (181.14–17). One page further on, Shaun adds the question: "how very many piously forged palimpsests slipped in the first place by this morbid process from his pelagiarist pen?" (182.2–3). What is striking is that these misdemeanors, forgery and plagiarism, are necessarily public. Neither plagiarism nor forgery are of any consequence unless the perpetrator convinces a sufficient number of people of an object's authenticity (forgery) or of the perpetrator's claim to having produced it (plagiarism). On the one hand, we are thus given a depiction of Shem's writing that has him remain within his own four walls to scribble over every available surface, including parts of his own body. On the other hand, we are presented with the image of him producing cheques and documents to get them into circulation. And although these are not mutually exclusive activities, as descriptions of what is wrong with Shem's literary activity, they do appear to be conflicting. Is his writing too private, too withdrawn, too idiosyncratic? Or is it too public, too predatory, too invasive?

The crucial move in aligning these two images is to relate them to Shaun's phallogocentric outlook. In both descriptions, Shem can be seen to violate notions of essence and authority. Shaun's understanding of a writer's role, to which he unfavorably compares his brother, casts the artist as the sole origin of a work which at no point of the creative process is outside its maker's express command. When referred to such an understanding of the artist, the two accusations made against Shem, plagiarism/forgery and introspective obsession, cease to conflict and take on the form of complementary images for Shem's readiness to be transformed both by the discourses he produces and by those that come to him from elsewhere. Which is to say: the problem, for Shaun, is Shem's readiness to surrender control. Shem's thefts and borderline insanity cast the artist's activity as neither an imperious expression of selfhood, nor an annunciation guided by objective truth, but as ongoing, productive, and dangerous negotiation. Shem is not the sole origin of his own discourse. Yet if his words are never truly his own, it is not because he derives them from some store of long-perfected expression, either. Consider the passage that describes Shem using "his own individual person" (186.3) in order to describe life in general, forging his personal experience "into a dividual chaos" (186.4–5). In the movement that leads from the undividable self of the writer as subject or "individual" to the written expression of their views, this expression becomes "dividual": divisible, divided from itself. Being expressed, it enters iterability and is divided from its ideal essence. We could say that in the process of writing, as in the process of reading, there is straying from purpose, a structurally necessary element of this process's inadequacy to itself.

In this view, Shem's out-of-control writing method can be seen to exemplify that the act of writing exceeds any settled knowledge, that it can only ever set things down by newly negotiating them. Shem's mode of production closely corresponds to a point Derrida makes in *Writing and Difference*:

> To write is to know that what has not yet been produced within literality has no other dwelling place, does not await us as prescription in some *topos ouranios* or some divine understanding. Meaning must await being said or written in order to inhabit itself.
>
> (11)

Meaning is not produced through activation of some already given understanding, but through a confrontation with what in Chapter 1 I describe as the real kernel of language's productivity. Writing, to proceed at all, has to risk failure. Shem's work exemplifies this confrontation and this risk. Like the Derridean or Lacanian subject, Shem is not so much a wielder of language as he is wielded by it. This destabilizes not only his literary output, but also his own self. For discourse belongs "to the Other: in other words, it is drastically at odds with the ego's urge to achieve final semantic self-appropriation" (Thurston, *James Joyce* 94). Indeed, Shem is deeply and dangerously involved in his literary production, to the extent of being transformed by it. His surroundings come to resemble his mental state, as out-of-control bits of language are inscribed on his living space and his body. He writes and he is written upon. His split between active and passive attitudes is rendered as the image of a body serving as ink as well as paper. He is the writer and the written, as his physical self extends into writing both in the sense of the inscription that applies ink and in the sense of the document that receives ink. In short, Shem's mode of writing as described in Shaun's account shows us both the danger and the productivity of affirming the sinthome as a nexus of unreadability and active formation. By abandoning himself to the aspects of language that go beyond Shaun's anxious notions of control, Shem fashions a discourse, but he fashions it by destabilizing and renegotiating both the symbolic and the self. This is the re-knotting of the sinthome, the decision-making that goes right through anxiety.

This practice resembles not only Joyce's own affirmation of the sinthome, but more generally the descriptions many artists give of some electrifying moment in their creative process when they no longer know what they will do next, when they break out of the ordinary by abandoning knowledge – and courting failure. Insofar as Shem can be identified with Joyce in particular, Shem's enmeshment in language corresponds perhaps most intimately to Joyce's use of non-words, through which Joyce's writing undergoes a demonstrative break with the notion of setting down controlled, undistorted meaning. The rampant borrowing that takes place in Joyce's networks of allusions "destroys the traditional oppositions of true/false, owned/stolen, and so on, and dislocates the eidetic model where a text's meaning would be guaranteed through an author's animating intention or will" (Mahon 349). By writing in a manner that does not try to limit the straying of language, to evade it or find a reasonably secure spot within it, but that instead puts the straying to artistic use, Joyce, like Shem, undercuts notions of the author as a figure of control.

Finnegans Wake would thus appear to perform the only way out of the deadlock of anxiety: namely, to acknowledge the non-existence of essential meaning and to make the Shem-type wager that writing can be at its most powerful and most productive where it most embraces risk and instability. Yet, crucially, not even this solution can evade the anxiety of language. It can merely decide to inhabit anxiety. The hermeneutic shift that Joyce demands of us is not one from an anxious denial of distortion to an anxiety-free acceptance of it, but rather one towards an acceptance of anxiety itself, if there can be such a thing. I argue, above and in Chapter 1, that no negotiation, no analysis, no signifying gesture of any kind can get underway without entrusting itself to the fictional ideal of essential meaning. In order to produce any text at all, a Shem-type sacrifice of mastery has to be breached by a Shaun-type desire for expression. Which is to say that in Shem's mode of literary production, the anxiety displayed by Shaun already has to be at work.

The binary opposition between Shem and Shaun is thus complicated by an element of correspondence and interdependence. Here, I take my cue from Finn Fordham, who suggests that "Joyce's characters can be seen to embody principles of the various processes of writing and rewriting" (*Lots of Fun* 217), and that

> Shaun's attack on Shem is partly Joyce's self-critique, objectifying the self that criticizes and reformulates his very writing, according to opposing principles. Artists are the first critics of their own work. Self-judgement which predicts criticism may be a painful part of the creative process. The opposition of Shem and Shaun is a means for producing the identity of opposites in the work, something produced by revision, and a correlative for auto-critique.
>
> (221)

I would emphasize, however, that we cannot imagine this process of dialectical opposition as one freely at the writer's disposal. Auto-critique – Shem taking on attributes of Shaun, being drawn into the task of communication – does not result from a sovereign decision to anticipate and debate one's future critics. It is a structurally necessary result of *all* signification's phantasmatic relationship to essence. Nor does auto-critique end when all predicted objections have been taken into account. It is precisely by attempting to exhaust all possible problems that auto-critique indefinitely rekindles itself, as the object of desire – some envisioned act of communication – becomes the object of too close scrutiny (Shaun's anxious corrections now reproducing Shem's lack of control). If the framework of writing projects the ideal of absolute precision, and if absolute precision can never be achieved, then writing will inevitably bring into play both the positions of Shaun (desire as desire for specific effects, anxiety as a struggle for control) and Shem (desire as productive affirmation of risk, anxiety as the confrontation with the void). Auto-critique, the dialogue between these two positions, necessarily accompanies writing; it cannot end before writing ends.

In particular, this dialogue cannot exhaust itself by reaching a constellation in which one of these impulses would finally dominate the other or in which the two would somehow cancel each other out. As soon as we feel a Shaun-type sense of mastery, a Shem-type lack of control insinuates itself (our freedom is curtailed as we say too much and/or not enough); as soon as we engage in the Shem-type encounter with the void, a Shaun-type communicative project, perhaps even longing for clarity, is at work in the background (unless we are proceeding in bad faith). The process of writing, although it is necessarily interrupted at some point by external means, and although it proceeds by combining Shem-type and Shaun-type impulses, cannot therefore be interrupted by that which would put an end to the need for revision: completely dividing Shem-type from Shaun-type impulses, using one to overcome the other, or else finding a balance between them that would lay to rest the productiveness of their difference.

Short of these options, writing remains, as the *Wake* puts it: "That letter selfpenned to one's other, that neverperfect everplanned" (489.33–4). Writing is an ongoing process that continues to fall short of its perfect form, and that therefore continues to divide the one who undertakes it, pitching them against their other. The motif of the twins' inseparability balances that of their conflict throughout the *Wake*, though not in the mode of a neat fusion. They are combined in ways that preserve some contrast between them, for instance in the amalgamation of a tree or "stem" (216.3, Shem) and a "stone" (216.4, Shaun) into Tristan: "a Treestone with one Ysold" (113.19). The dialogue at the end of I.7 similarly demonstrates the impossibility of thinking the twins in the singular – thinking either one on his own, or both in one pair that would neutralize splits and multiplicities. The chapter's concluding section introduces them as "JUSTIUS (to himother)" (187.24) and "MERCIUS (of hisself)" (193.31). It thus creates a mixture between a sense of speaking to the other and speaking to oneself, it refers each to the other, and performs a substitution and distribution that splits the word "himself" in half. There is no stable outcome, as the pronouns' suspension between identity, exchangeability, and separation indicates. Mercius says that "the days of youyouth are evermixed mimine" (194.4), yet there remains "a convulsionary sense of not having been or being all that I might have been or you meant to becoming" (193.35–6). As each is divided from his ideal self and mixed with the other, the result is not synthesis, but longing, lack, and tension.

Regarding another reiteration of the biblical fratricide motif, "And each was wrought with his other" (252.14), Roy Benjamin points out that, "By combining the murderous rage of Cain towards Abel (and Cain was wroth with his brother) with the synthesis of each with the other, Joyce suggest a never-ending oscillation between conflict and resolution" (218). In this view, the true peril of the writer's position expresses itself in the fact that Shem cannot be imagined on his own, diametrically opposed to or absolutely identical with his brother Shaun. He is instead caught in the Lacanian "paradoxical topology of self and other" (Thurston, *James Joyce* 119). The one always depends on the other, and this co-dependence means that neither of the twins' identities is ever truly settled.

I would argue that this is also how we should understand Derrida's footnote in "Plato's Pharmacy," in which he speaks of "the whole of that essay, as will quickly become apparent, being itself nothing but a reading of *Finnegans Wake*" (88 n.20). The probable referent for "that essay," when we consider the footnote in isolation, is a text by Bataille mentioned earlier in the note. In "Two Words For Joyce," however, Derrida infamously suggests that "that essay" could be read as referring to "Plato's Pharmacy" itself. Discussions of this suggestion frequently point to its willful imposition of meaning on an earlier text, yet just as frequently they pass over the explanation Derrida gives for his strange claim. In "Two Words For Joyce," he continues by stating that it is "between Shem and Shaun, between the penman and the postman," that *Finnegans Wake* stages "the whole scene of the *pharmakos*, the *pharmakon*" (28). Derrida is not speaking, then, of "Plato's Pharmacy" being a reading of *Finnegans Wake* in any general sense. He is concerned with a very precise point: the twins' interdependence as Joyce's expression of the mixing of opposites – a theme which is taken up in "Plato's Pharmacy" when Derrida argues we cannot neatly distinguish opposites that inhabit the same gesture. As with the meanings of Greek "pharmakon," Shem and Shaun depict the impossibility of separating "the medicine from the poison, the good from the evil, the true from the false, the inside from the outside, the vital from the mortal, the first from the second, etc." ("Plato's Pharmacy" 169).

Derrida thus links his own analysis of the heterogeneity at work in identity (pharmakon/pharmakon) to the *Wake*'s insistence that it is impossible to separate Shem/Shaun. Joyce's text, in turn, unambiguously identifies Shem and Shaun as penman and postman, making it clear that what is at stake in their inseparability is the relation between reader and writer. When we engage the numerous moments in the *Wake* at which the twins clash, exchange places, overlap, or collapse into a split identity, we should not lose sight of the fact that they are assigned these roles: creator and carrier, writer and reader. These characterizations mean that the twins' perilous co-dependence, which is never quite a synthesis, is the *Wake*'s representation of a mutability and reciprocity that afflict the activities of reading and writing.

Shem and Shaun: Oscillations

If Shem is a writer and Shaun a carrier or interpreter of words, but each of them tends to imply the presence of the other, this complicates the ideal of an author masterfully orchestrating their work. To make one more reference to *Writing and Difference*: "The 'subject' of writing does not exist if we mean by that some sovereign solitude of the author. [...] Within that scene, on that stage, the punctual simplicity of the classical subject is not to be found" (226–7). Instead, writing is from the outset caught up in the struggle between "the author who reads" (227), who reads what they write in an attempt to anticipate and control interpretation, and "the first reader who dictates" (227), this being the author as reader, a construct that nonetheless has the power, by hitting upon unforeseen effects, to interfere with what should have been a unilateral writing process. In this interference, the ideal writer, solitary and sovereign, disappears from sight together with the ideal written. We are left with a process of pre-emptive negotiation that always remains dangerous, in the sense that this process will tend to wrench the writer from whatever they originally thought their purpose was (before they thought about it by writing about it). We could say that as soon as writing is begun, it turns from the setting down of a single subject's thoughts into a negotiation between several perspectives: a negotiation fraught with all the risks that iterability introduces. The writer is already a reader, and writing is thus a process that takes place in the absence of essence, insofar as the writer, in their role as reader, cannot *fully* comprehend what their writing means.

In trying to make sense of this complication of the roles of writer and reader, I will now draw on the concept of *dictation* as discussed by Derrida. In *The Post Card*, Derrida explores the roles of source and exegete by discussing the image reproduced on the eponymous postcard, which shows a thirteenth-century illumination of Plato and Socrates by an artist called Matthew Paris. The depiction seemingly presents the philosophers in a reversal of their customary roles. In Paris's illustration, Socrates is portrayed as "the one who writes – seated, bent over, a scribe or docile copyist," and thus appearing as "Plato's secretary" (9). Plato, on the other hand, is shown standing behind Socrates, with his finger raised in a manner that makes him look "like he is indicating something, designating, showing the way or giving an order – or dictating, authoritarian, masterly, imperious" (10). Derrida suggests that this inversion, which threatens to undo chronology and hierarchy, can be seen as a paradoxical illustration of the fact that we know Socrates' philosophy from the writings of Plato. For this means precisely that Plato is not the scribe, but the one who dictates. Plato "has made him [Socrates] write whatever he [Plato] wanted while pretending to receive it from him" (12, and

90   The Penman and the Critic

see 146). Plato can effectively be understood to *ventriloquize* his teacher. I take this term from "Literature in Secret," where Derrida comments on a section in Kafka's *Letter to His Father* in which Kafka imagines and sets down his father's possible response. Derrida asks:

> What does this spectral father say to Franz Kafka, to his son who makes him speak like this, *as a ventriloquist*, at the end of his *Letter to His Father*, lending him his voice or allowing him to speak but at the same time dictating what he says, making him write a letter to his son in response to his own, as a sort of fiction within the fiction?
> (134, my emphasis)

The point here is not that the Socrates we know from Plato's writings may be a fiction. It is rather to investigate the attributes such a fiction possesses: attributes that are of interest because Plato's (imagined and perhaps imaginary) method is a model for any number of interactions with the past, including the acts of reading and of writing an interpretation. In creating his dialogues, Plato would appear to be setting down what he wants, and bestowing authority on it by claiming to have received it from an authoritative source. Yet this maneuver changes nothing about the fact that the authority in question remains with Socrates. If Plato's writing can partake in this authority, it is because, nominally, Plato receives the text from Socrates – a claim that destabilizes identities on *both* sides. In this scenario, Plato's dialogues would give their author a certain freedom to reinvent Socrates, to efface him and take his place. Yet this freedom comes at the price of Plato being in turn effaced by his invention, supplanted by the fiction whose voice we hear in the dialogues. Plato, Derrida writes, "has succeeded, moreover, by inventing Socrates for his own glory, in permitting himself to be somewhat eclipsed by his character" (49). The inventor is eclipsed by their invention. The fictional character, once invented, makes demands that must be fulfilled if the creation is to have any credibility. Far from possessing unrestricted control over the ensuing dialogue, the ventriloquist has to *speak in character* if the act of ventriloquism is to make its proper impression.

Like Joyce's Shem and Shaun, Derrida's Socrates and Plato thus illustrate that the roles of writer and reader cannot be neatly detached from one another. The link is pointed out by Derrida, who speaks of "Shaun, John *the postman*" and "The writer, Shem" as "Another fraternal couple" that can be added to his own: "Shem/Shaun, S/p" (142). This, although maximally condensed, seems to me a decisive clue to Derrida's thinking about the *Wake*. Like Shem and Shaun, Socrates and Plato become impossible to separate: "S. is part of p. who is but a piece in S." (132). Also like Shem and Shaun, this does not make them parts of a synthesis. "They are each a part of the other but not of the whole" (132). And they are as impossible to put in any kind of order (chronological, hierarchical, etc.) as the two sides of a postcard: "What I prefer, about post cards, is that one does not know what is in front or what is in back, [...] the Plato or the Socrates, recto or verso. Nor what is the most important, the picture or the text, [...] reversibility unleashes itself, goes mad" (13).

This should not be taken to mean that we can simply reverse the positions of reader and writer as they are conventionally understood. Reversibility is not activated once, or any precise number of times, either rotating the reader into the place previously occupied by the writer, and vice versa, or else returning everything to the original state. As reversibility goes mad, it troubles the very division between reader and writer. Not by making them interchangeable, either, but by making them interdependent, as each role contains aspects of the other. The author is struggling with an inexhaustible series of self-readings, which wield a power of dictation insofar as self-reading may uncover unforeseen possibilities, that is, interpretations the writing gives rise to without having intended to do so. The reader, in turn, cannot hope to produce meaning without making decisions of their own. If they do not want to abandon the text altogether, then the only option they are left with is that of speaking in character: of speaking in a manner that aims to do justice to the text even as one is aware that what is said nevertheless originates with the interpretation.

Far from viewing interpretation as arbitrary, this approach argues that the blurring of Socrates and Plato, of Shem and Shaun, results in a destabilization of identities on both sides such that it can become *genuinely difficult* to locate where the voice of a given interpretation is coming from. It can become difficult even for the one producing the interpretation. For interpretation, like any creative process, can produce unexpected results and divide itself from what its originator intended it to be. In the attempt to remain in character, the writer of an interpretation will therefore scan their output from the reverse angle. This writer, too, is already their own first reader and therefore subject to the effects of ventriloquism – hearing the voice of the interpreted author in what is in fact the writing of the interpreting author, and hearing this voice in the very reading that would test the authenticity of what is being said. The question of authentic and authoritative interpretation is thus transported away from the *accessing* of an authority already given somewhere (Socrates unilaterally dictating to Plato, having complete mastery over the situation, or Plato unilaterally dictating to Socrates, completely usurping the father-figure) towards a *negotiation* of authority (Plato dictating to Socrates, but speaking in character by already taking Socrates' voice into consideration, and thus also taking dictation from Socrates in turn).

This returns us to Shaun the Postman with a new appreciation of his role as the reader who would preserve a message in unchanged form, but who cannot avoid being drawn into Shem-type excesses. Our focus is shifting to an ever more initial moment in Shaun's defeat: before he can formulate a reaction to Shem, already at the point at which he reads Shem's writing, Shaun is partaking in a production that refutes purity.

As a reader, he himself produces meaning, he ventriloquizes, he hears his own speech or reads his own writing, baffled by its perverse mode of fidelity to Shem's text and its infidelity to Shaun's own maxim of absolute fidelity. Here, I draw on a reading by Andrew Mitchell, who links Shaun's plight to the function of quotation marks or of packaging that would allow the enclosed material to be transported without being altered. Mitchell writes:

> To bear a message and establish order: these are the roles of Shaun the Post, and he is those quotation marks. Their problem is his problem. Each attempts to contain postality and yet maintain separation, to envelope it and limit the extent of its effect.
>
> (149)

If "Throughout the text and especially in book III, Shaun is a mediator" (149), serving, for instance, as the postman who carries ALP's letter, this position is ultimately an impossible one, for any attempt to bridge a distance brings into play iterability and puts into question the idea of absolute fidelity, of noise-free transmission, of transporting meaning without affecting it. Mitchell argues that, to the extent to which Shaun can be identified with this impossible task, the letter he carries "is a rift in his being that divides him from himself, and it distances him from himself by interrupting his identity with himself" (149). This can be detected in the phrase "to isolate i from my multiple Mes" (410.12), which is pronounced by Shaun in the context of complaining about his task: "I am now becoming about fed up be going circulating about" (410.7), "since it came into my hands I am hopeless off course" (410.17–18). Yet in the end, nothing would be delivered, and Shaun could not inhabit the role of a carrier of messages, if such a division did not successfully wrench him from his own project: a project that in the radical form he envisions for it could only mean immobility, inertia, the ceasing of transportation.

Shaun's inevitable failure not only interrupts postal delivery (or communication more generally speaking) in the sense of the means by which one attempts to *access* a certain authoritative meaning. The split that divides Shaun from himself and introduces a Shem-type activity into postal delivery can be seen to threaten the very principle of a message's self-identity. If Shaun-type purity is impossible, and a mixture of Shem-type and Shaun-type processes informs every step along the way, then this merging threatens the very idea that meaning could *ever* be given in an initial and authoritative form – whether for reader or writer, for author, postman, or anyone else.

Consider that ALP's letter is repeatedly described as having been dictated to Shem. We read of the "Letter, carried of Shaun, son of Hek, written of Shem, brother of Shaun, uttered for Alp, mother of Shem, for Hek, father of Shaun" (420.17–19). And elsewhere: "The gist is the gist of Shaum but the hand is the hand of Sameas" (483.3–4). The letter, then, is not the work of one voice alone. Having been dictated by ALP, its writing appears to have required Shem's/Seamus's assistance, with contributions to its "gist" from either Shaun or Shem himself ("Shaum" being another example of the difficulty of distinguishing between the two, seeing how one is nearly the same as – "Sameas" – the other). In view of the above argument that the one who takes dictation is simultaneously the one who can dictate, this means that Shem's creative process, with all its implications regarding the lack of total control, impacts ALP's letter. The letter's purity is in question not only at the level of its being read, but also at the more constitutive level of its writing. This is also how I would read I.5's finding that the author of the letter is "possibly ambidextrous" (107.10–11). The presence of two hands might indicate two writers or two sides of the same writer – either possibility entails a split that distances the letter from anything like a masterful, self-sufficient source. Or, as Shari Benstock comments:

> The letter's content is not only influenced by the woman who dictates it, but by the son who pens it and the son who posts it; its message is full of gaps and uncertainties, at times is partially or wholly obliterated, is badly transcribed, is written in foreign languages, and is addressed to someone other than its recipient. The letter's route from writer to reader is circuitous, ambiguous, uncharted.
>
> ("Letter of the Law" 169)

Uncertainties flow into one another. Just as Shaun cannot be neatly distinguished from Shem, the question of a message's transportation is entangled with that of its doubtful nature and its creation. In the remainder of this chapter, I will argue that the problems of interpretation, interpretative authority, and writing are interrelated in the *Wake* in such a way as to suggest that authoritative meaning is not something pre-existing that waits to be accessed, but is negotiated in an interaction between reader and writer. To begin to explore this topic, I now turn to a scene that directly links the question of authority to Shaun's task as a messenger.

The Name of the Father

At the beginning of chapter III.3, Shaun acts in the role of "a medium at a séance channelling the voice of HCE" (Mitchell 149): that is, the voice of the ghost of the father. The un-deadness of HCE is, of course, a central motif of *Finnegans Wake*. The book's very title brings to mind Tim Finnegan's return from the dead as described in the ballad "Finnegan's Wake." As early as the first chapter, HCE turns into a version of Finnegan when he refuses demands to stay dead. "Now be aisy, good Mr Finnimore, sir. And take your laysure like a god on pension and don't be walking abroad" (24.16–17). "Drop in your tracks, babe! Be not unrested!"

(26.16–17). "Repose you now! Finn no more!" (28.33–4). The rise of the repressed, the lost, and even the dead is thus established as a theme from the outset (detectable also in the "wake" of the book's title, when read as a verb). It is important to note, however, that in the séance taking place in III.3, HCE does not fully return. His presence is conjured up, but it remains phantasmatic; like the "spectral father" of Kafka's letter, he is allowed to speak only by merging his voice with that of his son.

The séance begins with Shaun being either asleep, unconscious, or in a trance: "Yawn in a semiswoon lay awailing" (474.11). While he is in this state, the "four claymen clomb together to hold their sworn starchamber quiry on him" (475.18–19), directing questions at Shaun to which Shaun responds by channeling a number of different voices. The first thing to note about the ensuing exchange is that it features HCE as "this *Totem Fulcrum Est Ancestor*" (481.4–5). That is to say, HCE appears as the prehistoric father from Sigmund Freud's *Totem and Taboo*. The presence of Freud's book in *Finnegans Wake* has been variously commented on, for instance by Brivic (see *Joyce Between* 207, *Joyce Through* 165) and Rabaté (see "A Clown's Inquest" 98). But emphasis is typically given to the motif of patricide, and not to the other gruesome act featuring in Freud's narrative. Here is the relevant passage from *Totem and Taboo*:

> One day the brothers who had been driven out came together, killed and devoured their father and so made an end of the patriarchal horde. United, they had the courage to do and succeed in doing what would have been impossible for them individually. (Some cultural advance, perhaps, command over some new weapon, had given them a sense of superior strength). Cannibal savages as they were, it goes without saying that they devoured their victim as well as killing him. The violent primal father had doubtless been the feared and envied model of each one of the company of brothers: and in the act of devouring him they accomplished their identification with him, and each one of them acquired a portion of his strength.
>
> (141–2)

In *Cannibal Joyce*, Thomas Jackson Rice points out that there are numerous references in *Finnegans Wake* to HCE being eaten that can be linked to "the Freudian patricidal paradigm" (24). A darkly humorous one occurs in chapter I.1, where it appears that the mourners at HCE's/Tim Finnegan's/Humpty Dumpty's wake are served Humpty Dumpty (eggs) for breakfast, sunny side up: "And even if Humpty shell fall frumpty times as awkward again in the beardsboosoloom of all our grand remonstrancers there'll be iggs for the brekkers come to mournhim, sunny side up with care" (12.12–15). The trial scene in I.3 similarly conflates HCE as foodstuff with HCE as man (French: "homme") in the remark that if "you wish to ave some homelette, [...] Your hegg he must break himself" (59.30–2). The question in I.6 that is looking for the answer "Finn MacCool!" (139.14) includes among the characteristics of this avatar of HCE that he represents a complete set of meals: "is Breakfates, Lunger, Diener and Souper" (131.4). Finally, when the customers leave HCE's pub towards the end of II.3, they tell him: "We could ate you, par Buccas, and imbabe through you" (378.2–3). These references to cannibalism are significant because they transport Joyce's evocation of *Totem and Taboo* away from a straightforward motif of violence, towards Freud's more complex concern with the sons' assimilation of the father's power.

Freud's narrative is designed to accommodate a highly ambiguous attitude towards the father on the part of the murdering horde. Freud writes: "After they had got rid of him, had satisfied their hatred and had put into effect their wish to identify themselves with him, the affection which had all this time been pushed under was bound to make itself felt" (143). If the killing itself results from hatred, its subsequent interpretation as an act that must never be repeated – a codification Freud holds to be a founding moment of guilt, the law, and culture itself (see 159) – is the result of a resurfacing of more positive feelings. The retroactive judgement that declares the killing a crime and that bestows guilt on those who committed it is based on an impulse of wishing the deed undone: an impulse tied to a shift in the perception of the father. As Freud has it: "their longing for him increased; and it became possible for an ideal to emerge which embodied the unlimited power of the primal father" (148). Freud ventures that it is for this reason that "The dead father became stronger than the living one had been" (143) – more admired, feared, and eventually worshipped.

If we now turn to HCE's summoning in III.3, we find hints at a similar appropriation of the father's strength: an appropriation that even as it destroys the father establishes his all-powerful phantom. References to the killing can be found from the beginning of the scene onwards, for instance in the exclamation: "The cubs are after me, it zeebs, the whole totem pack" (480.30–1). It is with a view to this hostility, and the history Freud imposes on it, that I would read the question: "His producers are they not his consumers?" (497.1–2). This is sometimes taken as a self-aware comment on Joyce's part about the co-operative relationship between him and his audience. Although I would not want to deny the pertinence of this reading (and note the intriguing phrase "The author, in fact, was mardred," 517.11, that follows later in the séance), it also puts strain on the text by having it proceed from what is arguably the less obvious term (the producers: the readers as active participants) to the more intuitive, seemingly tautological term (the readers as consumers). As a question asked of *Totem and Taboo*, by contrast, it runs: "those who have created the idol or totem of the father, are they not those who *ate* the father in the first place?" This reading, in turn, gives a different inflection to a phrase that appears on the facing page: "you may identify yourself with the him in you" (496.25–6). If the "in" points to the psychological inside of internalization and identification, it also points to the physical inside of imbibing.

Freud's hypotheses about an elevation through assimilation of the father should thus be kept in mind when we read the séance's discussion of HCE. For instance, HCE's development "from the human historic brute, Finnsen Faynean, occeanyclived, to this same vulganized hillsir from yours" (481.12–14) resonates with the transformation of Freud's father-figure. Finn's/HCE's trajectory from human bully to natural phenomenon (volcano, hill) or god (Vulcan) resembles the idolization and naturalization that take place in *Totem and Taboo* and that cast the dead father in the role of a god, totem animal, etc. A few lines further down, we encounter a statement that engages in a similar dialogue with Freud's text: "That is a tiptip tim oldy faher now the man I go in fear of, Tommy Terracotta, and he could be all your and my das" (481.31–3). The figure who can appear in such sublime manifestations as a mountain, a god of fire, or King Midas ("my das"), the larger-than-life father one goes in fear of and who stands in a paternal function to everyone ("all your and my das"), is precisely the HCE who is no longer there, who has perhaps been killed and consumed and who, at any rate, is speaking at this point only through the medium of his son Shaun.

We can compare Joyce's rendering of Freud's myth to Lacan's interpretation of *Totem and Taboo*. Here is Lacan, writing in *Écrits* that Freud's investigation of authority

> led him to tie the appearance of the signifier of the Father, as author of the Law, to death – indeed, to the killing of the Father – thus showing that, if this murder is the fertile moment of the debt by which the subject binds himself for life to the Law, the symbolic Father, insofar as he signifies this Law, is truly the dead Father.
>
> ("On a Question" 464)

The father elevated to the position of absolute authority, Freud says, is the father no longer present. However, Lacan adds a twist: inverting the Freudian logic that proceeds from death to signification, Lacan ventures that in order for the absence of the father to allow for his return as a personification of the law, he need not actually be killed; it suffices that he be *named*. If "It is in the *name of the father* that we must recognize the basis of the symbolic function which, since the dawn of historical time, has identified his person with the figure of the law" ("Function and Field" 230), it is because naming, too, amounts to the removal necessary for subsequent idealization. In a no doubt unduly literal, but nevertheless illustrative reading of Lacan, we could imagine the occurrence of one of the first words in human language as the naming of the father in a prehistoric group or horde. If one of the members of this group sees the father and makes a sound, the sound is not a name, but an undifferentiated call attracting attention. It is a name only if another member, or the same member at another time, repeats the sound (repeats it in memory of one of them having seen the father and having made the sound) – or anticipates the possibility of repeating the sound in this function. What gives a name, then, is not the presence of the father but the possibility of a sound becoming a name by *recalling itself*, which is to say precisely by imagining not a presence ("here and now is the father") but an absence ("let me preserve this presence in a sound"). As Lacan puts it elsewhere: "the being of language is the nonbeing of objects" ("Direction" 524).

Here, I trail the line of another overlap of Lacan's work with Derrida's, for whom the absence typically attributed to writing already organizes speech, and for whom the proper name is by no means excluded from the dynamics of iterability and différance. Derrida writes that "the proper name was never possible except through its functioning within a classification and therefore within a system of differences" (*Of Grammatology* 109). On this basis, Derrida, too, associates the name with death. If your proper name is an iterable signifier, then it is not fully *yours* and not fully your *proper* name: "The name is made to do without the life of the bearer, and is therefore always somewhat the name of someone dead" (*Post Card* 39). Rabaté summarizes the Lacanian/Derridean thought: "the father is not, for all that, a presence embodying the legitimate succession. Language is a system of differences, a power of death and absence in which he too is caught up" ("A Clown's Inquest" 83). The *mortification* of the father, we might say, is not literal patricide; it consists in the father's entering a symbolic order in which he will inevitably fall short of the ideal that can henceforth be signified. Intrinsic to the name of the father is the idea that no-one quite succeeds in being its legitimate bearer.

This ideality of the name is what makes Lacan's analysis of paternal authority interesting to a discussion of the *Wake*. Drawing on the Lacanian concept, MacCabe points out that "the split between bearer and name is made absolute in *Finnegans Wake* as the father becomes the simple permutation of a set of letters" (142) – HCE. This is not necessarily to say that Joyce anticipates Lacan's reading of *Totem and Taboo*. It is to argue that *Finnegans Wake* stages a general disparity between naming and identity, and that both this disparity and HCE's Freudian cameo in III.3 are among the aspects of the text that indicate that for Joyce, the status of paternal authority is far from unproblematic, insofar as the very presence of the father is in question in various ways. Evoked through linguistic patterns, symbolic functions, and various substitutable avatars, the *Wake*'s father-figure is less a fictional character than a manifestation of fictionality itself, of what it means to be structured by fictions: "entiringly as he continues highly-fictional" (261.17–18) – e.c.h. More symbolic constellation than actual character and "more mob than man" (261.21–2), HCE is the abstract, over-individual concept of the father. At the same time, he is each one of the *Wake*'s individual father-figures who fall short of that concept. That is to say, he is each instance in which the fictionality of the correspondence between concept and individual reveals itself.

This last aspect can be read in correlation with the central theme of HCE's guilt. Chapter I.2 first introduces us to the mysterious events in Phoenix Park or "the people's park" (33.27), different versions of which are found all through the *Wake*. The descriptions vary with regard to the precise circumstances of the events, but one recurrent motif is the accusation, levelled against HCE, "of annoying Welsh fusiliers" (33.26–7) and/or "of having behaved with ongentilmensky immodus opposite a pair of dainty maidservants" (34.18–19) Since these are key motifs of *Finnegans Wake*, much could be said about the nature of HCE's deed, its repercussions throughout the text, and the conflicting information we are given about it. I will touch on the significance of HCE's culpability in Chapter 4; for the time being, I simply want to suggest that this narrative serves to undermine his role as quintessential father-figure (if by "quintessential" we mean the conventional idealization). Whether the story of the events in the park constitutes the true account of HCE's crime or the slanderous mode of his being made a scapegoat, in either case it shatters his identification with pristine symbolic authority. This, too, aligns him in significant ways with the fictional nature of paternal authority as Freud and Lacan conceptualize it. In Joyce as well as in Freud and Lacan, we find that the father's actual presence, far from lending to authority the full weight of unquestionable immediacy, effectively interferes with the ideality in whose image the father would like to appear. Ideality is more closely allied with absence, with the horde's longing for someone no longer present, with the possibilities of mythification and signification.

If the *Wake* can thus be seen to *oppose* paternal authority to the father, this is also a variation on a theme first sounded in *Ulysses*. There, Stephen Dedalus famously remarks that "Paternity may be a legal fiction" (9.844). If, as Stephen suggests, "Fatherhood, in the sense of conscious begetting, is unknown to man" (9.837–8), then there is no intrinsic (biological) truth to the (symbolic and legal) role of the father. Maud Ellmann comments, "It is only through the 'legal fiction' of the *name* that he can reclaim his dubious paternity" (92, my emphasis). Or, as Lacan phrases this: "the function of *being a father* is absolutely unthinkable in human experience without the category of the signifier" (*S III* 292). HCE, too, can be read as such a legal fiction. He is a name from which a certain symbolic role and authority are derived, but at the same time, he illustrates the fact that this role is more than the individual bearer of the name (in HCE's case, either a pitiful scapegoat or a sexual predator) authentically embodies. In the individual, we only ever meet an imperfect representative of the authority that ultimately resides in the name.

Based on my account of the peril of writing, I now want to argue that this contrast between fictional ideals and empirically present authority figures can be brought to bear on the role of the author. I should immediately address a possible misunderstanding of this proposition. If actual authors fall short of the power and control attributed to an idealization of the role of the writer, this should by no means lead us to believe that they do not enjoy any authority at all, that reading simply operates outside considerations of doing justice to sources and origins. If the law resides not in an empirical person but in the possibility of attaching to that person a name and a role – if paternity may be a legal fiction – then what is crucial is the fusion of the expressions "legal" and "fiction." The *OED* defines "legal fiction" as "an assumption of the truth of something, though unproven or unfounded, for legal purposes." In other words, a legal fiction takes a construct and *makes it binding*.

To argue the fictional nature of authority is not the same as saying that such authority is unimportant; it is to consider the efficacy and binding nature of something construed. Nor is constructed authority an arbitrary imposition: a fake, pure and simple. Fictions, in this view, are not there for us to unmask them so as to penetrate to the level of truth. Although we may challenge them and transform them, there is in a crucial sense nothing beneath the kind of fictions we are concerned with here – nothing supporting the fiction of authority, and the authority of fiction, but fiction itself. *That which is constructed is not discountable.* Do away with all that is constructed, and you do away with the symbolic order itself (and thus with reality as we know it). Therefore, to speak of authority as constructed or fictional is decidedly *not* to say that it falls short of being serious. In the following discussion on the construction of authoritative meaning, I want to keep in mind Freud's proposition that a construct – a specter – can become much more powerful than an actual presence could ever hope to be.

Spectral Authority

In "Ulysses Gramophone," Derrida links authority in interpretation to paternal authority when he speaks of the "filiation" mechanism at work in *Ulysses* (a concept that is applicable to *Finnegans Wake* as well): "The filiation machine – legitimate or illegitimate – is functioning well, is ready for anything, to domesticate, to circumscribe or circumvent everything" (70). Domesticating anything and everything: this is not to argue the banal and largely meaningless possibility of declaring legitimate even such filiations/interpretations as are known to be anything but that. It is to maintain the much more fundamental difficulty of knowing legitimate from illegitimate filiation/interpretation in the first place.

Derrida's position echoes Stephen's radical skepticism with regard to paternity. Michael Naas ventures: "as Joyce [...] once said and Derrida often cited, even 'paternity is a legal fiction,' which means, I take it, that it is the effect of discourse, of *logos*" (*Derrida From* 46). Stephen demotes biological fathering; it is through a legal/symbolic discourse that fatherhood is bestowed. This means, as we have seen above, that authority inheres not in the father but in a name. If no individual can make an absolutely legitimate claim to paternity, if that relation resides in a name, then we cannot make any distinction between legitimacy and illegitimacy without drawing on discursive effects. Naas goes on to cite Derrida: "it is precisely *logos* that enables us to perceive and investigate something like paternity" ("Plato's Pharmacy" 80). I don't take Derrida to be abandoning the concept of paternity here, or to be considering its functions any less important and binding. To put it simply: Derrida should not be cited by the defense in a paternity suit – on the contrary, according to Derrida, anyone named a father has the responsibility of that role thrust upon them. It is a discursive effect that gives us the *one* concept of paternity we can have. I cite these considerations because I hold that interpretative authority is constructed in much the same way. Like paternity as thought by Derrida and Stephen, by *Totem and Taboo*, and by Lacan – where the father "has never been the father except in the mythology of the son" (*S VII* 177) – authority in interpretation is fictional, without therefore being discountable. The fiction of authority gives us the only possible concept of authority.

We may undertake the Shaun-type gesture of trying to preserve an author's meaning unchanged, of trying to access the authoritative position directly. Yet in doing so, we find that such an articulation of authority is impossible. There is no mode of speaking that remains undistorted by iterability and ventriloquism; whenever it is consulted, authority's pronouncements emerge as the result of a negotiation that already mixes and confuses positions. And beneath this dynamic of displacement, there is a mechanism at work that divides even the author from any interpretative authority in the sense of total mastery over what they produce. We have seen this illustrated in Joyce's twin producers of discourse: Shem abandons control over his output, and Shaun's response to this output promptly replicates the Shem-type chaos. This is crucial, for if there exists no absolutely authoritative position for interpretation to displace, if production itself is afflicted by imperfection, then *the uncertainty introduced by interpretation is not sharply distinguishable from the uncertainty of the production*. If Shem and Shaun merge to the extent of becoming difficult to separate, then not only can a reader not access essential meaning, but neither can they approximate essential meaning by identifying authorial meaning and thus producing what amounts to a non-essential but indubitably legitimate filiation.

Authorial meaning is not present in a text as a solid stratum, side by side with effects of illegitimate meaning from which it can be told with total certainty. From the outset, from the moment writing is taking place, an *excess* of effects is at work. If I have suggested that a writer cannot exhaustively anticipate what their writing means, it is precisely because language refuses to codify a single, authentic intention without also dividing it, wrenching it from itself, and transforming it in multiple and unpredictable ways. This is the lack of control that Shem's and Joyce's modes of writing dare to affirm. As the process of writing oscillates between Shem-type and Shaun-type impulses, it creates possibilities of meaning in such a manner that the writer can only ever control a subset of them. And even if we grant that, once this process is interrupted, the author can adopt the role of reader and have a personal understanding of the finished product (which might then be termed authorial meaning, although any formalization or communication of this understanding would again be subject to the same mechanisms), what the lack of control during the process means is that in the resulting text, effects intended or noticed by the author are not – not necessarily – distinguishable from effects not intended or noticed. As the latter type of effect is by definition not governed by any control, there is also no guarantee that effects will be fashioned in such a way as to reliably allow for distinctions between the two types.

Therefore, the plurality a reader faces is an excess of possibilities. It is not a set of well-defined interpretative options awaiting elaboration or creative recombination; its contradictory nature undoes the very concept of a discrete and self-identical interpretative option. Derrida writes that in order to read (to inherit, as he says in this context), "*one must* filter, sift, criticize, one must sort out several different possibles that inhabit the same injunction. And inhabit it in a contradictory fashion around a secret" (*Specters* 18). In other words, the reader has to make decisions in confronting a certain irreducible unreadability, secret, or uncertainty. This is what, above, I describe as going through anxiety. In doing so, an interpretative act may want to direct itself towards the absent ideality that is the trace/*objet petit a*. We can now add that *authorial meaning, far from constituting a pragmatic solution that cuts through the paradoxes of those terms, is a concept structurally analogous to them*. We call something a meaning intended by the author with reference to certain textual effects. The impossibility of distinguishing legitimate from illegitimate effects with absolute certainty, therefore, means that the author, too, is a presence constructed by our interpretative decisions. This is what Derrida refers to as the *specter* of the author. Being "beyond the opposition between presence and non-presence, actuality and inactuality, life and non-life" (13), this specter embodies authorial authority in the same paradoxical manner in which the trace embodies essential meaning. Or, conversely, "In terms of [Derrida's] later work, we can say that the trace entails a general 'spectrality'" (Bennington 93).

The trace-structure both rules out essence and conjures up the promise or dream of essence. Essence, or rather the spectral trace of essence, which presents itself as the signifier's origin, is actually produced by the movement of signification. The specter, similarly, "while always legitimated by a performative context that precedes and exceeds it, [...] always attempts to elide or conceal these origins, to present itself as self-generated, as naturally and purely given" (Naas, "The Mother" 167). In the absence of any authoritative meaning that could simply be present, we hypothesize an authorial figure which is supposed to have produced a signifying gesture's singular structure, but which is actually a substrate that we ourselves derive from the operations of that structure. The specter, that is to say, is *a modulation of our voice*: an attempt we make at speaking in character, at internalizing the other and speaking from the elusive point that is the other's position.

This, then, is the specter to which we attribute the authority to sanction some meanings as authorial. As Colangelo puts it, "a reading of *Finnegans Wake* will construct a new version of Joyce to write the text it claims to interpret" (72). Which is once again not to say that construction can go anywhere. As the imperfect merging of Shem and Shaun indicates, the reader is not simply a writer, making up their own text. Nor is the writer simply a reader, at the mercy of effects that come to them from elsewhere. Rather, "one becomes a reader only through the act of reading, meaning that one *must* create these authorities in order to be actualized through them" (73). The force of my claim to be reading fully depends on my construction of a convincing authorial specter. A reader's active production thus draws on the work of a writer who *does* exercise some control over the possibilities opened up by their work – rendering any actual interpretation a bilateral effort. Yet "one must never forget that the Joyce through which one articulates one's reading is a hypothetical figure" (74). No formula can guarantee the success of this hypothesis, and no strategy can retrospectively assess its success if by assessment we mean discriminating with absolute certainty between authentic and inauthentic material.

This is why Derrida describes *Finnegans Wake* as a linguistic performance so intricate that "everything we could say after it looks in advance like a minute self-commentary with which this work accompanies itself" ("Two Words" 27), but then contrasts this statement with the assertion that, in spite of what it may *look* like, "the new marks carry off, enlarge, and project elsewhere – one never knows where in advance – a program that appeared to constrain them, or at least watch over them" (27). Derrida is commenting on the necessity for a reading to be a response to the text, but he expresses this necessity in a defamiliarizing mode in order to emphasize the *Wake*'s proliferating spectrality. Any reading (everything we could say) has to offer itself up to be reappropriated by the authority of the text. A reading that is found to entirely evade the retrospectively identified possibility of its prediction is not a reading, but an invalid deviation from the text, unconnected to it by any identifiable correspondences. Yet the possibility of prediction is identified *retrospectively*, by the reader, in an attempt to follow the guidance of the spectral interlocutor. If such a process of retrospective identification is different from an author's unilateral command, it is not because it has become the unilateral command of the reader, but because reading and command must reciprocally construe each other. Such construction may produce results not foreseen in advance by either reader or author (thus carrying off the program), and spectral authority extends to these unforeseen results (which is why authority can look total) precisely because they are not safely distinguishable from foreseen results.

This is also to say that spectral or constructed authority is not *opposed* to some form of "proper" authority. It is the only manifestation of authority there is. Hence Derrida's reference to "the specter as possibility," which is to say, the specter as that which "will have at all times conditioned, as such, address in general" (13). There is no reading without iterability, and no iterability without the bilateral inhabiting of voices. If reading is to be possible at all, then we cannot avoid the risk intrinsic to conversing with specters. Or, to put it differently, without specters, we would never even begin to read. Try to declare a reading legitimate without engaging in any construction, and you will have to refrain from *all* iteration, thus confining yourself to silence. On the one hand, to engage with the specter of the author thus requires our ability to think outside the automatisms of processes of reading that might as well happen without any intervention on our part. Conceptualizing authority as spectral underlines our implication in the text as producers of meaning. On the other hand, the powers that specters nonetheless wield – including powers of dictation – can tell us that if the meaning thus produced is not neatly divisible into elements that partake and elements that do not partake in the authority bestowed by an authorial blessing, this does not mean that the notion of authority is abandoned. What divides our readings from authority is the *uncertainty* of their relation to it, and this uncertainty cuts both ways. It perpetuates authority in the very act of putting it into question. Like Derrida's Plato, who in inventing Socrates takes on a debt and responsibility towards the fictional father-figure, the reader who is at risk of usurping the position to be consulted is also tied to this position as the one to be iterated and interacted with.

Let me return to the example of the séance with a view to these considerations. The voice that Shaun and the four old men conjure up in III.3 is precisely the spectral appearance of HCE, who moreover appears as a Freudian father-figure in this scene: as the idealized ancestor called upon to do away with present uncertainties. HCE is speaking through Shaun, so it is Shaun who can say: "I have something inside of me talking to myself" (522.26). He has assimilated or internalized the other and is now engaging in an exchange that is no longer limited to his own voice. Yet, crucially, the origin of the phrase "I swear my gots how that I'm not meself at all" (487.17–18) cannot be decided with equal certainty. It may be Shaun informing the four that he is speaking from the position of the other, that he is channeling the voice of HCE. However, it may also be the manifestation of HCE produced by this channeling, pronouncing a warning that the channeled voice is not in fact him, that it is not his true and authentic presence. It may, finally, be both of these voices at the same time: HCE ventriloquized and ventriloquizing, HCE dictating and taking dictation. This would be the specter in the Derridean sense, caught between being an inauthentic construct and being the most authentic reference point there is.

III.3's play with voices and perspectives may convey something about the workings of the rest of *Finnegans Wake*. After, all, one of the titles given in I.5 to ALP's letter – and thus to the *Wake* – is: "Suppotes a Ventriliquorst Merries a Corpse" (105.20). The text's multiplicity of voices results from interactions that *are and are not* instances of displacement: interactions that speak for that which is not by itself a living presence, which is not in a positon to speak for itself, which will not speak at all unless it is given a ventriloquized voice. The voice of HCE, along with many others, would not emerge in III.3 without Shaun's act of ventriloquism (no manifestation would be produced without spectrality). At the same time, this act also threatens to usurp HCE's voice. But in order for the ventriloquism to draw on the authority of the other – and this is how usurpation is achieved – there has to be some discernible remnant of the position of the other left in the ventriloquized voice. Which means that there may just be enough of HCE's voice coming through for him to be able to say: "this is not me." The position of this voice, I suggest, is analogous to that of textual authority. The voice that says "I am not myself, *I* am *not I*" (and that precisely in saying this preserves the notion of an original "I" able to say this) is also the voice of the text itself. It is the voice of any text, divided from its essence and preserving the ideal of this essence as it is being iterated. But in particular, it is the voice of this text, *Finnegans Wake*, which directs this message at us with every non-word we read, with every instance of a non-word's *non-identity* with any of its readable forms.

A double bind thus emerges. The peculiar form in which *Finnegans Wake* is written catalyzes excess. It transports us even further away from unilateral authorial mastery than regular texts already are. Yet the decision to give *Finnegans Wake* this form is Joyce's. An echo of this decision, and thus a spectral remnant of Joyce's authority over his text, is inscribed in an unusually broad variety of interpretations (though by no means any and all interpretations), because it resides with the very plurality of voices and interpretations. By writing the way he does, and writing *about* writing the way he does, Joyce lends his name and his authority to the excess that does away with the purity of the single voice. Consider the complication of voices and identities in this exchange in III.3: "– Are you in your fatherick, lonely one? // – The same. Three persons" (478.28–9). Where one voice is speaking from within another, the notions of identifying and counting identities become uncertain. Sameness may turn out to involve inhabiting the position of another ("are you in"). Loneliness no longer excludes the multiplicity of several persons. Brivic comments that "III.3 is a major demonstration that the discourse of the *Wake* speaks for multitudes" ("Daughter" 256), since "the typical phrase of the *Wake* has several meanings that speak for several voices" (257).

I will argue in the following chapters that this dissemination into multiple layers of meaning is a key effect of Joyce's affirmation of excess. Even Brivic's multitude of meaning would fall short of Joyce's plurivocality if it were taken to designate a group of distinct, separable voices. Joyce's writing undercuts the self-identity of any given voice. Precisely insofar as a reading of *Finnegans Wake* attempts to read the text for what it is – for what Joyce in fact wrote – interpretation thus faces the impossibility of reducing the *Wake*'s excess to stable configurations. Yet far from serving the purposes of interpretative freedom for the sake of itself, this multiplication of meanings forms part of a much more specific gesture or program on Joyce's part. Joyce achieves an excess of expression that is both *more volatile and more powerful* than that of more conventional texts. The *Wake* thus problematizes the conventionally assumed opposition between, on the one hand, precision in language, and, on the other hand, the failure of language. In defiance of a monovalent ideal of purity, the *Wake* celebrates the richness and expressive power inherent in imperfection, in imprecision, indeed in so-called failure.

Regarding the séance in III.3, Anne Cavender notes that Shaun's discourse – or that of the specters talking through him – eschews giving any concrete answers to the questions asked by the four, and she points out that "the Four are so frustrated at their failure to come to grips with Shaun that their tempers begin to flare" (671). Cavender links this aggressiveness/anxiety to an attitude that informs both I.5's examination of ALP's letter and the four's interrogation of Shaun, driven as it is by a "desire for order and fixity" (665). The four are an example of a Shaun-type interpretative effort; yet like Shaun (who in this scene is again wrenched from his own ideal), they are confronted with the fact that their search for a fixed answer cannot accommodate the complexity of what they encounter. Their failure also throws into relief that III.3 presents us with another, arguably more successful figure of the reader. This, Cavender suggests, is the donkey that draws the four's cart and that appears in the séance as another listener or interrogator, one who "exhibits genuine sympathy for Shaun" (678) and who, Cavender argues, derives from Shaun's talk a hermeneutic pleasure that the four sacrifice in their effort to reduce Shaun to stability. Joyce's positing of such an alternative is crucial. In view of such moments in the text, we should take seriously Joyce's critique of the fetishization of clarity and his vision of different artistic and hermeneutical procedures.

This vision does not settle on either hermeneutical pleasure or hermeneutical anxiety as an absolute goal. As we will see in the next two chapters, it accepts a certain simultaneity of the two, a simultaneity that renders difficulty productive and productivity difficult. This simultaneity is not unique to the *Wake*; it is a constitutive feature of signification. What is remarkable is the *Wake*'s active embracing of this simultaneity – the text's self-deconstruction by means of non-words – as well as Joyce's insistence on making mechanisms such as anxiety, dictation, ventriloquism, and spectrality his own subject matter. It is scenes like the examination of ALP's letter, Shaun's vilification of Shem, the four's questioning of Shaun, or Shaun's channeling of HCE that make Joyce a theorist. If, in reading *Finnegans Wake*, we are to take our cue from Joyce's hermeneutics, then I believe we need to exercise caution in any appeal we make to ideas he problematizes in these scenes: decency, clarity, purity, control, or presence. This caution can only increase when we consider how Joyce's use of non-words fashions a language that pushes the excess of writing towards its uttermost potential, that reveals the ventriloquism which inhabits and activates this excess during reading, and that thus confronts us with a Shem-type text to which it is impossible to coherently apply Shaun-type distinctions between completely legitimate and completely illegitimate filiations.

The *Wake*'s meta-textuality, in combination with its non-words, calls on us to become aware of the logocentric axioms on which we base our critical enterprises whenever we equate the critic's task with the production of a knowledge that can only be monovalent. By contrast, in order to do justice to the hermeneutic agenda that Joyce pursues both in the content and the form of the *Wake*, we have to acknowledge the text's excess and its explicit break with monovalence. This is a double injunction, through which Joyce's ordering authority is paradoxically both present and not present in our manipulations of his text. The next chapter will be concerned with examining how we can conceptualize the pluralities of meaning that arise from such a double imperative.

3 Tower of Babel

The Linguistic Fall

If interpretation can be conceived of as a dialogue with the specter of the author, and if Joyce's specter partly manifests as his decision to give *Finnegans Wake* its singular form, then his authority resides with a plurality of interpretations more than with any individual reading. In this view, interpretation is not exactly denied by Joyce's unreadable text. The non-words' referentiality without reference continues to call us into the text and to tease us with the prospect of subjecting the text to a reading. Yet these readings branch out into a plurality of approaches that explore Joyce's singular creation. The present chapter examines how such pluralities are structured, and what role they play in the *Wake*'s hermeneutics.

In "Two Words for Joyce," Derrida's watchword for Joyce's strange authorial gesture is that it constitutes a "double commandment" (39). *Finnegans Wake* demands of us that we read it, but that we do so without falsifying it for the purpose of reading. "Change me – into yourself – and above all do not touch me, read and do not read, say and do not say otherwise what I have said" (34). Needless to say, such a demand (produce meaning, but without ventriloquism) cannot be met, particularly with regard to non-words. According to Derrida, the result is that interpretation is *perpetuated*, for the double bind of a double commandment eliminates the possibility of the interpretative process ever producing a reason for coming to a halt. Derrida describes his own experience in reading Joyce thus: "the endless diving in throws me back onto the bank, on the brink of another possible dip, *ad infinitum*" (26). We should be careful here not to infer from indefinite repeatability a freedom to champion whatever interpretation takes our fancy. As I will argue in more detail towards the end of this chapter, the fact that the movement of reading cannot stop does not mean that it goes everywhere, indiscriminately. What it does mean is that even careful and thorough readings, *all of which* are in violation of the double commandment, are positioned in a complex state of equivocality.

Joyce's double bind puts competing interpretations on much more of an equal footing than would be possible with a standard text. In a

DOI: 10.4324/9781003361411-4

manner so fundamental we almost stop noticing it, *all* our interpretations are off target, insofar as they refer to words Joyce did not quite write. The difficulty of divining such a reading's "degree" of imperfection, as it were, complicates the exegetical impulse to distinguish between central and peripheral meaning. It complicates this impulse – it does not undo it. With the *Wake*, we are not in a situation where all interpretations are equally acceptable or equally inacceptable. We find ourselves in a context of heightened difficulty, where attempts at sorting readings according to a *hierarchy* of their importance are troubled by the *simultaneity* of their importance. This is what inhabiting the anxiety of language means: to find in difficulty itself a precarious and unpredictable productivity. By contrast, once we conceive of Joyce's non-words as expressions that merely demand particular care in the identification of their meaning, we lose sight of the way in which the *Wake* rethinks the very connection between signification and meaning in the singular.

This rethinking informs one of the *Wake*'s recurring themes, whose importance I discuss in this chapter: the mythological motif of the loss of a once perfect language. Derrida draws our attention to the presence of this mythological register when he cites the following passage from the *Wake*: "And shall not Babel be with Lebab? And he war" (258.11–12). Derrida relates "Babel" and "he war" to the declaration of war God pronounces at Babel: "And the Lord said [...] let us go down, and there confound their language" (Gen. 11.6–7). This declaration is an "act of war which consisted in declaring" (Derrida, "Two Words" 33), insofar as the divine judgement both announces a resolution to act and also coincides with the action itself. This ultimate disruption of speech through speech provides a template for Joyce's impossible double imperative. Both condemn their addressees to haplessly negotiate the effects of a disruption articulated in an ineffable language.

The traditional reading of the biblical narrative has it that the divine act at Babel, the destruction of the tower and the dispersion of language, reaffirms original sin by punishing a transgression that results from this sin. The language confusion chastises the Babylonians for their hubris in creating a cultural work to rival divine greatness. It also confirms mankind's fallen status by confining it to a corresponding linguistic condition. The events at Babel thus complete Adam and Eve's fall into the corruption of culture, so that we can think the linguistic confusion as a *second fall* to complement the first and decisive one. In particular, the linguistic fall destroys the language Adam creates when he gives a name to each animal (see Gen. 2.19–20), an event retold in the *Wake* as Adam putting "his own nickelname on every toad, duck and herring" (506.1–2). Since each name miraculously corresponds to the essence of the named animal, the language invented in this process is ideal: it constitutes the original and immediate mode of expression to which, according to this narrative's tradition, we have been trying to return ever since it was lost at Babel. We will see, however, that this account is complicated by an alternative also presented in the biblical report.

The *Wake*'s immersion in sheer linguistic performance, which is also an immersion in evocative condensation, is occasionally likened to an attempt to press language back to the Adamic idiom. This appears to be Deane's position in his introduction to the Penguin edition, in which he comments on the "directness of communication" (ix) displayed by the *Wake*'s language. The notion that Joyce's text is charged with *direct* significance, rather than with connotations bestowed by convention, also informs approaches that think Joyce's non-words as being self-reliant without communicating anything at all – a view first expressed in Beckett's famous comment that "[Joyce's] writing is not *about* something; *it is that something itself*" (14). I would read Beckett's statement along the lines of Tim Conley's suggestion that to derive from Joyce's unreadable non-words a normalized, "semantically sensible middle text," a translation sandwiched between Joyce's writing and the reader's interpretation, is to betray "The primary text and its central negation of meaning" (244). This negation, without mediation through semantic codes, draws attention to the signifiers themselves. These readings thus construe the *Wake* as a book that rejects conventions, to rely instead on its own system of signification or non-signification.

Conley's line of argument is close to my own insistence on the difference between words and non-words. However, I would subscribe to a "negation of meaning" only if it is understood as the negation of *one* meaning, not as an inhibition to interpret at all. Here, the ready availability of meaning remarked on by Deane comes into play. Not in the guise of direct signification (in the sense of a self-sufficient, intuitively decipherable symbolism), but rather in the form of the irresistibly productive communication achieved by the double commandment. What I would criticize in both of the above approaches is the notion that anything in the *Wake* happens plainly or effortlessly, be it effortless signification or a plain denial of signification. I maintain the importance of the gap that opens up between ideal, effortlessly precise language and human, imperfect language. In view of the productive oscillation between Shem-type and Shaun-type impulses that *Finnegans Wake* depicts, we should consider the possibility that to Joyce's writing, this gap between ambition and capability is not an impairment to be overcome, but a dialectic tension that enhances the text's creative power. What is more, the *Wake* not only embraces postlapsarian language as a catalyst at the formal level. At the level of content, Joyce can be seen to relate linguistic chaos and confusion to a Judeo-Christian tradition that has examined these issues in some detail. In doing so, *Finnegans Wake* bestows a thematic significance on its opacity. I will argue that in his dialogue with the interpretative tradition surrounding the linguistic fall, Joyce ultimately casts that event as an enabling one.

It is important to note that the Judeo-Christian account of language confusion contains more than one particular story to be read in one particular way. The biblical account describes a repeated event or a *split* event, since the linguistic fall occurs at two separate moments. It happens with God's announcement at Babel, but it also happens with the dispersion of Noah's descendants into separate nations after the flood. The two incidents do not complement each other. Each of them presents a self-contained explanation of the linguistic fall, which therefore annuls the alternative explanation and is annulled by it. The better-known story is the destruction of the tower at Babel, the event in which humanity causes the wrath of God and brings upon itself the loss of ideal language. It is the instant of God speaking:

> Behold, the people is one, and they have all one language; and this they begin to do: and now nothing will be restrained from them, which they have imagined to do. Go to, let us go down, and there confound their language, that they may not understand one another's speech.
>
> (Gen. 11.6–7)

The language that is lost through this divine punishment is explicitly identified as a tongue shared by all mankind: "And the whole earth was of one language, and of one speech" (Gen. 11.1). Without explicit legitimation from the biblical text, this original and common language is usually taken to be the Adamic one, meaning that the dispersion at Babel is cast as the explanation for both the plurality of human languages as well as their inferiority to the ideal nomenclature invented in Eden. I will refer to the notion that mankind speaks Adam's language up to the fall of Babel, at which point that language is dissolved into a multitude of inferior idioms, as the *babelian hypothesis*.

This hypothesis conflicts with information given in the preceding chapter of the Bible. In Genesis 10, we read that the various lineages originating from Noah's sons, Japheth, Ham, and Shem (a trio the *Wake* frequently invokes), form different nations that are scattered over the earth to repopulate it after the flood. The variations of the formula repeated for each genealogical line are as follows: "every one after his tongue, after their families, in their nations" (Gen. 10.5); "after their families, after their tongues, in their countries, and in their nations" (Gen. 10.20); "after their families, after their tongues, in their lands, after their nations" (Gen. 10.31). The contradiction to the babelian narrative and its initial declaration that "the whole earth was of one language" is evident. If at this stage of pre-babelian history, each racial or tribal group has already developed its own linguistic variety, by which its members can be identified "after their tongues," then linguistic unity has already been lost. Nor is there reason to believe that the languages spoken by Noah's descendants are not roughly equal to each other (and to latter-day language) in their expressive capacity. There is no indication given in the biblical text that of the tribal idioms, one was a continuation of the pure language of Adam. Of the numerous questions this raises, the one that particularly interests me here is posed by Umberto Eco: "[Genesis 10] is a chink in the armour of the myth of Babel. If languages were differentiated not as a punishment but simply as a result of a natural process, why must the confusion of tongues constitute a curse at all?" (10).

The account in Genesis 10, which I will call the *diluvian hypothesis*, has two major consequences for an inquiry into biblical myths of the origins of language. First, it invites a description of our present, post-lapsarian and multilingual condition in terms that are not entirely pessimistic. After all, as Eco points out, the emergence of multilingualism appears to be a development that occurs quite unspectacularly among the descendants of Noah – a notion that also encourages us to emphasize the extent to which the flood constitutes a new beginning. Secondly, Genesis 10 invites us to revisit the story of Babel with a view to aspects other than the punitive dispersion of language. In the light of the several nations already founded by Noah's sons, it becomes possible to read Babel as the preservation of multiculturalism, rather than the thwarting of human civilization. The split of the linguistic fall into two events thus complicates the fall's meaning and opens onto a variety of alternative readings of the biblical histories involved – not least because the *Wake*'s treatment of the linguistic fall borrows from the biblical narratives but also reimagines them in various ways.

The Flight of the Scribe

In a densely packed passage in the first chapter of *Finnegans Wake*, we read the following:

> Somewhere, parently, in the ginnandgo gap between antediluvious and annadominant the copyist must have fled with his scroll. The billy flood rose or an elk charged him or the sultrup worldwright from the excelsissimost empyrean (bolt, in sum) earthspake or the Dannamen gallous banged pan the bliddy duran.
>
> (14.16–21)

Campbell and Robinson are the first critics to point out that "*Ginnunga-gap* ('Yawning Gap') is the name given in the Icelandic *Eddas* to the interval of timeless formlessness between world aeons" (p. 45 fn. 1). It is a gap interrupting history itself, and in the context of this passage, it also takes on the form of a breakdown of continuous tradition. Ignorance inserts itself, in the shape of a cataclysmic event, between ourselves and the memories whose passing down cultural continuity is meant to ensure. The precise nature of this interruption is unclear, since we are offered four competing explanations for it. Whatever has happened, the record is now lost: "the copyist must have fled with his scroll." This loss of recollection is so comprehensive that not only the manner, but also the moment of the loss is nearly forgotten. We cannot date it more precisely than as having occurred "between antediluvious and annadominant," at any point in a stretch of time that reaches from before the flood right up to the birth of Christ. The reference to the flood also recalls another cultural loss: that of the Adamic language as portrayed in the diluvian hypothesis. For if we now turn to the four different explanations offered for the copyist's flight, it becomes apparent that the linguistic fall is indeed at stake in this passage.

Let us consider the alternative histories: the flood, the elk, thunder, and the bird (I will presently explain what a bird has to do with the fourth history). I will gloss them out of sequence – bird, flood, elk, thunder – in order to develop a thematic interpretation that links the motif of disrupted tradition to the interference of an aggressor, a link most explicitly sounded in the last of the four histories. This version, which we therefore need to consider first, contains an allusion to "Biddy Doran" (112.27) or "Belinda of the Dorans" (111.5), the hen that in I.5 scratches up "on that fatal midden" (110.25) an object that "looked for all this zogzag world like a goodish-sized sheet of letterpaper" (111.8–9) – ALP's letter. This literary bird, associated with the recovery of the recorded past, is here "banged pan" – presumably killed, fried in a pan, and eaten – by "the Dannamen," a coinage that incorporates a reference to Danish men, that is, to Viking invaders. Read in this way, the account adds to the many parallels between ALP's letter and the *Book of Kells* (for instance, ALP's letter and the *Book of Kells* share the fate of being lost and subsequently found under a heap of earth). Joyce's chief source for constructing these parallels is Edward Sullivan's introduction to his facsimile edition of the *Book of Kells*, a paradigm of scholarly analysis both painstakingly detailed and wildly speculative, to which chapter five of the *Wake* makes frequent, often parodic reference. The description I.5 gives of different punctuation marks found in ALP's letter (see 121.12–13 and 123.33–124.5) echoes a similar analysis Sullivan provides of punctuation in the *Book of Kells* (see 26 and 49–50). The violence towards Belinda Doran, and the hurried escape that the scribe makes with his scroll, would then evoke the history of attacks on the abbey of Kells that Sullivan describes. He lists the Danes as one of the nations that most frequently pillaged the abbey, and states that "How the Gospels of St Columba [i.e. the *Book of Kells*] survived this century of violence and spoliation it is impossible to say" (21).

In the version we are concerned with here, ALP's letter proves less fortunate than the illuminated manuscript on which it is modeled. The mother-bird personifies both the unearthing of the past and the creation of future generations to engage with that past: "she just feels she was kind of born to lay and love eggs (trust her to propagate the species)" (112.13–14). With her destroyed (killed and eaten), the letter remains undiscovered and barren: it takes on the role of the part of heritage that is lost in violent cultural transitions and intersections. This reading is reinforced by other renderings of the passage. As "banged upon the bloody door," the phrase makes use of Danish "døren": "door" (McHugh 14), which contains another hint at the invaders' nationality and links the intruders to the "cad with a pipe" (35.11) who late at night tries to gain entrance to HCE's house by breaking down the door (see 63.20–64.21). McHugh also identifies "Danny Mann" (14) as a character from Dion Boucicault's play *The Colleen Bawn*, in which Danny attempts to murder the title heroine Eily O'Connor: another example of violence against a female character. Similarly, the word "gallous" echoes a key line from J. M. Synge's *The Playboy of the Western World*: "there's a great gap between a gallous story and a dirty deed" (act 3, lines 572–3). This statement refers to Christy Mahon's attempt to kill his father – an instance of violence against heritage or the past. In addition, "gallous" also conjures up a rooster (Latin "gallus"), further gendering the violence against Belinda the hen.

Yet all of these relatively straightforward interpretations of "the Dannamen gallous banged pan the bliddy duran" are destabilized by the proximity of the phrase "the copyist must have fled with his scroll." If invasion, plundering, and murder are amongst the themes echoed in this history of Belinda the hen, then a scribe's flight could be taken to signify the opposite of what I have so far suggested its meaning to be: it would not indicate that the written record ends, but that it continues (with the scribe hastily abandoning the abbey under assault to save himself and his precious document). In the context of the linguistic fall, the very event that apparently represents destruction may contain an element of creation. This motif is only hinted at in the sentence about the scribe – in the form of a possible preservation that may catalyze future development; it is evoked more explicitly in two of the other three histories.

As it is imagined in the other versions, the catastrophic event that interrupts history and jeopardizes remembrance of the past may indeed take on an ambiguous shape that combines destruction with suggestions of a new beginning. The first explanation offered for the copyist's flight is a "billy flood." In this version, it would be God who sends a global, punitive disruption, a "biblical flood" (which might be irreverently identified here as a "silly flood," perhaps the divine equivalent of someone losing their temper). This proposition repeats the diluvian motif already sounded in "antediluvious," linking the disappearance of the copyist's scroll to the violent new beginning of the flood that reduces antediluvian culture to a nearly clean slate. We should ask what happens to the copyist and his scroll once this "billy flood" rises. After all, the tale of Noah is that of an infinitesimal but all-decisive *departure* from the destruction of all else: the preservation of that which allows a new start.

Joyce refers to this story, and its relevance to linguistic matters, in Book IV, the part of the *Wake* most concerned with disappearances and returns. At the moment of dawn, a personified bringer of light addresses "the cowld owld sowls that are in the domnatory of Defmut after the night of the carrying of the word of Nuahs" (593.20–2). These are cold old souls, but they are also animals – cows, owls, pigs – that evoke the catalog of animals assembled on Noah's ("Nuahs") ark. As night is ending, these animals and/or people find themselves in a "domnatory." This echoes "damnation" and the "dominion" of the damned. It thus concerns the theme of afterlife. That same theme is sounded by the combination of the passage's particular wording and its references to the Ancient Egyptian deities "Tefnut" and "Nu" (McHugh 593). Between them, these elements suggest the presence of the *Book of the Dead*, a strand of Egyptian mythology to which the *Wake* frequently alludes. Then again, "domnatory" could also contain a reference to a dormitory, a reassuringly ordinary place in which to find oneself at dawn. The dormitory in question is the "domnatory of Defmut," which, via the dialogue between Joyce's Neanderthals Jute and Mutt (see 16.10–18.16), alludes to Giambattista Vico's mute prehistoric giants (more of which presently). And since Joyce takes on board Vico's theories about our mute forebears without giving much consideration to people with impairments of hearing or speech, the "dormitory of deaf-mute" may here indicate the absence not only of spoken language but of all expression, even of understanding in general. Yet if these readings emphasize death (the afterlife) and silence (the mute giants), the night that has passed is, nonetheless, "the night of the carrying of the word," indicating the *persistence* of logos, language, knowledge, spirit, etc. Moreover, "Nuahs" is "Shaun" backwards (McHugh 593), summoning the character who, as Shaun the Postman, is a carrier of words. In view of the presence of Noah's ark, the night in question could then be interpreted as the metaphorical darkness of the flood; it is the darkness of a catastrophe that extinguishes nearly all of life (plunging it into damnation), but through which one decisive word is nevertheless carried: the essential formulation of life as it is preserved aboard the ark, and from which a new (Irish "nua") civilization emerges.

As with the flight of the scribe, there is a *split narrative* to be found here that indicates both ending and continuation. We should therefore consider the possibility that a "billy flood," too, is charged with ambiguity as to whether it is destructive or creative, whether it refutes or confirms the capacity of the word to transcend disruptions. Bear in mind also that in book IV, where this description of Noah's carrying of the word is found, ALP figures not only as the river Liffey, but also as the biblical flood. At the beginning of her monologue, we read: "Folty and folty all the nights have fallen on to long my hair" (619.20–1), a statement partially echoed three pages further on in the phrase: "Afartodays, afeartonights" (622.15). Both passages recall the apocalyptic rainfall reported in the Bible: "And the rain was upon the earth forty days and forty nights" (Gen. 7.12). This complicates the symbolism of ALP's river-form. Book

IV's description of the river Liffey joining her "cold mad feary father" (628.2), the sea, represents the fading away of one generation as life makes its cyclical return in the next – in ALP's daughter Issy, who is ready to rise from the sea in the form of a cloud (see 627.3–13), to return to the earth, and the cycle of life, as rain. In this context, ALP personifies procreation (as we have also seen with regard to Belinda the hen) and the flows of life-force that travel across individual lives and historical shifts. Yet ALP's association with the biblical flood also identifies her with the cataclysmic *violence* that accompanies each turn of history's wheel.

This merging of opposite meanings directs our attention towards the destruction that constitutes an inherent part of each new beginning. In view of the *Wake*'s famous cyclical structure, which ends and begins with the river, ALP is herself an end that contains a beginning and a beginning that contains an end. Her role is split in a manner that reproduces the split of the flood myth itself, in which both divine wrath and divine mercy manifest themselves. In an unpublished paper, John Bishop furthermore points out that ALP's monologue combines references to the development of a foetus with references to old age and failing health ("Joyce's Last Word;" referred to in Slote, *Joyce's* 152). The *Wake*'s motif of cyclical recurrence is thus linked, in multiple ways, to the split between ending and beginning, between renewal and violence. Via the biblical flood, this split echoes in the simple phrase: "The billy flood rose."

To the growing list of potential sources of violence – which so far includes humans and gods – the next alternative history adds another entry when it gives the reason for the scribe's disappearance as: "an elk charged him." I admit that if there are relevant mythological implications to this particular version, they escape me. Deer feature in Christian, Greek, and Norse mythology, yet there seems to be precious little mention made of elk. (I will not undertake a discussion of the question how much freedom the *Wake* might grant us to travel along the metonymical lines provided by taxonomic relationships.) Perhaps, this is a Darwinian variant on the broader theme of attack and destruction, included to remind us that violence is present among non-human animals as well.

That these various forms of violence – cultural, natural, and divine – are all linked to the problem of language is made evident by the last remaining history, the one centering on the theme of thunder: "the sultrup worldwright from the excelsissimost empyrean (bolt, in sum) earthspake." This explanation is a reference to yet another theory on the origins of language, put forward by eighteenth-century philosopher Giambattista Vico in his *New Science*. Joycean readings of Vico's philosophy typically privilege his idea of the cyclical return of historical ages. If I want to focus on Vico's history of language instead, it is because we find there yet another split narrative that appears to have gone into the making of the *Wake*. Discussing this narrative will initially lead us away from the passage on the scribe and the "ginnandgo gap"; I will return to it, however, for a number of closing remarks.

According to Vico, the first instance of words spoken by early humans is a manifestation of religious awe that our prehistoric ancestors felt for the phenomenon of thunderstorms. Vico argues that "When people are ignorant of the natural causes that produce things, and cannot even explain them in terms of similar things, they attribute their own nature to them" (§180). Observing thunder and lightning, prehistoric human beings, whom Vico pictures as brutish giants, therefore instinctively anthropomorphized the phenomena. They concluded that an immensely powerful being, a god, "was trying to speak to them through the whistling of his bolts and the crashing of his thunder" (§377). Whether it was because they tried to answer the god who was thus earth-speaking from the empyrean heavens through his bolts, or whether they wanted to contain the terrifying phenomenon by taking possession of it through replicating it, "articulate language began to take shape in onomatopoeia" (§447). That is, speech began at the precise moment at which the giants attempted to imitate the sound that had frightened them. In so doing, they invented the first word of human language: the name of the thunder-god, "initially called *Ious* after the sound of crashing thunder," "*Zeus* after the whistling sound of lightning," or "*Ur*, after the sound of burning fire" (§447).

Finnegans Wake makes frequent reference to Vico's theory of onomatopoeia, for instance where it comments on "The hundredlettered name again, last word of perfect language" (424.23–4). The name or word of one hundred letters (or one hundred and one letters in the case of the word that immediately precedes the phrase I cite here) is a thunder-word: a distinctive feature that occurs ten times in the *Wake* and that, in its prolonged rumbling, onomatopoeically represents the sound of thunder in a way similar to the awestruck stuttering of Vico's giants. The notion that thunder is the "last" instance of "perfect language" highlights a critical difference between Vico's theory and the two biblical hypotheses. To Vico, articulate language does not begin with Adam adequately naming each animal, thus demonstrating his perception of the true nature of each being. It begins with the giants inadequately imitating thunder (inadequately because thunder is a sound the human vocal tract is unable to reproduce), a phenomenon of whose natural cause they remain ignorant. "Perfect language" ends with the meteorological event. Once the thunder-god has spoken his awe-inspiring name, what follows is a history of misunderstanding and feeble mimicry. Contrasting Vico's account with the biblical one, we therefore find that Vico argues mankind has at no point lost a perfect idiom, but has always used language of an inferior nature, all the way back to the hardly articulate shouts and grunts sprung from the first giants' state of unreason.

It is possible to still read this as an updated version of the biblical narrative, as a translation of the biblical portrayal of mankind's humiliation into the terms of an aspiring natural science. For whether fallen language originates from the imperfect imitation of thunder or from God's thundering announcement at Babel, the linguistic fall would appear to be associated with human failure. In either narrative, our expressive capacity is measured against a sublime ideal that, in its unrivaled power, demonstrates nothing if not the feebleness of our own language. I would argue, however, that Joyce's implementation of Vico is more subversive than such a fitting of Vico onto traditional readings of the Bible. In the phrase cited above, Joyce does not cast "perfect language" as an object purely of admiration, but associates it with thunder as a perceived threat to humanity. The aspect of Vico's thought brought out in this application is not only the idea that speech begins imperfectly, but also the decisive reason for its beginning at all: a perception of danger. In Vico's opinion, the giants' hardly articulate first expressions were motivated by *fear*.

Vico's theory, that is to say, is yet another instance of a split narrative, yet another account in which destructive and creative forces are subsumed in one and the same influence. The thunderclap that initiates Viconian history is a catastrophic limitation of the giants' freedom. As it causes them to stutter in helpless imitation, it also sends them to live in caves, henceforth afraid of the sky that has manifested itself as the sphere of the frightful divine being. As Vico puts it: "Now, with his lightning bolts, which were the source of the greater auspices, Jupiter had laid low the giants, driving them underground to live in mountain caves" (§491). There is, however, an enabling element to the thunder-god's rage: "By laying them low, he brought them good fortune: for they became the lords of the ground in which they dwelt hidden, and so emerged as the lords of the first commonwealths" (§491). Mary Reynolds comments that "Vico's psychology finds men escaping the bestial primitive state only when the superstitious fear of thunder drives them into caves. Seeking shelter, they begin to form families; thus, the first step is taken toward the City, toward civilized human life" (118–19). It is in response to a perceived threat that the giants first discover the concepts of home and community. The shattering of their narcissistic self-image becomes part of the process that allows them to overcome their ignorant state.

The cultural achievement marked by what Vico calls the first cities remains itself a profoundly ambiguous one. As Vico imagines them, the organization of these proto-households is violent and cruel (see §510). In Chapter 4, I will discuss how Joyce, too, presents the problem of the city as that of a critical mass where progress may deteriorate into chaos, and where accelerated change may collapse into violence. Thus, of the four alternative histories, it is in this one that we find the most striking coincidence of constructive and destructive forces. In Vico's account, it is not the fall from an Edenic ideal that contains the seed of present-day existence. Vico's view is thus opposed to the Christian interpretation of history as the loss of perfection. At the same time, his description of our forebears also opposes itself to such Enlightenment philosophies as posit human rationality as the attribute that fertilizes prehistory's clean slate. As Bishop observes, Vico's philosophy "completely breaks with such forms of Enlightenment belief as Cartesian rationalism and Lockean empiricism, both of which regarded 'Reason' as an eternal manifestation of laws of nature" (*Joyce's Book* 177). In Vico, civilized life (which is not always so civilized) results from the human ability to use palpably *imperfect* means of cognition and communication in order to develop forms of social organization that aspire to improve on an originally brutal situation. Given said imperfection, these forms are not guaranteed any success. That this lack of certainty entails not a carte blanche, but a number of serious tasks, will be at the heart of the next chapter. The divine/real register (the thundering of the fall, the absolute demand, the unreadable intrusion) opens up a space in which the human/symbolic register may try to do its best: I will therefore want to ask, in Chapter 4, how we can think the category of "best."

History, in this view, proceeds through what are essentially limitations imposed on an otherwise bestial state. This aspect of Vico's thinking, Bishop proposes, can explain Joyce's somewhat peculiar proposition "that Freud had been anticipated by Vico" (Richard Ellmann 340). Bishop suggests that the Viconian "crash of thunderbolts [...] operates like the thunder of the patriarchal 'NO!' in Freud's accounts" (191), providing the template for an internalization of law that becomes the basis of self-imposed limitations. I would add two things. First, as in the Freudian history of specters, totem animals, and divinities discussed in Chapter 2, most of the heavy lifting in Vico's explanation is done by a fictional construct (the thunder-god). Both Freud and Vico thus provide Joyce with descriptions of the potentially formative – even law-giving – powers of fictions. Secondly, Vico's theorizing of the thunder-god, like the Freudian narrative of prehistoric patricide, explains the origins of culture through a dialectic of crisis and response. I would therefore read the phrase: "Now their laws assist them and ease their fall!" (579.26) as another one of the *Wake*'s reformulations of Vico's theory. It is only after their fall from self-absorbed supremacy that the giants develop the fictions and formalizations that underpin culture. Vico maintains that a fall, precisely because it creates a need to be eased, is also the starting point without which there would be no human response at all, no struggle, and therefore no foundation for civilization or language as we know it.

Re-reading Babel

This reading of Vico allows us to return to Derrida's "Two Words for Joyce" with an adjusted focus. At the beginning of this chapter, I cited Derrida's definition of God's declaration of war at Babel as an "act of war which consisted in declaring" (33). We should now consider Derrida's description of that declaration as a statement in which all that needs to be declared is God's own, ineffable, name: "the vocable of his choice, the name of confusion" (33). For Derrida, the act of declaring war, the divine name, and the process of confusion are all one. The three aspects come together in the two words Derrida extracts from Joyce's text: "he war" (258.12). As "he wars," these words report an act or a declaration of war: "he wages war, he declares war, he makes war" (22), as Derrida puts it. As "he was" (from German "war"), they are the name of God, the name of him who says of himself: "I am he who is, who am, I am that I am" (22–3). But as "he war," they are the symbol and the symptom of the dispersion of language: a multilingual pun (summoning, at least, English and German), suspended between meanings that can never be reproduced in their full range and their full ambiguity by any expression employing only one language.

Derrida's description of God's declaration of war thus parallels Vico's description of Jupiter, who in his thunder speaks his own name and who through this very announcement condemns humankind to linguistic inferiority. If we now apply Vico's insight that this ruinous event can be the starting point for a *beneficial* development, it quickly becomes apparent that Derrida's text goes even further in overturning traditional evaluations of the fall. Derrida suggests that God's "act of war is not necessarily anything other than an election, an act of love" (33). For when God declared war, "he declared war in tongues [*langues*] and on language and by language, *which gave languages*" (23, my emphasis). This motif of giving through waging war is repeated towards the end of the lecture, where Derrida proposes that God, by speaking his name at Babel, puts in place both the law and the "gift of languages" (39). To Derrida, the babelian act of war gives something in the same gesture in which it takes something away. He comments again on this simultaneity of gestures in "Des tours de Babel," an essay on translation the first part of which is a companion-piece to "Two Words for Joyce." Here, Derrida observes that

> the text of Genesis links without mediation, immediately, as if it were all a matter of the same design, raising a tower, constructing a city, making a name for oneself in a universal tongue that would also be an idiom, and gathering a filiation.
>
> (195)

These, then, are the things that God's intervention is going to disperse, in one and the same gesture. Further down, we read:

> Can we not, then, speak of God's jealousy? Out of resentment against that unique name and lip [idiom] of men, he imposes his name, his name of father; and with this violent imposition, he initiates the *deconstruction* of the tower, as of the universal language; he scatters the genealogical filiation.
>
> (195–6, my emphasis)

The traditional answer to the question Derrida poses is yes. The Babylonians' vision of "a city and a tower, whose top may reach unto heaven" (Gen. 11.4) represents an act of hubris that God cannot tolerate. But the actual words that the Bible reports are more ambivalent: "they have all one language; and this they begin to do: *and now nothing will be restrained from them, which they have imagined to do*" (Gen. 11.6, my emphasis). The Babylonians' universal language is a source or at least a symbol of their growing power. It is part of an empire and of a lineage that is ambitious about perpetuating itself. We should even say that the universal Babylonian idiom is part of an aggressive political agenda: of a project as intolerable to the rest of humankind as it is to God. With this in mind, it becomes possible to interpret the story of Babel in the way Derrida reads it: as a gift of languages and an act of deconstruction that "ruptures the rational transparency but also *interrupts the colonial violence or the linguistic imperialism*" (199, my emphasis) of the Babylonian project – all in one and the same gesture. There are elements of preservation and new beginning in the babelian confusion even as there is also devastation and chaos.

This reading makes sense in the myth's historical context. Nicholas Ostler comments that in its standard interpretation as a cautionary tale about linguistic confusion, the biblical narrative "is bizarrely ill placed as a fable of Babylon, which was notable throughout its history for the leading role of a single language. For almost two thousand years this language was Akkadian" (59). From about 2000 BC to about 500 BC, the entire region of Mesopotamia was "periodically unified under Akkadian-speaking dynasties ruling from Babylon in the south or Assyria in the north" (40). Ending in approximately 500 BC, the politico-military supremacy of Akkadian extends up to or indeed beyond the setting down of the biblical story of Babel. This section of Genesis is attributed to a source known in compositional studies as the Yahwist or "J" (see Baden 68–9), typically dated to about 900 BC, with some critics arguing for other dates as late as about 600 BC (see Campbell and O'Brien 5–6). One defender of a late dating, John Van Seters, proposes that J wrote "within a particular sociohistorical environment – that of the Judean exiles in Babylon" (287). That is, Van Seters holds that J lived as a deportee or a slave in the Babylonian empire. On this basis, Van Seters reads the Babel story as "a deliberate effort to lampoon this massive royal construction and all that it stood for" (32–3). Ostler does not propose an altered reading of Babel, but he repeatedly discusses the regional dominance of Akkadian with a view to political, economic, and military power. Together with what we know of the Pentateuch's composition, this suggests a connection between, on the one hand, the time and place from which the Pentateuch's portrayal of Babylon emerges, and on the other hand, the privileged position of a single language as a result of jingoistic politics. For the author or authors of Genesis 11, the link between linguistic diversity and political liberty may have been very real.

In theology, interpretations that conceive of the Babylonian empire as a menacing force whose destruction is a welcome event go back to antique sources (though removed from the original setting down of the biblical text by more than half a millennium). One of the earliest exponents of this approach is the first-century historian Flavius Josephus. In his *Jewish Antiquities*, Josephus identifies Nimrod as the Babylonian king who ordered the construction of the tower, and writes that Nimrod "little by little transformed the state of affairs into a tyranny, holding that the only way to detach men from the fear of God was by making them continuously dependent upon his own power" (55). As far as liberation from Babylonian oppression is concerned, current scholarship thus finds itself in agreement with the traditional view. But only a recent line of argument suggests that the positive inflection of the events at Babel, far from residing in the necessity of the imposed punishment, consists in a divine act that is not a punishment at all.

The first efforts in theological studies to revisit the narrative in this manner are about contemporary with Derrida's tentative attempt in the same direction. The interpretation flies in the face of the established (but not intrinsic) significance of God's action, for the revisionist approach sees liberation in the very *multiplicity* of languages – what Derrida refers to as the deconstruction of the limitations of a monolingual culture. One early account that argues for this political reading is an essay by Latin American theologian José Míguez-Bonino published in 1999. There, Míguez-Bonino suggests that Babel's linguistic uniformity is a symptom of totalitarian co-optation, and that the Babylonians' power is that of a hegemony threatening not so much divine supremacy as individual human freedom and cultural diversity. The purpose of the myth of Babel, writes Míguez-Bonino,

> is *not* primarily the explanation of the origin of diverse languages, *but* the condemnation and defeat of the imperial arrogance and universal domination represented by the symbol of Babylon. God's action, then, is twofold: the thwarting of the project of the false unity of domination *and* the liberation of the nations that possess their own places, languages, and families.
>
> (15)

It is the second of these two aspects – the setting free of individual characteristics – that constitutes a significant reinterpretation of God's destruction of the tower. If the dispersion of language is read as an act of decentralization and democratization, this means that the act of war opens up a field of cultural undertakings which not only deviate from the centralized, overpowering, and megalomaniac project of the single language and the single tower, but which actually profit from entrusting themselves to that project's opposite: a state of chaos.

I go into some detail about all this because I want to suggest that the *Wake* makes use of the Babel myth in this revisionist sense. The goal here is not to retrofit a theological framework that is alien to Joyce's concerns.

Joyce's rethinking of linguistic confusion takes place in an ongoing dialogue with the Judeo-Christian tradition. Biblical references figure large in the *Wake*'s intertextuality, prompting, for instance, the examination by Derrida from which I here take my cue. The Tower of Babel and the babelian confusion of tongues are alluded to throughout the *Wake*, with Babel being cast as something of a mythological shorthand for imperfect and postlapsarian language. Yet since Joyce's response to this imperfection is to amplify it, his reliance on the biblical narrative takes on a revisionist hue. Any traditional, non-revisionist reference to Babel (any allusion to it that is content to grant that the destruction of the univocal idiom is indeed a punishment) implicitly holds up univocal clarity as a lost ideal. Joyce does not do this. Joyce affirms imperfection and thereby builds a diversity of meaning that in some respects outperforms attempts at univocality.

If Joyce shifts emphasis away from control and towards openness, Babel in the revisionist reading makes sense of this shift, helping us gauge the political significance of the *Wake*'s form. Derrida invites us to imagine a scene in which translators attempt to capture the meanings of "he war" in a monolingual unification – an enterprise Derrida declares to be futile. "Their very success cannot but take the form of a failure. Even if, in an improbable hypothesis, they had translated everything, they would by that very fact fail to translate the multiplicity of languages" ("Two Words" 34). The translators' project, aiming to confine every aspect of "he war" to one translated expression, is in some ways akin to the scheme of the single tower that would unify all ambition and all work into one structure. But Joyce's "he war" escapes translation of this kind. By creating a scope of meaning that exceeds any single expression in any single language, Joyce makes sure "he war" cannot be pinned down in a monolingual, univocal explanation. Which means that Joyce's articulation may be read as an implicit critique of the protocols of comprehending words in a single, towering, transcendental interpretation. As Slote puts it, "Derrida argues that this translinguistic confounding, as registered in the word 'war', is highly *polemical*" ("No Symbols" 196). Whereas Slote underlines that "*Wakean peregrinism* (exile; use of foreign linguistic elements) registers ontological disarticulation" (195), I would emphasize not ontology but politics, following Philippe Sollers's argument that the staging of (linguistic) differences is how *Finnegans Wake* opposes itself to all uniform thought.

On this basis, I would add Babel to the list of myths in *Finnegans Wake* that remain suspended between destruction and creation. Like Noah's ark, Vico's thunder, and the flight of the scribe, the Tower of Babel is a split narrative. What all of these myths have in common is that they describe the linguistic fall as a deeply ambivalent event. They speak of destruction, fear, loss, and confusion. But they also open on the very aspects of language whose productivity Joyce's text so powerfully demonstrates: multilingualism, imperfection in language, the plurality of perspectives and of attempts at making sense. By staging how cataclysmic interruptions coincide with narrow escapes, turns of the wheel, historical progress, and the gift of tongues, these myths inscribe the *Wake* in a counter-tradition of interpreting the linguistic fall: a counter-tradition that conceives of ambiguity and plurality as of something other than a failure. As Avital Ronell summarizes: "*Thank you for giving us Babel, baby Babel, as your language of choice, thank you for the gift of unreadability, for the complaint that was thundered on the myth of transparency, the urge toward one meaning*" (*Complaint* 62).

Pentecostal Plurality

There is another biblical narrative we should consider here, since it can be read as already forming part of the counter-tradition of re-reading Babel. It constitutes a New Testament response to the Old Testament challenge posed by Babel, and it aligns itself with the idea that the destruction of a domineering center can liberate a vibrant multitude of endeavors. This is the narrative of Pentecost: the moment at which the Holy Spirit descends on a gathering and miraculously enables speakers of different languages to talk to each other. The biblical account describes this moment in a rhapsodic enumeration of nationalities that bears quoting at length:

> Now when this was noised abroad, the multitude came together, and were confounded, because that every man heard them speak in his own language. And they were all amazed and marvelled, saying one to another, Behold, are not all these which speak Galileans? And how hear we every man in our own tongue, wherein we were born? Parthians, and Medes, and Elamites, and the dwellers in Mesopotamia, and in Judea, and Cappadocia, in Pontus, and Asia, Phrygia, and Pamphylia, in Egypt, and in the parts of Libya about Cyrene, and strangers of Rome, Jews and proselytes, Cretes and Arabians, we do hear them speak in our tongues the wonderful works of God.
> (Acts 2.6–11)

I cite the passage in its entirety because its juxtaposition of ethnicities and nationalities creates an impression that a summary would, by definition, ruin. The catalogue shows that Pentecost is a moment of plurality, not unity. The people in this narrative are from different cultures and speak any number of different languages. What changes during the miraculous event is their ability to understand one another. The Pentecostal miracle thus answers the babelian dispersion not in the mode of a re-convergence into a single position, but in the mode of a dialogue between numerous and divergent positions. Whereas we may or may not read Babel itself as a positive event (and the norm, until recently, has been not to), the counterpart represented by Pentecost unquestionably takes place within the post-babelian diversity of languages and just as unquestionably turns this diversity into a source of wonder and delight. People with different backgrounds can suddenly communicate with each other, peacefully and in a fruitful manner, while still occupying a rich variety of individual positions. In short, Pentecost affirms the babelian diversification rather than undoing it. In particular, there is no single Pentecostal language temporarily granted to all interlocutors in this scene. The text states that "they all heard them speak *in their own language*" – in Greek: "ὅτι ἤκουον εἷς ἕκαστος τῇ ἰδίᾳ διαλέκτῳ λαλούντων αὐτῶν" (Acts 2.6 in Aland et al.), with "ἰδίᾳ" meaning "own" (as in "idiolect"). Whereas every participant still speaks in their own language, they also hear all others speak in that same language. The experience of the event thus miraculously *varies* from speaker to speaker, and the overall effect is a bustling disarray confusing enough to be mistaken by outside witnesses for drunkenness (see Acts 2.13).

On the basis of these considerations, I disagree with the description of Pentecost that Laurent Milesi offers when he writes that "le miracle de la Pentecôte, le don divin des langues venant racheter la confusion babélienne, permet de restaurer l'unité linguistique" (178), which I would translate: "the miracle of Pentecost, the divine gift of languages that undo the babelian confusion, allows the restoration of linguistic unity." A few pages further on, Milesi adds that in the Pentecostal event, "L'universalité et l'intelligibilité sont restaurées localement" (186): "universality and intelligibility are locally restored." Milesi is not arguing for the presence of a universal idiom at the Pentecostal event; in fact, the terms "unité" and "universalité" can be understood to indicate the sort of joyful capacity for exchange I also have in mind. Still, this way of phrasing matters, particularly the double stress on restoration, overemphasizes a story-arc in which the destruction of the tower is finally overcome by Pentecostal unity, and underemphasizes the thematic link between defeating the oppressive project of the tower and celebrating the chaos of Pentecost. In the Pentecostal gathering of voices, the diversification initiated by the erasure of the tower is not reversed; it reaches a momentary zenith of communicative productivity. I therefore propose to conceive of this event along the lines described by theologian Letty M. Russell, who writes: "This is a different kind of world than the one envisioned by the builders at Babel. Here the unity comes, not through building a tower of domination or uniformity, but through communication" (463–4). The miracle of Pentecost gives the ability to communicate; what it does not do is to remove the element of chaos inherent to postlapsarian speech. On the contrary, what Pentecost adds to the babelian confusion is an unreserved toleration of plurality and chaos.

This description aligns itself with Joyce's mode of expression in *Finnegans Wake*. Milesi, based on his definition of Pentecost as a restorative gesture that redeems confusion, argues that "L'avènement de la Pentecôte est sans cesse déjoué et la réconciliation n'apparaît pas derrière la fusion formelle des langues dans le moule de l'idiome wakien" (178): "the arrival of Pentecost is constantly prevented and no reconciliation manifests itself behind the formal fusion of languages in the cast of the Wakean idiom." Also citing this description, Slote comments: "Languages are fused, but, as such, do not point toward a syncretic, whole, and pure language" (*Joyce's* 146). This absence of a whole or a definitive synthesis I agree with, but I do not think it indicates that "*A linguistic Pentecost* – ALP – is always to be awaited" (Slote, "No Symbols" 203). I would instead suggest that the language of the *Wake* is already Pentecostal precisely because of its indefinite suspension of a monovalent reconciliation: a suspension through which the text affirms chaos, plurality, the other, the unknown, uncertainty, and so on.

However, if we are to translate "Pentecost" from the name of a mythological event into a term describing a certain way of writing, a number of qualifications are needed. First, although the *Wake* is a multilingual text, I am not specifically referring to that multilingualism when I discuss the *Wake* as Pentecostal writing. The remarkable feature of the Pentecostal event is that in bringing together heterogeneous and possibly contradictory outlooks, cultures, and languages, it generates a productive if not entirely harmonious discourse. Where we would expect to find either conflict or else a disintegration into the flat meaninglessness of white noise (the usual result of a merging of too much information) we instead find an abundance of meaning. It is this abundance on the brink of total confusion – an effect that is prominent in the *Wake* – that I propose to label "Pentecostal." Although the *Wake*'s multilingualism contributes to its production of this effect, a text does not have to be multilingual to partake in Pentecostal heterogeneity. I use "Pentecostal" to mean the presence of multiple levels of meaning in a disunity that is more precarious and more heterogeneous than the conjunctive multiplicity of ambiguity.

For similar reasons, Pentecostal writing is not related to the project of artificial languages like Esperanto. These constructed languages aim to meet the challenge of linguistic diversity by means of unification. Where they synthesize existing languages, it is to make themselves available to an international community of speakers by providing one system accessible to all. The Pentecostal event, by contrast, maintains the differences between those present and allows each to communicate using a different system. Pentecostal writing intertwines various layers of signification, but it does this in a manner that invites juxtaposition and reseparation rather than levelling and once-and-for-all fusion. Norris remarks that

> Unlike artificial or "auxiliary" languages whose purpose is to overcome the Babelian diversity of national languages, Joyce's "muttering pot" (20.7) in the *Wake* appears to be a dump or rubbish heap like ALP's scavenger sack, in which the fragments merely mix and mingle to be distributed anew.
>
> (Decentered Universe 129)

The essence of Pentecostal writing as I understand it hinges on the capacity "to be distributed anew." The various meanings that co-exist in the *Wake*'s Pentecostal utterances, although they productively interact, cannot be subsumed under a single heading and defy complete synthesis. As Jesse Schotter puts it in a discussion of Joyce's take on Babel: "Joyce provides in his own version of a universal language not the solution to the problem of Babel but Babel itself: a radically impure cacophony of different languages" (100). Which is precisely how this mode of expression remains a multitude of effects and avoids collapse into the single, overwhelming note of white noise.

Finally, in proposing to dub the language of *Finnegans Wake* Pentecostal, I am not suggesting that we should read Joyce's text for a particular exegesis of that biblical story (even less for any affinity with Pentecostal forms of Evangelicalism). My application of this theological framework to the *Wake* is intended to demonstrate that we should not hastily term Joyce's text a *babelian confusion* without problematizing what is meant by this shorthand, Babel, that perhaps somewhat too readily presents itself when we talk about what *Finnegans Wake* does with the plurality of languages. To contrast Babel with Pentecost in the classical manner – as fall and redemption, punishment and resolution – cannot do justice to the *Wake*'s split retellings of the fall, nor to its sheer enjoyment of the linguistic condition which may be subsumed under that name. Rather than holding on to a traditional understanding of Babel that can only overemphasize the myth's negative connotations, we should think Babel in Pentecost and Pentecost in Babel. In multiplicity, chaos is implied; in turn, a certain chance is part of the fall (as we will also see at the end of the next chapter, where I discuss *Felix Culpa*, the fortunate fall, of which the linguistic fall at Babel can be regarded as one version).

This is not to say that the story of Pentecost is absent from the *Wake*. Beryl Schlossman discusses HCE's being made a Christ-like scapegoat whose triumph or "pentecostal jest" (99.21) follows shortly after his resurrection (see 83.4–6) in much the same way as Pentecost follows Easter in the liturgical year. That connection is also discernible in the quiz of I.6, where HCE appears as "Mr Easterling of pentecostitis" (130.8–9). The sacred aspect of "Pentecost [as] the *presence* of the Word, reunited with the Father" (Schlossman 158) features again when HCE (channeled by Shaun in III.3) mentions "Paas and Pingster's pudding" (550.12–13), "Pa" evoking the father and "Pfingsten" being German for Pentecost. And the link between Pentecost and intoxication is mentioned when ALP speaks of someone "losing her pentacosts after drinking their pledges" (624.34–5), as well as when Shem indulges in inebriated writing, dealing in "fermented words" (184.26, qtd. in Schlossman 168). My terminological choice, however, is not a response to such narrative or thematic implementations of the Pentecost story. I take my cue from a more latent affinity between Pentecost and Joyce's linguistic experimentation: an affinity Schlossman refers to when she suggests that "Pentecost is the symbolic core of the Joycean reading of Judeo-Christian tradition; [...] it enables him to engage in the plurality of tongues" (159). My use of "Pentecostal" is intended to draw on instruments from theology that go beyond the standard version of Babel in an attempt to make sense of how Joyce reimagines Babel's multilingualism and plurivocality. If we read Joyce's treatment of Babel as one of his strategies in problematizing language, then the revisionist style of his approach requires a wider-ranging theological toolkit than has so far largely been applied to his text.

We can now return to the flight of the scribe and consider again the four alternative histories presented in that section. Their listing constitutes an instance of Pentecostal plurality, for the gesture of offering disparate accounts, without giving any indication that one of them is authoritative, is a strategy that abolishes hegemonic singularity. We are presented with a multiplicity of interpretations, none of which can be singled out as the central one. To call this multiplicity Pentecostal is to note that the passage offers several answers that should exist in a state of mutual exclusion but instead exist in a state of simultaneity, and it is to suggest that this very simultaneity takes on an importance of its own.

Another such simultaneity can be found in the phrase "the copyist must have fled with his scroll." I have already argued that this flight may be taken to signify either the loss of information or its rescue. We can now add that this split between collapse and preservation is a Pentecostal one. In fact, this particular ambiguity between creation and destruction is characteristic of all Pentecostal plurality. The overload of meaning already contains the breakdown of meaning, and this flaw in turn contains its productivity. If we take "the copyist must have fled with his scroll" to mean that the handing down of information has been interrupted, that we have no access to the knowledge recorded in the missing document, then what we nevertheless *have* knowledge of is this lack itself, which we immediately begin to interpret. There is something like an oscillation here that touches on both versions of the split narrative. Something has been lost, but it is a *partial loss,* for although we cannot say what has been lost or how (or even when), we know about the loss itself – loss itself has been salvaged – and thus loss and preservation come together in one and the same event.

What, then, of my claim that Pentecostal language defies synthesis? Is not the notion of a partial loss a quintessential synthesis of the flight of the scribe? My answer is that although the idea of a partial loss combines some of the text's connotations, it is far from exhausting the text. The multiplicity that splits the narrative of the scribe does not disappear once this synthesis, the story of a partial loss, is found. On the contrary, the split nature of the narrative remains present as *the result brought about by a partial loss.* A partial loss or a noticeable lack (which amounts to the same) is what makes a split narrative possible. In order for such a narrative to exist at all, some remainder of referentiality needs to persist and be noticed, some interest needs to be aroused so as to get underway a series of varying hypotheses regarding that remainder, however distorted by lack it might be. Yet if we could remember, communicate, or otherwise summon into presence the precise details of that lack, it would cease to be lack, and with it would cease to exist any space for multiple interpretations. Here, destruction and creation of meaning are truly interdependent.

The flight of the scribe can thus be read, in several different ways, as a passage *mise en abyme*. First, the passage addresses the conditions of its own existence as a split narrative – as a story that could recount either preservation or loss – by reflecting on how a partial loss of information leads to a state of uncertainty.

Secondly, the text also addresses the conditions for the existence of non-words, which are possible only if the record has been disrupted, but not completely, not beyond a point at which the knowledge *that* something is absent still comes to us and entices us to interpret this lack itself. A Joycean non-word is not a word, but it is close enough to being one to have us look for words it resembles: referentiality persists. In the resulting plurality of interpretations, each of the *Wake*'s non-words (like the history of the copyist's flight) is split into several meanings that cannot be gathered under the heading of one translation or one interpretation, and which nevertheless all communicate with each other as we indefinitely oscillate between them.

Thirdly, the flight of the scribe also comments on issues that go beyond the difficulties of the *Wake* in particular. The split meanings of non-words are the result of a state in which something is missing, a state in which we encounter a palpable lack or an absence made present. But what if the missing thing is the copyist's scroll, his document, perhaps we could even say his letter – or indeed ALP's letter? There is more at stake in this identification than a superficial resemblance of images. The scroll that is missing and the letter that is absenting itself are representations of one and the same thing. They both symbolize that which would remove uncertainty and provide a conclusion. The loss of this possibility destabilizes language by introducing into it the problems of equivocality, plurality, and excess. And this loss afflicts all forms of linguistic capability. The *Wake*'s Pentecostal writing, then, is not fundamentally different from other language use. Its plurality is the exemplification and radicalization of what could be called the fallen state of all language – it makes palpable a loss and an opening that all signification subliminally feels. What is particular about Joyce's procedure, as I have been arguing throughout, is that in the *Wake*, the postlapsarian split between losing meaning and opening up to meaning is not buried, hidden, or suppressed. It is made explicit in a text that challenges us to engage in a plurality of meaning even if, in order to do so, we have to acknowledge that this plurality results from the anxiety-inducing loss of the letter/scroll.

A Pentecostal plurality is not a totality, set, or pattern that controls or summarizes its components; it does not branch out from the semantic center of an equivocality, but from a distortion or loss that interferes with the very concept of such a center. We can clarify this by considering some examples. Is "he war" an expression in German or in English? Does "Nuahs" mean Noah, Shaun, or new? And is there any common denominator to these meanings? What exactly does "Allmaziful" mean, and how many languages does it mean it in? Does it mean the same in all of these languages? If not, which meaning is the most important? Or, to give an example not based on a non-word, what kind of fusion or confusion is taking place between Shem and Shaun? A co-operation? A conflict? A supernatural merging of their existences? A split identity? Or simply a difficulty in telling one from the other? And how, stranger still, are we to unite Issy the girl and Issy the cloud? My point is that we can no more integrate these instances of plurality into a neat synthesis than we can subject them to a hierarchy or an "either/or." As I will argue in the following, our task is neither to find some hidden correspondence that would gather together all these meanings, nor to hit upon criteria by which we can decide between them. What we are left with, then, is the "and" of an open-ended list without a clear center and sharp margins.

The excess of this list is not necessarily a question of quantity or magnitude. It is not the meaningless chaos of all-inclusiveness, but a more intriguing state – an intensification of the excess of writing – in which chaos stems from the fact that what *is* included does not naturally divide itself into discrete units. This division has to be undertaken in an identification that already changes the material it distributes. To appreciate the role Pentecostal diversity plays in the *Wake* is therefore not to abandon all caution and to indiscriminately accept any interpretation we care to invent. We can always construe inapplicable readings of a non-word. Yet a serious consideration of the material manipulation that *any* reading of a non-word requires shows that what readings are in fact applicable is not easily decided. The counter-intuitive nature of this admission can hardly be overstated. In our critical endeavors to make sense of the *Wake*, we more or less by definition tend to treat the unreadability of this text as if it were an underlying but (after a period of initiation) unobtrusive principle. That is, we run the risk of nominally acknowledging unreadability only to subsequently exclude it from our readings, which it could only serve to destabilize. I am sure the very interpretation I am developing here falls prey to this temptation. Still, whether we acknowledge it or not, *a non-word destabilizes the interpretations it provokes*. It subjects each reading to the double commandment: "create, and then doubt, scan again what you created, pluralize it, and combine it with alternatives." In this sense, Derrida's notion of the double commandment can summarize for us the effects of an authorial voice that does not proclaim its own monovalent purity, but affirms the excess of language brought about by what we could call language's postlapsarian imperfection.

It is by having us grapple self-consciously with our search for common denominators and stabilizing centers that Joyce has us comprehend the extent of his text's resistance to such systematization: the extent of his refutation of purity and univocality as the proper realms of literary production, and his defiant reliance, instead, on postlapsarian fallibility. There is much more at stake here than Joyce flaunting his technical brilliance. Shaun-type modes of writing – which strive to approximate univocality by controlling, as far as possible, each expression's scope of meaning – subject themselves to a limitation structurally akin to that of the monolingual project of Babel. As they fight for some minimum of much-needed clarity, they also tend towards an impoverishment of Shem-type imaginative daring and range. To this vision, Joyce's Pentecostal writing opposes an audacious agenda that finds in ambiguity itself, in the very flaw that separates us from the ideal state, a force creating new opportunities for expression.

Finnegans Wake not only subscribes to this theory of meaning, it details it: describing (as discussed in Chapter 2) the excess that writing brings about, and articulating (in the mythological register examined here) how this excess opens up new possibilities. Joyce's concern with these issues is one reason why it is useful to read him as a theorist. If we want to take his hermeneutics seriously, we need to be careful not to cast Joyce's non-words as obstacles to a clarity well-informed criticism would be tasked with bringing about. If we posit that the partial and provisional nature of our readings can be overcome through sufficiently accurate interpretation, if we aim to identify one translation (or a given number of translations) of a Joycean non-word as the one whose overriding likelihood can hold at bay all alternatives, and if we venture that in this process, we overlook no relevant possibility and exclude only such readings as are demonstrably invalid or minor, then the very first step of this exegetical procedure is *to undo Joyce's decision* to use a non-word rather than a word. Thus, we return the outrageous otherness of his text to the rigidity from which Joyce has risked to sever his writing.

The emphasis that my interpretation places on this severance, my insistence that any reading of a non-word is not in fact a reading of that non-word but of a word Joyce did not quite write, must raise the question whether the account of Pentecostal plurality I give here may not be a misapprehension that sees unfathomable conundrums where there are merely disguised words. That is, my interpretation finds itself in direct opposition to approaches which argue that criticism's job is clarification, and that clarification happens by narrowing things down: by *identifying* the words Joyce used. Since meaningfulness is deeply connected to specificity, I hold this to be a serious challenge to the reading I present here. In order to address it in sufficient detail, I will devote the final subsection of this chapter to a discussion of Geert Lernout's article "The *Finnegans Wake* Notebooks and Radical Philology." My reasons for responding to this particular text (rather than a more recent contribution to genetic criticism) are as follows.

First, Lernout's article distinguishes between two attitudes that inform diametrically opposed strategies of reading. One sets itself the goal to identify, for each of Joyce's inscriptions, the precise meaning it draws on. The second perspective, to which Lernout explicitly opposes the first approach, is Derrida's notion of iterability, which holds that meaning is plural and that we never succeed in pinning it down. Since Lernout criticizes Derrida's analysis as tending towards relativism, a theoretical approach which, like mine, relies on this analysis can illustrate its *difference* from relativism by plausibly refuting such criticism, which in the following I will attempt to do. I will be concerned to show how and why talk of irreducible plurality, open-ended interpretation, and even infinite possibilities is not opposed to an exploration of authorial intention.

I partly agree with Lernout's proposition: "Take away intention and context, and the only thing left to say about a text is that it can mean anything at all" (47) – which is of course tantamount to saying that it means nothing whatsoever. For reasons outlined in Chapter 2, I think it is impossible to univocally identify an author's intentions. They cannot serve as an unmovable basis of interpretation. But I do believe that authorial intention should form part of what is at stake in interpretation. The process of interpretation can be thought of as an interaction with the author's spectral presence that is both origin and trace of a creative and (at least partly) intentional process giving the text its shape. It is only through a response to the specific operations of Joyce's writing that we are able to read this writing's pluralities without producing meaningless isotropy and universality ("anything at all"). Nonetheless, the nature of reading is necessarily bilateral. The notion of listening to Joyce's own voice is complicated by the ventriloquism that lends to this voice the only vitality it can possess: a spectral vitality. To deny the risk that accompanies spectrality does not put us on safe ground, it does not return us to Joyce's text. Rather, such a denial effaces the text itself; it denies the risks Joyce's non-language requires us to take. I will therefore argue that it is precisely a consideration of authorial intention that demands not a narrowing down, but a pluralization of interpretations.

Secondly, Lernout chooses the term "private" reading to describe the act of making up anything at all (as opposed to the shared endeavor of identifying Joyce's intended meaning). Although I ultimately disagree with some of Lernout's conclusions, I fully subscribe to the ethical overtones present in this term, which raises such questions as how our interpretations partake in *public* discourses, and what responsibility we might therefore have not only towards the text we are studying, and its author, but also towards other readers of it. Another reason for discussing Lernout's article, then, is that doing so allows me to set up part of my argument in Chapter 4 concerning the *interdependence* of the private and the public.

Finally, Lernout's text is the clearest articulation I have been able to find of a concept that I believe informs the approaches of many other readers of *Finnegans Wake*: the rivalry of meanings. According to the precept of the rivalry of meanings, readings are subject to unified comparability. They can and should be evaluated on a single scale of correctness, which will tell us which readings are the best ones. This leads to arguments we frequently encounter in debates on the *Wake* (think of reading groups, for instance): that some non-word or phrase probably does not mean A, because it is probably safer to say that it means B. Lernout calls this one meaning being *true* in a sense that is different – more profound – than the truth of another reading. I hope to show that settling on meaning in this manner is a reading strategy that stops too soon. It cuts short the process of engaging with Joyce's complex intention and with the intentional weirdness of his text, in which an appeal to the legitimate nature of one particular reading is not a sound basis on which to infer the lesser relevance of other readings.

Intentional Complexity

To approximate the singular creative event of Joyce's writing, Lernout proposes to consult the notebooks in which Joyce jotted down textual building blocks for composition. Drawing on these notebooks serves as a homing beacon that protects us from losing sight of the focal points and likely scope of Joyce's creative labor. "It is only when we refer to the notebooks and the drafts that we can decide with some degree of probability which parts of the world went into the book and which parts probably did not" (45). Specifically, referring to the notebooks takes the form of identifying the standard expressions underlying Joyce's non-words, as well as, where possible, tracing these *source-words* "to the text from which they were taken by Joyce" (37). This identification promises to reveal in some detail "the chaos of ideas out of which *Finnegans Wake* developed" (34). By contrast, "If we decide to ignore the notebooks – and maybe we have every right to do so – we can only continue to read as much of our world into the *Wake*: each reader will then inevitably create his or her own private *Wake*" (45). The *private text*, in this sense, is something like the text filtered through our own individual chaos of ideas. Insofar as it can be understood as Lernout's term for the isotropy of an interpretation that can go absolutely anywhere, it is a term that requires careful analysis.

First of all, if an isotropic or relativist reading is *private*, then what are we to make of the claim that a reading in good faith, a radically philological reading, is to be based on Joyce's notes? It would be crude to simply insist here that Joyce's notebooks constitute private records. I agree with Lernout, who writes: "I do not believe that the notebooks are private documents in more than the most pedestrian of meanings" (46). As archival evidence of the creative process, the notebooks partake in Joyce's authority and in criticism's public enterprise. I hope to show, however, that there is a problem here, namely the notebooks' being different from the book published as *Finnegans Wake*. This difference means that rather than constituting one homogeneous space, the public realm is traversed by fault-lines, raising the question of how various manifestations of public knowledge relate to each other.

In addressing this relation of avant-texte to text, Lernout takes on board an axiom adopted from Danis Rose, who proposes that "*Finnegans Wake* is an ordered aggregate of elements each of which can be identified with a unit entered in one of the notebooks" (xiii, qtd. in Lernout 30). Lernout thus resolves the relation between two public archives – *Finnegans Wake* and the notebooks – by concluding that this relation is one of correspondence. Although the source-words undergo a process of transformation, which necessitates some detective work in identifying the source-word corresponding to a given element in the *Wake*, the fact remains that each unit in the *Wake* "can be identified with" its source-word (or in some cases source-words). If such an identity between text and source-material can indeed be assumed, then it is curious that Lernout still concedes that we may have "every right" to ignore the notebooks. Here is the explanation that directly follows in this section of Lernout's text:

> The difference between the two approaches is one that is familiar from recent practice in the performance of classical music. Either we attempt to play the Brandenburg Concertos or the Goldberg Variations or the Ninth Symphony in the way Bach or Beethoven would have wanted them performed, or we play them our own way. The two approaches are irreconcilable because we have set ourselves different tasks.
>
> (45–6)

In one case, it is our privilege to explore the creative range of personal readings – what Lernout calls the private approach. In the other case, the case we can label *public*, our job consists in the reconstruction of the author's intention. This strikes me as an interesting but problematic distinction for a number of reasons.

Consider what is perhaps the most straightforward case: an "illegitimate" reading, a reading in which the knowledge of the reader can be seen to displace the knowledge of the writer. I would argue that this need not manifest as what Lernout terms "textual solipsism" ("James Joyce" 96), that is, as an interpretation primarily interested in its own hermeneutical or aesthetic powers ("look at what I can do with this text by removing it from all its realistic concerns"). Interpretations that subject Joyce to their own exegetical priorities may do so in order to explore social, political, and ethical questions of considerable real-world importance. Where this is the case, reading "our own way," even along the lines of procedures that many readers will deem to transgress the boundaries of authorial meaning, constitutes an interpretative enterprise anything but confined to a solipsistic or private realm. One could argue that it is more truly public than readings concerned exclusively with what one person – Joyce – thought and wrote. This is a point I also make in the Introduction: treating a literary text as strictly a means to an end is often diametrically *opposed* to a solipsistic approach totally disinterested in the world.

Moving away from the crassest examples, it is often difficult to distinguish between legitimate and illegitimate interpretations in the first place. It is not obvious that reading with our own concerns in mind – playing our own way – is necessarily opposed to what Joyce would have wanted. Interpretations may inherit from Joyce's thought in order to think about our own questions in his spirit. Where, in these cases, should we draw the line between Joyce's meaning and ours? There is no two-step process here of Joyce's "original" meaning and our application of it, for as I discuss in Chapters 1 and 2, essential meaning and authorial meaning are useful notions, even necessary ones, but *they do not exist*, not as immutable presences. Essential meaning and authorial intention are ghostly ideals, always co-constructed by the reading that tries to respond to them. For this reason, it can be difficult to draw a sharp line between Joyce's contribution and the reader's. We can see this in the case of musical performances. The distinction between playing the original and playing our own way may be straightforward when the question is whether you want to hear Beethoven's Ninth Symphony as conducted by Sir Simon Rattle or as performed on the synthesizer by Wendy Carlos on the soundtrack of Stanley Kubrick's *A Clockwork Orange*. But it is less straightforward when you ask whether you want to listen to Olivier Messiaen's *Turangalîla* Symphony as conducted by Sir Simon Rattle or as conducted by André Previn. Does one of these versions represent the truth of how Messiaen would have wanted the symphony performed, and the other one an aberration? If not, if both are good performances, why do they differ in subtle ways? Is there room in public performances for deviation after all? Where does this residual uncertainty come from? Can it be *distinguished* with any certainty from the uncertainty of whether one has indeed found the composer's intention?

We have thus returned to Derrida's point that the problem is not one of free choice ("I will read this notation however I please"), but one of a pervasive uncertainty that menaces even the best interpretations with the possibility of their incompleteness, their partiality, their *in-conclusiveness*. It is significant, then, that in "The *Finnegans Wake* Notebooks and Radical Philology," Lernout links the essay in which Derrida develops the concept of iterability, "Signature Event Context," to a strictly "private form" (Lernout 46) of language use: the randomized production of meaning in which all that comes about is the private text created by a particular reader. Lernout cites Derrida on the

> possibility of disengagement and citational graft which belongs to the structure of every mark, spoken or written, and which constitutes every mark in writing before and outside of every horizon of

semio-linguistic communication; in writing, which is to say in the possibility of its functioning being cut off, at a certain point, from its "original" desire-to-say-what-one-means [*vouloir-dire*] and from its participation in a saturable and constraining context.

("Signature Event Context" 12, qtd. in Lernout 46)

With regard to this *possibility of citational graft*, Lernout states that "A radical philology simply does not see its relevance. I don't think there is such a thing as a private language in this fundamental sense" (46–7). That is to say, it is hard to see the relevance of meaning cut off from the original intention. We should dismiss such meaning; in fact, it is questionable whether something this fundamentally private still constitutes language. The problem with this way of putting things is that by referring to citational graft as "private language," we end up applying the term "private" to something that is a universal feature of language because it is *inevitable*. The grafting that "Signature Event Context" is concerned with is not an unrestrained interpretative power that interrupts transmission and self-importantly decides to enjoy its own, private (i.e. irrelevant) meaning. Derrida is arguing the opposite: that a subtle but irreducible uncertainly results from any reader's all too limited powers vis-à-vis the task of relevant interpretation. This limitation is iterability. No legibility can come about without iterability, yet iterability divides us from essence.

Citational graft entails the *inaccessibility* of essence, not a belated change interfering at will with an essence that is otherwise secure. As Derrida puts it in the passage Lernout cites, citational graft "belongs to the structure of every mark, spoken or written," and it defines this structure *"before and outside* of every horizon of semio-linguistic communication," since it represents the mark's very functioning as a mark. From the start, and from before any essence can be secured, the possibility of a signifier's being iterable, and legible in its iteration, is the same as the possibility of its being wrenched from one usage and sliding into another. Signification and this risk are one and the same: *"writing, which is to say* [...] the possibility of its functioning being cut off." A few lines further down in Derrida's text, we read: "This does not imply that the mark is valid outside of a context, but on the contrary that there are only contexts without any center or absolute anchoring" (12). Derrida is not presenting an alternative to, or giving a recommendation against, contextualization (asking what the author intended, what the text was doing in its original context, etc.). He is arguing that even the best contextualization we can carry out still depends on decisions made by the reader in ways that cannot be exhaustively controlled (there is no "absolute anchoring"). If citational graft is a possibility, it is so in the sense of an underlying condition such that we can never be quite sure to what extent grafting has taken place and in what direction it may have taken us.

The reason we cannot be sure of these things is that the origin we are trying to access does not exist. Essence is conjectural and phantasmatic. It isn't there. There is no *vouloir-dire* as it would have existed outside any context and outside the mutability and permeability of even a single signifying gesture's original contexts. Nor can original context(s) be inscribed in a signifying gesture in such a manner as to ward off the fact that the gesture's legibility will consist in its appearance in other contexts whose relation to the original one is imperfectly knowable. *To read or write is to lack perfect control* (though it is not to lack *all* control). By contrast, Lernout goes on to suggest that "A radical philology limits the inquiry to the original desire-to-say of any form of writing *and* to its participation in a saturable and constraining context" (47). There is a sense here of wanting to approximate a center, which I would argue is similar to Derrida's notion that reading directs itself towards the gestalt image of essence that is the trace. Lernout's critique of Derrida thus misses its target, since his rejection of relativism marks an agreement between the two. At the same time, Lernout's position seems informed by the notion that original *vouloir-dire* and original context are available to us. This implicates him in a form of logocentrism. Meaning and intention appear as solid presences, publicly accessible without any risk of interpretation – but only because logocentrism leaves unexamined the private coordinates of this very appearance. I will presently discuss the particular perspective that radical philology brings to bear on Joyce's text.

Our reading of a text is always already our co-constructing the text. The uncertainty that radical philology attempts to banish by subsuming it under the category of the private thus returns to haunt public discourse. If citational graft, and the possibility of misreading that comes with it, are to be regarded as instances of private language, then private language is at work within public language, indeed private language is what makes public language possible and what is thus at the core of public language (a point I will elaborate in the next chapter). To be clear, the blurring of this distinction does not mean that intentionality counts for nothing. To acknowledge that we lack a language that would be *perfectly* public does not result in a facile voluntarism in which signification has no meaning apart from whatever a reader wants it to mean – and in which, consequently, no reader can ever reasonably speculate about an author's intentions as evidenced by their text. (I myself am constantly referring here to what I take other authors to be saying.) In order to clarify this crucial point, let me draw attention to a potentially confusing passage in "Signature Event Context," where Derrida talks about the signifying gesture "[breaking] with every given context, engendering an infinity of new contexts in a manner which is absolutely illimitable" (12). The claim that interpretation goes on indefinitely and produces a potentially infinite number of different readings is not the same as saying that a signifying gesture can be made to mean absolutely anything.

It is possible to misread a text, to construct a reading whose claims are not sustained by the meaningfulness of its response to the text. Above, I argue that Lernout misconstrues Derrida. I am therefore clearly assuming that not every reading of Derrida is acceptable, as well as that my reading of Lernout is somehow related to his intention. The point is that things like acceptability or relation are measured not as the distance between the meaning produced by a reading and the actual, given meaning (this is impossible because no meaning is given without production), but by examining whether an act of meaning-production has successfully iterated some of the text's network of signifiers. Of course, that examination's understanding of success will depend on the examiner's own iteration of the text and of the interpretation – but this dependence *preserves* the link between acceptability and reference to the text. It moreover opens on an examination of the examination, and so on, ultimately grounding the notion of acceptability in intersubjective communication and debate. This way of putting things holds on to the text as shaping its interpretations, while getting rid of the idea of a stable core meaning to which interpretations are to be compared and of which they form either variations or deviations. It is precisely this lack of unified comparability that accounts for the potentially infinite number of acceptable readings. Readings are not placed on a single grid, on which they could only ever differ from each other by providing diverging answers to the same questions. They differ from each other in more subtle ways, expressing various perspectives that may not even share a taxonomy.

To assert that meaning is not guaranteed by a stable center, that it divides and subdivides into an infinite plurality, does *not* contradict the necessary assertion that there are meaningful responses as well as cases outside the acceptable range of reading. The distinction between infinite plurality and meaningless universality is crucial. An infinity does *not* cover a universal ground. Consider, for instance, the series of even numbers: 2, 4, 6, 8, 10, etc. This series is infinite, yet we can easily name a number not included in it: 1. The number 1 is found outside the series of even numbers, and so are 3, 5, 7, and so on. Banal as it may seem, this example is all that is required to understand that an infinity can include certain cases and excludes others. Analogously, the potential infinity of readings is a question of unending addition, but *not* a matter of undifferentiated extension. We know this, of course. Scholarship on Joyce has been going on for decades, scholarship on Shakespeare for centuries, scholarship on biblical texts for millennia. Yet we do not expect any of these exegetical processes to come to a halt anytime soon. One of the advantages of Derrida's model of signification is that it can explain this.

To summarize: the fact that essential meaning is an ideal, not a presence, pluralizes readings in such a way that any particular reading we develop can be more or less rigorous, more or less successful, more or less convincing, while also always remaining minimally but irreducibly inconclusive. *Even if what we say about the text is highly appropriate, there will always be more to say.* Now, it would be one thing for Joyce's text to be subject to this effect. But I would argue that the effect is deliberately amplified by Joyce's Pentecostal pluralities, in which interpretations that should be mutually exclusive can be seen to co-exist. That is the last and most important reason why I question a distinction between private and public readings of *Finnegans Wake*. If we define "public" as "authorial" and "private" as "randomized" and "plural," we are confronted with the fact that what the author appears to be doing, in this case, is dialing up language's propensity to conjure up plurality. This authorial manipulation complicates the notion of reading the work in a scientific mode not afflicted by private fickleness, for the fickleness in this case appears to be Joyce's.

Consider the *Wake*'s non-words, its most effective tool in the creation of Pentecostal pluralities. Regarding the interpretative conjectures we engage in when we normalize non-words, Lernout attributes a privileged status to normalizations based on Joyce's notebooks. "Findings that derive from a radical philological approach belong to a different category: they are true in a different sense for the simple reason that *they can be proven wrong*" (48). Therefore, they belong to "a type of research that is *falsifiable* and therefore scientific in Karl Popper's sense of the word" (48). The problem with this argument is that where this approach resolves the conundrum of a Joycean non-word – where the notebooks can indeed provide, or point to, a standard word on which the non-word can be seen to be based – that source-word is, by the same token, different from the non-word found in the *Wake*. Disregarding that difference, treating it merely as a gap between text and explication that scientific criticism has to close, the reverse engineering that radical philology engages in sidesteps a major portion of the text it wants to interpret.

This is a problem. On the one hand, genetic criticism is grounded in an appeal to authorial intention. Joyce's notebooks are a valuable resource because they illuminate Joyce's process, the scope and nature of his plan. Reading the notebooks, we gain a better idea of Joyce's intended meaning. On the other hand, the notebooks are not the final product. They stop short of unveiling the entirety of the authorial intention – and the full complexity of the authorial intention – that went into the published text. That is, while a source-word gives us a good translation or normalization of a non-word, we do not know that the author intends only this one thing, or mainly this one thing. What gets in the way of a source-word exhausting a non-word in this manner is precisely *the difference between source-words and the non-words Joyce formed from them*. Although this difference is not separately recorded, as identifiable source-words are, it is just as concrete. It consists in the changes that source-words undergo: the distortion produced by Joyce's empirically verifiable addition and/or deletion of letters. Joyce has introduced this distortion at some point. Consequently, the distortion is part of the authorial intention that goes into the formation of the text and part of the linguistic material to which criticism is required to respond. Nor is the situation fundamentally different where Joyce combines several source-words into one non-word. The resulting non-word does not contain these source-words in an unproblematic manner; any meaning to be gained from the non-word is again produced by a normalizing conjecture that counteracts a distortion.

My point, then, is this: if we assume that a distortion is a kind of detour ultimately returning us to the source-word, we will have a hard time accounting for what all these distortions are actually *doing* in *Finnegans Wake*. It appears to me that as long as we hold on to the idea that the source-word is the main or only meaning of a non-word, we can only repeat that despite all his distortions, Joyce is ultimately using normal words in a normal manner – in a roundabout way. And this does not strike me as a convincing explanation of what *Finnegans Wake* does with language. I fully share Attridge's view that "Joyce did not spend some sixteen years weaving multiple threads into his work only to have a single one emerge as supreme over all the others" (*Joyce Effects* 150). What I would criticize in the approach of radical philology, and indeed in any approach that seeks to reduce Joyce's non-words to their "correct" meaning, is the unspoken assumption that the authenticity of a source-word, or indeed of any kind of interpretative clue, can outweigh the authenticity of a distortion.

A translation based on a source-word is not "true in a different sense" from any other translation: as a normalizing transformation of the illegible non-word, it is as incomplete as any other. I agree that the interpretation provided by a source-word is *different* in the sense that the likelihood of its relevance is singularly hard to deny (likely and incomplete: this is Joyce's double commandment in full action). A source-word, once it has been found, will hardly be placed outside the non-word's plurality of meanings at any subsequent stage. Yet to call this "*true* in a different sense" is to identify *how safely* we can affirm an interpretation's significance within the authorial design with the *extent and centrality* of this significance. A source-word will then appear to provide the meaning on which everything hinges since, compared to its virtually assured importance, other interpretations are seen to be less certain and therefore more conjectural, less authoritative. There is, however, a subtle confusion of categories involved here, for the definiteness with which we establish an element's presence in Joyce' scheme is not the same thing as the importance of that element. To have found one translation of a non-word of whose inclusion we can be almost certain is not proof that the non-word has a hierarchical or monovalent structure centered on this one translation, bestowing on this translation a power that uses up the non-word's scope and renders other translations not merely tentative but secondary and less than serious. In short, when the philological approach convinces itself to have demonstrated a source-word's *central* place, it has in fact demonstrated the source-word's *place*. The source-word's centrality remains problematized by Joyce's distortion. That is the explanation I propose of what his distortions are doing.

The source-words are the only thing of whose significance we can be reasonably sure in *Finnegans Wake*, yet Joyce renders the manner and extent of their significance problematic. Denying this simultaneity, holding on only to its first part, Lernout's dividing line between what is reliable and what is unreliable about Joyce's text includes on the side of alleged reliability such meanings as Joyce literally tears apart. If a different translation violates the authorial intention contained in the source-words, the *translations based on source-words violate the authorial intention contained in the distortions*. We are dealing with more than one univocal authorial intention. This is not an unduly radical assumption to make about a text as weird and difficult as *Finnegans Wake*. And it becomes an altogether reasonable assumption in view of Joyce's meta-textual comments on difficulty and certainty. In arguing against the absolute authority of source-words, I am therefore not questioning the relevance of authorial intention. Nor am I taking recourse to the wholesale rejection of avant-textes that Van Mierlo comments on when he notes "how sticky the debate can get as critics question the relevance of evidence not provided by the text itself" ("Reading" 53). I am arguing that Joyce's creative process, as it emerges from the public archive in total (published text, available manuscripts and notes), reveals a complexity of his intention that is given short shrift by reduction to monovalent elements. In its very attempt to secure the essential and authentic parts of Joyce's creation against private deviation, such reduction introduces hierarchies that run counter to Joyce's pervasive program of generating interpretative impasses, and indeed of demonstrating the hermeneutic value of such impasses.

As I put it in the introduction, an appreciation of Joyce's authorial intention in *Finnegans Wake* ushers us towards a theoretical perspective, not away from it. This theoretical perspective finds itself in agreement with Van Mierlo's observation that "The works and the manuscripts" are not placed in opposition, but on a continuum on which they "share a state of incompletion with each other, revealing that there is no well-wrought urn but only a coming-into-being of the text through an intricate process of trials, errors, hesitations, reconsiderations, coincidences and so on" (56). Van Mierlo advances this as a critique of the poststructuralist position, whose emphasis on "the text itself," he argues, conceptualizes the work of art as a self-contained entity. This, I would venture, is the myth of poststructuralism and theory as formalism. Significantly, there is nothing in Van Mierlo's description here that differs from Derrida's, Lacan's, and Joyce's approaches, which likewise posit the writer as the subject of a process whose excesses they never fully control (as discussed in Chapter 2). Joyce's creative gesture paradoxically affirms and implements this lack of control, and neither theoretical nor genetic procedures can return his writing to monovalence and well-wrought wholeness. As Van

Mierlo has it: "Each step along the discontinuous path of composition involves a new intentional moment" (56).

It seems likely, then, that we cannot assert any hierarchical relationship between the intentional moment represented by a source-word and the intentional moment represented by a distortion. Not without making assumptions about the discontinuous path of composition that are as far-reaching as they are unfounded in evidence. Again Van Mierlo: "What is falsifiable seems limited to a few applications: the dating of notebooks, identification of sources, location of notebook units in the drafts of 'Work in Progress'. Beyond that every part of the game involves interpretation" ("Indexing" 176). In nevertheless asserting that the source-word is the only answer not based on unscientific conjecture, radical philology reveals itself to be – like all interpretation – an example of what I call ventriloquism. It speaks in Joyce's voice, it modulates its own voice through references to the avant-textes of *Finnegans Wake*, in order to claim to be listening to this voice, the voice of authority itself, when, actually, what ventriloquism speaks is pervasively structured both by the authorial material considered and by decisions originating with the purported listeners.

In a non-word, authorial intention is itself uncertain, plural, split. It is because of this plurality that all interpretations of the *Wake* are necessarily partial. If we cannot subject what I call the Pentecostal plurality of Joyce's writing to a final either/or, if we cannot exclude an interpretation solely on the basis of having shown another interpretation to be convincing, it is because no single interpretative strategy can simultaneously do justice to all authorial manipulations operative in this text. There is no reading of *Finnegans Wake* without a minimum of conjecture – and in this, Joyce's text is an exemplification and indeed an examination of virtually any act of reading.

Every decision we make to negotiate the plurality of Joyce's non-words imposes some partiality or limitation that violates their double commandment to be read and read in full; yet where we follow the command to read, we cannot but make such decisions. In the next chapter, I explore how these forced decisions relate to questions of responsibility. Effectively, the *Wake* has the potential to transform any exegetical discourse we construct around it into a meta-discourse: a discourse about the formation of discourse, and therefore also a discourse about certain problems of ethics.

4 Making Do

Productive Chaos

The absence of hegemonic centers interferes with hierarchies of meaning and with syntheses that gather meanings under a single heading. In the present chapter, I keep exploring the ethics of interpretation by looking at the challenges posed by such plural meanings without closure. We cannot simply assume that such meanings are "good" (whether we take this to designate legitimacy, relevance, usefulness, ethical soundness, or any other quality we wish to focus on). Instead, we need to ask how we navigate the complex textual space of Pentecostal pluralities.

The first thing to note here is that the uncertainty brought about by non-words is rarely an isolated phenomenon surrounded by a stable context. Attridge points out that for many non-words, "the context *itself* is made up of puns and portmanteaux [i.e. non-words]" (*Peculiar* 202). This means that Pentecostal pluralities often remain undecidable even where we look for meanings sustained over sentences, paragraphs, or entire passages. Far from providing one central theme that helps us sort through our readings, such textual units frequently support multiple themes and narratives at the same time. As one non-word offers up several meanings, it also offers several contexts for the non-words in its vicinity. Thus, "a 'contextual circle' is created whereby plurality of meaning in one item increases the available meanings of other items, which in turn increase the possibilities of meaning in the original item" (202). Even readings that carefully respond to what we find in Joyce's text may thus branch out into multiple possibilities that are largely independent of each other. Slote suggests that "the complexity of the *Wake* is primarily syntactic rather than semantic in that glossing, or unpacking, the portmanteaux is only of small (but not insignificant) help" (*Joyce's* 131). Syntactic complexity (which may or may not include convoluted grammar) is another way of saying that Wakean plurality destabilizes more than the univocality of individual expressions; it extends to the relations these expressions establish among each other. As a result, reading becomes what Slote terms "linguistically parallactic: multiple perspectives are allowed, which complement and subvert each other" (131).

DOI: 10.4324/9781003361411-5

Given that Joyce's non-words often fuse together expressions whose phonetic or orthographic similarity is coincidental rather than etymological, the layered perspectives made possible by a non-word need not be semantically compatible. Accordingly, phrases and passages that make use of non-words can generate multiple senses that remain linguistically parallactic: "sometimes harmonious, sometimes discordant, often both" (131). These layers of meaning exist in Pentecostal simultaneity. They may speak to each other, but they do not compete for validity on a single universal grid. Which is why I suggest that we should not ask whether a given reading succeeds at integrating all of a non-word's meanings into one. Although a non-word's range of meaning is not boundless, not only do we not know where precisely its boundaries are (since we can neither anticipate nor exclude the possibility of future discoveries of relevant readings). There is also no "rule" or linguistic feature dictating the semantic compatibility or comparability of such readings as we do have. I therefore propose that no single reading is tasked with bringing all discovered meanings into agreement – or indeed with drawing on all discovered meanings. Different readings of a non-word explore different meanings or sets of meanings.

Let me clarify these considerations with an example from the first generation of *Wake* criticism which illustrates a syncretic approach still in evidence whenever interpretation aims to reduce linguistic parallax to semantic agreement. In 1939, Jorge Luis Borges published a review of *Finnegans Wake*. Borges explains his disappointment in Joyce's "*calembours*" (195) by glossing the non-word "ameising" (417.28). "*Ameise*, in German, means 'ant.' Joyce [...] combines it with the English *amazing* to coin the adjective *ameising*, meaning the wonder inspired by an ant" (195). The semantic unity posited by this interpretation (the non-word's two sides feed into the same overall meaning: amazement *caused by* an ant) is a strategy often found in monovalent readings: "When you put all the elements together, what do they actually say?" Yet this approach is not supported by anything we know about non-words. There is no rule-book inside or outside *Finnegans Wake* that tells us this is how non-words behave, and the assumption runs contrary to the sheer heterogeneity of Joyce's materials.

The ant that is bugging Borges can probably be read in conjunction with other aspects of "ameising," as the various layers of a non-word resonate with each other. But they need not collapse into the kind of neat solution that would merge ant and amazement into a single statement. For one thing, the non-word's context, "He was ameising himself hugely" (417.28), provides at least one additional overtone ignored by Borges: "amusing." A reading of "ameising," then, should perhaps take into consideration the relation between amusement and amazement. Furthermore, since the "He" in question is the ant-like "Ondt" (417.24), there is an added circular structure of an ant "ant-ing" itself. How does this fit in with the idea of amazing oneself or amusing oneself? And what, to return to Borges's manner of synthesis, is so amusing about an ant? My point is that Joyce's non-word gives rise to a linguistic parallax in which none of these meanings need to be compatible at all, though they may produce interesting harmonies and tensions.

Interpretative strategies that knowingly or unwittingly equate rigor with an ideal of monovalent synthesis undo precisely this simultaneity and disunity of meanings: a more peculiar effect than an opening up to arbitrary interpretation. Even careful readings are ultimately destabilized by virtue of being one among many responses to Joyce's text. This destabilization undermines the identification of a single, central, or overall meaning, but it does so without eradicating Joyce's role in structuring his text or undoing the specificity (and thus ultimately the meaningfulness) of individual readings. Instead, interpretation cuts into an excess of possibilities from which specificity is gained through decision-making, thus locating any specific reading in a space of alternative possibilities. As Slote has it: "Joyce is developing a writing strategy in which nothing could be correct since any and every element is short-circuited by another" ("Imperfect" 148). Such writing raises the question of how you are to articulate your own position against a background of incessant change, how you should negotiate encounters with *other* articulations, and what results can possibly be worked towards within a fluctuating, short-circuiting plurality. The very form of non-words should have us consider how discourse can function in the absence of certainty and stability.

In addressing these issues, I take my cue from a meta-textual image in the *Wake* to which the themes of unruly plurality, cohabitation, and interaction with others are central: the building of a city. In the "Haveth Childers Everywhere" section (532.6–554.9), which forms the ending of III.3 (and thus of the séance already discussed in Chapter 2), HCE presents himself as a builder of cities, or of one city, which he has constructed in honor of his wife ALP. Stuart Gilbert gives an intriguing account of Joyce's method in writing this passage. Here is Gilbert describing Joyce's literary workshop:

> Five volumes of the *Encyclopedia Britannica* on his sofa. He has made a list of 30 towns, New York, Vienna, Budapest, and Mrs. [Helen] Fleischman has read out the articles on some of these. I "finish" Vienna and read Christiana and Bucharest. Whenever I come to a name (of a street, suburb, park, etc.) I pause. Joyce thinks. If he can Anglicise the word, i.e. make a pun on it, Mrs. F. records the name or its deformation in the notebook.
> (*Reflections* 20–1, insertion in original)

Gilbert disapproves of this method, which to him appears random and confusing. It does not create what he calls "appropriate" (21) puns: puns playing on a predetermined central meaning, deepening or inflecting it.

Instead, the procedure generates deviations that have nothing to do with what – according to Gilbert – Joyce is actually writing. As he puts it, "The system seems bad," for "The insertion of these puns is bound to lead the reader away from the basic text" (21). The underlying assumption here, a variation on Borges's, is that there has to be a fundamental level of meaning which holds together all of the text's various complications. Even more reductive than Borges, who at least starts by considering several meanings, Gilbert locates this fundamental level in the undistorted English of a core text assumed to antedate Joyce's textual confusion. As Rabaté puts it, "Gilbert's position corresponds to that of the reductive reader who imagines that a first-draft version of *Finnegans Wake* would be written in 'normal' English and would provide a 'basic text'" ("Fourfold Root" 395), with puns and neologisms forming a secondary – and therefore negligible – layer. Holding that the manipulations which "lead the reader away" from all those nice place-names are inappropriate, Gilbert skips over the significance that Joyce's distortions have in their own right. He believes that "When, as in this case, we have retrieved almost all the sources from which the text is constructed, [...] the meaning of the text is finally provided" (Rabaté 399), as knowledge of the sources allows us to undo the distortions and return to the basic text.

Contrary to this exegetical dream and to Gilbert's suspicion, Joyce's compositional method does add important functions to the source material. Rabaté suggests that Joyce "was interested in adding overlays of meaning applied to the text in an almost mechanistic manner. And yet it is in this very method that he gained access to a different and original generation of meaning" (398). As Joyce builds more and more allusions into HCE's tale, the "sheer excess of references" (401) begins to take on significance. It not only serves to evoke certain places and edifices (whose inclusion in the text, if Gilbert's account is to be believed, is a disconcertingly offhanded matter), it also creates an effect not present in any individual source: the theme of chaotic city space. On the one hand, the passage's "endless piling up of textual debris" (404) comes to evoke the chaos and filth of big cities, thus problematizing HCE's achievement. On the other hand, this image of the urban jungle functions as meta-textual comment. The complex make-up of social spaces illuminates Joyce's strategy of implementing excess itself as a compositional tool – using it as the very element that allows him to rework his material into pluralities from which specificity is gained only through an exploration that remains *partial*, not through the *authoritative* reduction dreamt of by Gilbert.

The patchwork language of the *Wake* resembles a busy city-space in that neither one of them is parceled out into items serving only one project and one possible path. Instead, Joyce's non-words open onto what III.3 calls a "parapolylogic" (474.5) – conjuring effects of parallax, parallel processes, and polysemy. Whereas a city's topography can be conceived of as a grid organizing discrete units, its topology is characterized by how the lives of its inhabitants overlap: sometimes supporting each other,

146 *Making Do*

sometimes interfering with each other, sometimes simply co-existing. To give just one example: a park bench might serve not only as a resting place and an opportunity to take in one's surroundings, but as the magical site of a couple's first kiss, an obstacle on which to pull off a skateboarding stunt, a homeless person's way of spending the night, a castle defended against pirates in a children's game, or an improvised office space for an afternoon's studying. Similarly, in Joyce's linguistic parallax, self-containment is displaced by the plurality, even the simultaneity, of uses.

Like a city that subdivides and reorganizes itself, however, Pentecostal plurality operates within certain limits. If Joyce's writing were to indiscriminately embrace any and all possibilities, it would capsize into meaningless white noise. This is the link I chiefly want to explore in reading the city-building passage as another one of the *Wake*'s instances of meta-textuality. HCE's city shares with the text in which it appears the quality of being a productive chaos that pushes dangerously close to this edge of collapse. City-building, as Joyce presents it, constitutes yet another activity split between production and destruction. We can thus take the achievement boasted of by HCE as a self-reflexive comment on how the *Wake*'s language is cluttered, bursting at the seams, constantly on the brink of overload and implosion. The negative aspects sported by HCE's city include prostitution ("daughters-in-trade being lightly clad," 532.25–6), contagion ("oppedemics," 539.36; "tuberclerosies," 541.36), overpopulation ("fair home overcrowded," 543.22), insufficient sanitation ("shares same closet with fourteen similar cottages and an illfamed lodginghouse," 545.2–3), waste ("house lost in dirt and blocked with refuse," 543.32–3), and poverty leading to the deterioration of the city space itself ("copious holes emitting mice," 545.8). Most of these issues arise from a city's sheer complexity, from the subdivision of spaces to accommodate more and more people, from the adding on of new materials and technologies, from the palimpsest-like overwriting of uses. This is a different world than that of the single tower, a world richer and more varied, but also prone to generating its own forms of violence.

At the beginning of "Haveth Childers Everywhere," we read: "Eternest cittas, heil!" (532.6). The evocation of the eternal city, Rome, is followed by the Nazi salute, suggesting that HCE (appearing as E.c.h.) encompasses both the splendor of great cities and what Joyce identifies as their brutality. HCE's rhapsody of cultural achievements, which ranges from the seven wonders of the Ancient world (see 553.9–11) to the modern wonder of electricity (see 549.14–16), is thus complicated from the start by a sense that "the 'eternal city' can embody all cities only if it carries its onus of guilt, betrayal, and totalitarianism" (Rabaté, *James Joyce* 179). This is echoed in HCE's declaration: "Seven ills so barely as centripunts havd I habt" (541.1), transforming into "ills" the seven hills on which Rome is famously built. Given Joyce's reference to fascism, one might conclude that the greatest risk presented in the city-building passage is not chaotic excess but the totalitarian ambition to achieve perfect order. The hubris and brutality of great cities moreover establish a thematic connection to the Tower of Babel, which appears at least twice in the passage: first, when HCE speaks about a "Babbyl Malket" (532.25), and again when he talks about someone "confused by his tonguer of baubble" (536.8). Yet the second mention already leads us away from the overbearing tower, evoking the "confusion of tongues" that reduces mighty Babylon to the dimensions of a mere "bauble." The power-hungry aspect of these cities, then, is far from self-sustaining or self-stabilizing.

In *Ulysses*, Babylon features as one in a series of examples that go through Bloom's mind when he thinks about the finitude that catches up with even the most bombastic cultural projects: "Cityful passing away, other cityful coming, passing away, too: other coming on, passing on. [...] Piled up in cities, worn away age after age. Pyramids in sand. Built on bread and onions. Slaves Chinese wall. Babylon. Big stones left" (8.484–90). This interior monologue occurs in "Lestrygonians," the chapter concerned with eating and (via the Homeric parallel) cannibalism, evoking entire populations and indeed entire cities devouring each other; one edifice built on the ruins of the last. This theme features in the *Wake* in the form of the "Quinet sentence," a quotation from Edgar Quinet that is alluded to throughout the text and that spells out the eventual fate of cities and their inhabitants: *"pendant qu'autour d'elles les villes ont changé de maîtres et de noms, que plusieurs sont entrées dans le néant, que les civilisations se sont choquées et brisées"* (281.7–10). McHugh translates: "while around [the flowers] the cities have changed masters & names, while some have ceased to exist, while the civilisations have collided with one another & smashed" (281). City-building sooner or later undoes the project of Babel with its single inert center. It feeds into plurality and change, into structures that are shared, modified, connected, divided, and put to new purposes, that influence each other and edge each other on – if always as part of processes that involve many clashes and ultimately end in collapse.

The hermeneutic upshot of approaching HCE's city as a meta-textual image is that doing so cautions us not to idealize Pentecostal pluralities. Plural meanings are neither "inherently" good, nor are they made so by way of opposition to the authoritarian project of the one. They allow for a wealth of useful possibilities, but the split between creation and destruction that characterizes city-building reminds us that the usefulness of pluralities goes hand in hand with an excessive productivity potentially violent in its sheer intensity, as well as with the production of results that are anything but lasting. Regarding the first aspect, the building of pluralities can be compared to the self-destructive chaos of Shem's house described in I.7. Production that actively relies on instability and imperfection is naturally perilous. A consideration of the second aspect, the impermanence of achievements, means instable pluralities also tie in with the questionable morality of the Quinet sentence. From a sufficiently abstract macro-perspective, cultural achievements appear as a kind of ebb and flow which masks the brutality of each change undergone by cities and civilizations. Alison Lacivita points out that a similar issue is at work in the loss and discovery of ALP's letter. "The decomposition and recomposition of the letter in I.5 mirrors the burial and unearthing of HCE in I.4" (73) indicating that "All human endeavours and creations become compost, fertilizer for the next generation of lives, legible in the remains buried in the ground" (82), with human beings simply "being humus" (18.5) as the *Wake* has it. This reading finds in the transience of our cultural and biographical projects the source not only of inevitable ruination, but more specifically of violent *reappropriation* further down the line.

All of this might imply an unsavory trade-off which bases intensity of production on the willing destruction of what came before. This dynamic resembles an interpretative move often considered to be a particularly unattractive aspect of theoretical readings: that theory appropriates and redistributes inherited symbolic material in order to provide the fuel for its own reading and writing, at the expense of the original historical contexts and concerns of the texts theory is dealing with. Joyce's writing fits this description in two ways. On the one hand, one of the central themes of *Finnegans Wake* is the change that decomposes and recomposes social and individual life in order to provide the fuel of history. On the other hand, as I argue in chapters 2 and 3, Joyce's use of his source material subjects it to such excess and distortions as severely interfere with any notion of utilizing pre-existing meaning. In order to address what may at this point appear like a particularly brutal logic of *sacrifice*, I now want to think the spaces of HCE's city, so dangerously yet productively open to a plurality of lives and meanings, in connection with an ethical problem of impermanence: a theme that Derrida conceptualizes under the name *hospitality*.

Openings on the Unknown

That which gives hospitality, that which allows someone to offer hospitality to someone else, may at first appear to be the space of a certain privacy. I am hospitable by welcoming the other within the space that is mine: the space that I, by right, inhabit. Yet, as Derrida points out, welcoming and indeed inhabiting already imply publicness: "There is no house or interior without a door or windows. The monad of home has to be hospitable in order to be *ipse*, itself at home, habitable at-home in the relation of the self to itself" (Derrida and Dufourmantelle 61). There is no way to refrain from offering hospitality in Derrida's sense, and no fundamental difference between the hospitality offered within an apparently private space and the hospitality offered within a public space – say, the hospitality of a city. Either constellation consists in opening up towards an outside whose public nature, whose possibilities of communication, exchange, economy, infrastructure, law, and so on, already structure the inside of the seemingly self-contained subdivision. Once hospitality becomes sufficiently continual, sufficiently busy, sufficiently hospitable, it reveals the *already prevailing* frailty of the boundaries that we draw to divide up space – an idea that may be present when the city-building passage speaks of a "staircase continually lit up with guests" (543.31–2).

Privacy is on the contrary found in the secret, in the unknown, in the stranger who is granted hospitality. It is here that hospitality signals its relevance to how we deal with texts. A text, too, is anything but cut off from the economies and interactions that surround its writing and its reading. Yet at the imaginary center of these interactions, there remains a secret into which none of them can tap. It remains secret not because it is hidden away more cunningly than other meanings. A secret is not part of a text, which is why a text cannot be made to divulge it. Attridge writes: "A work of art states what it states, presents what it presents, no more, no less; and it refuses to say anything further; no matter how hard we press it" (*Work* 256). There is, for each case, no text but the text itself, or no archive but the archive – to which I would add that a text or archive can *never* say enough. As I argue in chapters 1 and 2, a text always ends before essential meaning is pinpointed. Add more information, and the boundaries shift, essence withdrawing once more. The secret thus resembles the vanishing point marked only by the slipping away of the trace. It is the purely conjectural essence around which a text is presumed to be structured. As Miller posits: "The reader cannot go behind [the literary text], or beneath it, or before and after it. Literature keeps its secret, but on the surface" (*Topographies* 310). The secret is that about which the text has nothing left to reveal, that which would remain secret even if everything offered by the text had been made visible, brought to the surface, at which point it would become apparent that the text engenders conundrums it *still* refuses to resolve. The secret is the question raised but never answered: "with no other basis than the abyss of the call or address" (Derrida, "Literature in Secret" 157).

In short, any signifying gesture conjures up the phantasm of something no reading can find. That thing is illusory, but it is before us as soon as we read a signifying gesture and perceive in its weave of meaning such nodes as look like promises of a stable core. As Derrida has it, the secret is "infinitely private because public through and through. It is spread on the surface of the page, as obvious as a purloined letter" (*Given Time* 170), where a purloined letter is that textual surface at which we glance only to continue our quest for what we have not found yet. In middle Lacan's reading of Poe's story, he gives the example of a mislaid library book: "even if the book were on an adjacent shelf or in the next slot, it would be hidden there, however visible it may seem there" ("Seminar on 'The Purloined Letter'" 17). Anyone spotting it would be likely to continue their search for an object expected to be "elsewhere." Analogously, when the policemen in Poe's story look at the openly displayed letter, its visibility prods the continuation of a search for something presumed to be hidden. From this, Lacan continues: "what is hidden is never but what is *not in its place*" (17); it is hidden by virtue of not presenting itself where we would expect it to do so. A letter/signifier, then, is never fully in its place: "it will be *and* will not be where it is" (17). The very presence of a signifier conjures up a certain absence or secret: the signifier's essence, which remains an imaginary center that no search can actually access.

One might object that, in Poe's story, the letter is eventually retrieved. But Lacan makes it clear the letter's material presence at that point should not be taken to represent the signifier's phantasmatic essence. That which asserts its presence is not the symbolic but the real: "the real, whatever upheaval we subject it to, is always and in every case in its place" (17). When it is found, the letter can be seen to switch its position in Lacan's reading, from the signifier as an element of the symbolic to the real kernel at the heart of the signifier. "What now remains of the signifier when, having already been relieved of its message for the Queen, its text is invalidated as soon as it leaves the Minister's hands?" (28). The answer Lacan gives is: a manipulation of desire. The letter is the *objet petit a*, the object of both desire and anxiety. Turning away from the perfectly visible letter in order to keep looking for a secret presumed elsewhere, the police in Poe's story act not as readers for whom a matter-of-fact answer is not good enough, but rather as readers who continue a search for a fictional absence because they shun away from the presence of the real kernel. What is ultimately retrieved is this kernel: the remainder of referentiality that resists identification and that consists solely in the anxiety caused by a secret.

Rather than contrasting public communication with a private sphere understood as the personal idiosyncrasies of reading, we can thus conceive of the private as the dimension of the secret, of the real, of that which *withdraws* from any reading and leaves any reading in anguish. This is the private in the sense of *privation*, of something that is taken away. We encounter this element in amplified form in Joyce's non-words, whose distortions exemplify that at the heart of intention itself, there is illegibility and privacy: that a manipulation of measurable extent raises questions it may refuse to answer. Yet as I have been arguing throughout, this is but the radicalization of the secret at work in all signification. As we have seen in Chapter 2, meaning-production consists not in the accessing of a solid presence, but in the active interpretation of an excess of possibilities, about which Derrida says that they are organized "in a contradictory fashion around a secret" (*Specters* 18).

We can now circle back to the Derridean problem of hospitality. Hospitality, too, is about a confrontation with a secret. Derrida gives the example of a stranger whose name and status one does not know, and who may not even have a name and status: "absolute hospitality requires that I open up my home and that I give not only to the foreigner (provided with a family name, with the social status of being a foreigner, etc.), but to the absolute, unknown, anonymous other" (Derrida and Dufourmantelle

25). Since absolute hospitality is hospitality to alterity itself, it undoes the concept of hospitality as calculable, negotiable, or controllable. Derrida continues: "The law of absolute hospitality commands a break with hospitality by right, with law or justice as rights" (25). That is, absolute hospitality breaks with hospitality as a negotiated pact or as an object of legal or ethical duty. In view of Derrida's comment that a home is necessarily open, I would add that this is because absolute hospitality is effectively an exposure to alterity that is *always already* at work in the home and the self (rather than an agreed-upon contract). On this basis, a discussion of hospitality provides insights relevant to signification, where the encounter with the secret is likewise inevitable: not a matter of choice, but an irreducible risk that destabilizes our interpretative efforts. Naas gives a helpful pointer when he describes Derridean hospitality as

> a welcoming of an other whose identity and character are thus not assured, an other, therefore, who may in fact pose a threat to us, who may cause us *to question our right to what we call "our home,"* or who may in fact try to evict us from that home and from everything we consider "our own."
>
> (*Derrida* 22, my emphasis)

Despite the name, hospitality is by no means a benign concept in Derrida. Hospitable spaces are at least potentially dangerous. What is crucial is that this danger should not be read as an invitation to phobic thinking. The various outsides that phobic thinking wants to exclude cannot be kept at bay. We are always already exposed to alterity; all spaces are *necessarily* hospitable. The danger in question should instead be understood as a challenge to our preconceptions regarding ourselves and the space we assume to be ours.

Thinking through the encounter with the other means considering the changeability of one's space and one's self. As Attridge puts it: "when I encounter alterity, I encounter not the other as such (how could I?) but the remolding of the self that brings the other into being as, necessarily, no longer entirely other" (*Singularity* 24). With regard to the unreadability of a text's secret, we can say that although no reading can fathom the secret (the secret remains outside the trace-structure), a reading can try to allow the secret to *act on* the trace-structure and to reconfigure the conceptual and discursive categories of the self that does the reading. Again Attridge: "In order to acknowledge the other, I have to find a means to destabilize or deconstruct the set of norms and habits that give me the world – my idioculture, in short – in such a way that the force of that which they exclude is felt" (*Work* 71). However, if the production of new meanings is thus linked to the transformation of the self, I want to hold on to the *threat to the self* this necessarily poses. As with Derrida's concept of hospitality, there is no safety here in simply welcoming the new: no guarantee that the new constitutes an improvement or an enrichment. The new meanings I take on board in an encounter with a text may be disorienting, detrimental to my conceptualizing abilities, useless to myself or others, caricatures of the text I am trying to understand. Hospitality towards the unknown or the unpredictable is a split state that is productive and destructive in one and the same gesture, in a simultaneity that cannot be broken up. The question of hospitality thus corresponds to the question I pose at the end of the previous subjection: whether we are right to engage in destabilizing productivity, or whether this constitutes an ultimately insupportable logic of sacrifice.

Derrida insists that despite the positive connotations of hospitality, hospitality in an absolute form undoes itself as a regulatory ethics or a series of concepts codifying ethical responses to the other. He draws attention to the biblical narrative of Lot and his family, to "the moment when Lot seems to put the laws of hospitality above all" (Derrida and Dufourmantelle 151). The moment in question is the horrifying scene in Genesis 19 when Lot seeks to protect the guests to whom he has offered his hospitality (two angels disguised as men) against the citizens of Sodom by telling the latter:

> Behold now, I have two daughters which have not known man; let me, I pray you, bring them out unto you, and do ye to them as is good in your eyes: only unto these men do nothing; for therefore came they under the shadow of my roof.
>
> (Gen. 19.8)

The aftermath of this offer is that the angels defeat the citizens and enable Lot's family to escape into exile. There, it is Lot's daughters who think of yet another desperate measure: "Come, let us make our father drink wine, and we will lie with him, that we may preserve seed of our father" (Gen. 19.32).

Rabaté points to this narrative's affinity with motifs of *Finnegans Wake* (see *James Joyce* 163–4). In particular, both sexual violence and incest may figure in the *Wake* in the form of HCE's crime, which can be interpreted as HCE sexually abusing his daughter Issy (see Shari Benstock, "Nightletters" 224–5; Eide 134–7; and Shelton). I emphasize this connection because Derrida's invocation of Genesis 19 lends itself to what I consider two serious misinterpretations. On the one hand, one could take Derrida to be retracting here a notion of hospitality whose catastrophic self-destruction in the face of actual threats the biblical reference is supposed to demonstrate. I have already indicated that this is not Derrida's point, since hospitality according to him is not something that can be retracted. Our spaces are always already open. On the other hand, it could be suggested that Derrida is in fact urging us to *accept* the unspeakable violence committed by Lot as a necessary cost of hospitality. Transposed onto my discussion of *Finnegans Wake*, the implication of such a reading would be that any violence done in the course of creating the new is a necessary price to be paid, and that HCE's abusing Issy is part of a fall into greater cultural complexity we should accept. Such an interpretation is to be categorically rejected. The key issue here is the connection between postlapsarian existence and *responsibility*.

After his discussion of the biblical scene, Derrida asks: "Are we the heirs to this tradition of hospitality? Up to what point?" (155). I read these questions (which appear on the final page of the text) as a rejection on Derrida's part of any notion of violence as an acceptable means to an end in the context of hospitality. Instead, Derrida maintains that we can never exclude violence as simply extrinsic to the problem of hospitality. If the encounter with the other entails a transformation of the self, then we cannot reassure ourselves that this transformation will automatically be for the better. Yet Derrida is not arguing that hospitality puts us at risk by making us the passive recipients of a transformative event that is already pre-programmed and awaiting us. The most shocking brutality committed in Genesis 19 does not come from an outside, but originates with Lot. What the encounter with the other sets in motion is a transformation of the self that is also a reconfiguration or reinvention of the public realm, in the sense of our ethics and our interactions. And it is precisely because, depending on *our* choices, this reinvention can take us in different directions – violent or humane, just or horrifying – that it inscribes us in responsibility.

This understanding of hospitality aligns itself with Martin Hägglund's reading of Derrida. Hägglund shows that Derrida's analysis of the encounter with the other does not provide any straightforward ethical prescription. The problem of hospitality "does not refer to an ethical obligation to be open to the other, since it is not a matter of choice. The exposure to the coming of the other – which is inseparable from the coming of time – precedes every decision and exceeds all mastery" (126). Interacting with alterity is not so much a marker of goodness as it is an inevitability. As Derrida has it:

> The coming of the event is what cannot and should not be prevented; it is another name for the future itself. This does not mean that it is good – good in itself – for everything or anything to arrive; it is not that one should give up trying to prevent certain things from coming to pass (without which there would be no decision, no responsibility, ethics, or politics).
>
> ("Deconstruction" 94)

If Derrida's discussion of hospitality does not provide an ethical program, in the sense of a prescription regarding how one should act, it therefore nevertheless formulates an ethical *problem*: the problem, in fact, of ethics itself. Hägglund, in countering such misreadings of Derrida as see in hospitality an ideal to be aspired to, is somewhat too eager to be done with the ethical side of this formulation. He so forcefully opposes the idea of a Derridean ethics as to risk sidelining hospitality in the sense of what Derrida, in a phrase cited by Hägglund, calls "The nonethical opening of ethics" (*Of Grammatology* 140, qtd. in Hägglund 75). Hägglund describes this opening as giving rise "to both the desirable *and* the undesirable, to every chance *and* every menace" (97), yet even though he is clearly aware of the implications, he does not follow them to their logical conclusion.

If hospitality is at the basis of any event, it is "precisely the operation of the logic identified by Hägglund that makes ethics possible" (Attridge, *Work* 303). As the structure underlying all events, hospitality is what makes ethical interaction possible – along with any other form of interaction. What is more, this opening on all possibilities places on us a demand to *affirm* this opening, to acknowledge and respond to openness itself. Hägglund takes this into consideration when he writes about the necessity of making decisions: "the law of unconditional hospitality [...] requires one to make precarious decisions from time to time. The only unconditional law of hospitality is that one will have been forced to deal with unforeseeable events" (105). This is precisely the problem of responsibility, which comes into being where a decision has to be made that no preliminary reflection, rule, or convention can quite take care of for us. Hägglund writes that to empty this risk out of decision-making, "to deny this inevitable risk, to deny the essential corruptibility of responsibility or to project its consummation in an ideal future, is to deny the condition that makes responsibility possible in the first place" (106).

Hospitality towards the unpredictable is not ethical, it opens up the *possibility* of the ethical; yet in drawing this preliminary conclusion, we have to keep in mind that the possibility in question is not one in the sense of an option that could be rejected. The risk is inevitable; we are placed in a position of responsibility no matter what we do. A denial of this position cannot create a safe space outside responsibility. What it effectively denies is an understanding of the precariousness of the *only* available space. Relying on a stability that is not given, it fails to address the demand placed on us. In this view, what Derrida calls hospitality also takes on the meaning of an affirmation of these demands. It is an affirmation not in the sense of embracing any event that may take place (this being the naïve reading that Hägglund addresses and refutes), but in the sense of a contemplation of responsibility's underlying structure, a willingness to engage with the precariousness of the ethical, and an attempt to do justice to the demands placed on us by the coming of the other – including the potential threat of the other.

In asserting that this is an ethical obligation, I find myself in disagreement with Hägglund's vocal opposition to "those who want to turn Derrida into an ethical philosopher" (105) – an opposition Hägglund himself complicates in the passages I cite here. But I fully agree with Hägglund that the Derridean concept of hospitality is neither an encouragement to engage in reveries and utopian ideals, nor a fatalistic judgement that declares violence a fact of life to be accepted. What Derridean hospitality demands is decision-making, including political decision-making. Again Hägglund: "Far from absolving us from politics, it is the undecidable coming of time that makes politics necessary in the first place, since it precipitates the negotiation of unpredictable events" (171). The key term here is "negotiation": this is politics not as a once-and-for-all rule, but as a continuous effort. What Derrida shows is that *even though we cannot but offer hospitality, we are responsible for how we do this*. Hence, as Attridge writes, "the never-ending interaction and negotiation between the unconditional and the conditional" (*Work* 302), as each individual case is a response to a demand that is infinite.

There is perhaps less at stake in the act of reading a literary text, yet some problems in interpretation are analogous to those outlined in this discussion. Like the unpredictable event, a text's secret makes an absolute demand on our hospitality. It confronts us with the question of how we are to do justice to its radical alterity. In order to be meaningful, our response cannot be entirely removed from common ground, a purely private gesture of making the text say whatever we want it to say (as with the hospitality of spaces, such absolute, self-contained privacy disqualifies itself from being a space/response at all). At the same time, the response cannot consist in the application of an objective program already established, already outlining for us the meanings we should create (such a dream of stability can only proceed by perceiving its own response as no response at all, at which point it has rendered itself blind to the demands placed on it). We are left, then, with the option of making a decision: of actively producing a meaning that we see as a response to the text. As I have argued throughout, such an *iteration* of the text is not random; still, any iteration involves moments beyond total, public calculability.

Referring these moments to the continuous effort of negotiating public spaces and discourses – life in the *polis*, in other words – we can now venture that readings, also, do not inhabit a public discourse simply opposed to individuality, nor indeed a public discourse subject to limitless plurality, but a public discourse in which each reading is an individual contribution that potentially helps *shape* public discourse. We all shape a public realm whose precarious instability is the only discursive space there is. Where we attempt to leave everything the same, to create a public space unaffected by the private, secret, unknowable, or incalculable, this gives us not a different kind of iteration or a safer way of doing justice to a text, but no iteration at all, no production and exchange of meaning, and thus no public discourse. This is not to argue some hidden, menacing hypervolatility that somehow disproves public communicability as we know it. It is to recall that the public realm as we know it is nothing but the sum of the ways in which we inherit, interpret, interact – and in which we are responsible for these inheritances, interpretations, and interactions precisely insofar as they are neither totally objective nor totally subjective. As with hospitality, precisely *because* public discourse is open, we can shape the contributions we make to it and be held accountable for these contributions.

This way of putting things enables us to approach from a different point of view the relation between impermanence and sacrifice previously mentioned. In chapters 1 to 3, I have already established that even though we can imagine a state of prelapsarian lucidity (a state in which we would be capable of sharply distinguishing between the productive and the destabilizing aspects of iteration), in actual reading, there is never any question of occupying and subsequently sacrificing this state. We can only think this state as a state outside iterability. Impermanence in iteration is a fact. By drawing connections to Derridean hospitality, we can now add that this necessary exposure to impermanence and risk does not sacrifice *agency* or *accountability* in iteration, either. The decision we face is not whether we want to risk engaging in discourse; but the question remains *how* we choose to engage in the discourses we already inhabit. Plural, imperfect readings are not opposed to the articulation of specific and meaningful positions. It is in fact our very response to imperfection, impermanence, unreadability, etc. that bestows on us an active and meaningful part in discourse-formation.

Creation and Original Sin

I will now argue the compatibility of the above view with Lacan's thinking, before examining how it also features in *Finnegans Wake*. In chapters 1 and 2, we have seen that from a Lacanian perspective, Joyce's writing disturbs our discursive habits by presenting distortions on whose absenting and covering-up symbolic codification is typically based. Joyce's undoing of legibility may thus strike us as something that does not form part of our world as it ordinarily decodes itself, instead confronting us with what Thurston calls "something outside the discursive bounds and bonds of social reality" (*James Joyce* 96), which "refuses to be subject to the constraints that constitute that reality" (96). Yet our reaction to the presence of these distortions is not (usually) a descent into a psychotic unraveling of meaning. The nature of the symbolic is such that we strive to interpret even transgressions of it: to reconstitute it in new forms where it has been transgressed (the instances in which this fails are by definition traumatic ones).

When it comes to Joyce's act of affirming the unreadable, "an act of this kind is always a masked act, its transgressive edge blunted by an implication in social discourse; its exposure of jouissance is limited to an anamorphic instant, a momentary glimpse of the forbidden Thing" (Thurston, *James Joyce* 196–7). Responding to the Joycean distortion, we are compelled to move from the literary thing to the reconstitution of discourse: we reconfigure the symbolic. In fact, we do so indefinitely and in ever-changing forms, since we can never quite catch up with or truly repeat Joyce's "unspeakably innovative" (210) gesture. If this failure "dooms literary criticism to an eternal recurrence of misreading and misappropriation" (80), I would argue that this is first of all a productive mechanism – albeit along the lines of an anxiety-inducing productivity. Moreover, the inventiveness we are doomed to need not break with responsibility. Where our construction of readings leads us to reflect on how these readings inevitably constitute misreadings and misappropriations, the result may be a heightened awareness of the role that active interpretation plays in discourse-formation: in the production of the symbolic realm.

This view closely corresponds to the Derridean argument outlined above; it is also one of the tenets of Lacan's thinking about the *sinthome*. We have seen in Chapter 1 that the sinthome turns the symptom from an effect into a cause: instead of a leftover not symbolized, it constitutes the idiosyncratic braiding of the three orders that forms a subject's singular topology. Yet idiosyncrasy does not transport us beyond accountability, to a realm where (symbolically, psychologically, ethically) anything goes. Re-knotted and reshaped, the symbolic instead returns us to discursive bonds and to accountability precisely because it can be seen to depend on our decisions, rather than simply being imposed on us. As Thurston writes, in late Lacan, "What ties the knot of human subjectivity is therefore not some universal patriarchal law of signification, but an *act*" (*James Joyce* 196). Even as our social existence takes place in the symbolic order and therefore in this order's constitutive deficiency, we still have some freedom in deciding how to live in that deficiency. Therefore, even though the deficiency itself is not the result of any choice of ours, our mode of living in it is our responsibility. Again, this is structurally similar to Derrida's notion of a self that actively gives form to a necessary hospitality. The sinthome resembles hospitality in that both require us to see the secret, the private, the real – that is, the non-computable and unpredictable – as a necessary part of the legible, the public, the symbolic.

Another connection we may note is that, like Joyce, Lacan proposes to think of this constitutive deficiency of the symbolic in terms of the postlapsarian condition. It is not lost on Lacan that the sinthome, by way of an Anglophone pun, can be taken to suggest the biblical fall. Early on in *The Sinthome*, he states: "This is the fault, the *sin*, which my *sinthome* advantageously starts with" (5). The sinthome, the psychological manifestation of not being perfect, already carries within it an echo of the fall from grace (and perhaps Lacan is implicitly keeping in mind here the etymological root of "symptom" – "falling together"). Since the fall is an important motif in *Finnegans Wake*, it is worth examining this brief aside of Lacan's.

Speaking of Eden and original sin, Lacan refers these issues to Joyce via the palindrome found in *Ulysses*, "Madam, I'm Adam" (7.683) – "in keeping with the joke that Joyce makes" (5), as Lacan puts it, with the added twist (or is it a lapse in Lacan's recall of Joyce's joke?) that in Lacan, Adam is himself said to be a madam. This identification conjures up the familiar, problematically gendered image of castration. When Adam invents language by naming the animals, he gives rise not to a perfect language but – if his being a madam is any indication – to an idiom already subject to symbolic castration. Yet Lacan suggests that it is Eve who first uses this language: "she was the first person to put it to use, in order to speak to the serpent" (5). This act of speaking to the snake, in a language already imperfect, proves immensely productive. Lacan goes so far as to state that the "so-called Divine Creation is thus redoubled by the parley of the *parlêtre*" (5): the *parlêtre* indicating the speaking being, the symbolically constituted subject.

On one side of this doubling of the creative act, we have divine creation, the making of the perfect world that is Eden. On the other side, we have original sin, which Lacan presents as Eve using the symbolic order to strike up a conversation with the snake. As soon as there is the symbolic, there is sin, which means that the parley redoubles creation, revealing the world as we encounter it through the symbolic, with all the various imperfections this implies. Here, Lacan imposes on the linearity of the biblical narrative (paradise, then fall) the paradoxical circularity of symbolic and real. The symbolic is not simply added to a divine and whole real which it would merely fail to represent. The addition of the symbolic doubles the act of creation, creating the real of the postlapsarian world. We should recall here that Žižek posits the real both precedes symbolization (in the above example: paradise before original sin) *and* constitutes a left-over produced by the symbolic (which is always necessarily imperfect). This split means that once Eve has spoken, making us symbolically constituted subjects, we are no longer in the presence of the prelapsarian real. Thinking back to my argument about nudity and clothes in the first chapter, I would suggest that nudity corresponds to the real, while the symbolic corresponds to clothing that covers the real. I argued that postlapsarian nudity is different from prelapsarian nudity in that it is no longer entirely spontaneous but *tainted*, as it were, by the possibility of wearing clothes, thus displacing the innocent state instead of returning to it. In much the same way, the postlapsarian real – the real we encounter in the margins and blind spots of symbolization – displaces whatever access to the real may be possible for beings that exist outside the symbolic. As soon as the symbolic order is so much as possible, its possibility changes the real.

The fall, in this view, is not a delayed exclusion from a divine world available in principle. The fall, for Lacan, is the fact that for *parlêtres*, beings living in the symbolic order, the world cannot exist in a state of self-presence and stability in the first place (further parallels to the Derridean ideas of différance, iteration, and hospitality may be noted here). This casts a new light on the fact that the sin to which the snake tempts Eve consists in eating from the tree of knowledge, whose fruit opens Adam's and Eve's eyes to their own predicament, namely their nudity. Harari comments that "Lacan marks a certain inflection in the story of the Bible: the point that highlights how a site of castration or lack is linked to a certain knowledge" (28–9). In Lacan's retelling, the insight to be gained in the fall is precisely the realization of the *parlêtre*'s originary and necessary exclusion from perfection. Or, as Žižek puts it, the " 'Fall' is the first step toward liberation – it represents the moment of knowledge, of cognizance of one's situation" (*Parallax* 96). In a reading of the fall as fortunate (more about which presently), "The loss is thus not recuperated but fully asserted as liberating, as a positive opening" (127). As he puts it elsewhere: "We rise again from the Fall not by undoing its effects, but in recognizing in the Fall itself the longed-for liberation" (*Ticklish* 79): the liberation, but also the responsibility, that comes with our recognition of the opening that always already characterizes our situation.

Lacan's reformulation of the symptom as the sinthome is driven by this recognition. The sinthome, to return to Harari's conclusion cited in Chapter 1, means that "there is a degree of freedom in the way that each speaker organizes the marks of the Other" (300). We cannot undo the imperfection of the symbolic, but this predicament itself opens on opportunities for reinventing the symbolic. In rewriting the symptom as the sinthome, one of the issues Lacan is concerned with is thus that public, symbolic codification is not an already given framework that individuals are simply thrown into, but is negotiated by individuals, especially where they confront the limits of existing codification. This, according to Lacan, is exactly what Joyce did – hence the sheer weirdness of Joyce's writing. As with Derridean hospitality and discourse-formation, such negotiation is a far cry from mastery and prelapsarian infallibility. We can by no means be sure that addressing a certain aspect of the symbolic will automatically entail a change for the better. Yet these considerations take place where otherwise there would only be symbolic frameworks just as indebted to the particularities of their production, but untested for their adequacy to the task of responsible agency (historical heritage taken for divine order, ideologies accepted without reflection, etc.). Like Derrida, Lacan can thus be seen to insist on a crucial difficulty in the manipulation of the symbolic or public, as the problem once again manifests itself as a degree of freedom that is substantial enough to place on us certain responsibilities and demands, yet limited enough to make meeting those demands a considerable challenge.

Here, *The Sinthome* is also taking up some of Lacan's much earlier reflections on the topic of responsibility. In *The Ethics of Psychoanalysis*, he states: "Moral experience as such [...] puts man in a certain relation to his own action" (3). And he continues: "moral experience is not limited to that acceptance of necessity, [...] to that slow recognition of the function [...] of superego" (7). Instead, Lacan relates moral experience to the Freudian dictum "*Wo es war, soll Ich werden*" (7), which he glosses in the following way:

> That "I" which is supposed to come to be where "it" was [...] asks itself what it wants. It is not only questioned [by the superego], but

as it progresses in its experience, it asks itself that question and asks it precisely in the place where strange, paradoxical, and cruel commands are suggested to it by its morbid experience.

(7)

Even as experience bombards us with all kinds of demands (difficult and often enough impossible), Lacan associates the sifting and interpreting of this experience with an active and responsible self.

The reference to Joyce in *The Sinthome*'s discussion of original sin is offhanded enough, and not specifically presented as an examination of *Finnegans Wake*. Yet by conceptualizing a connection between original sin, the problem of the real, and the subject's capacity for articulating their own attitude, Lacan delineates a position that is relevant to the freedom generated by the linguistic distortions of the *Wake*. The *Wake*, too, relates the efficacy of imperfect language to the biblical framework of the fall. Lacan's discussion of the fall as constitutive moves along similar lines to James Atherton's proposition that, in *Finnegans Wake*, "creation is the original sin" (32). And like Joyce's implementation of uncertainty in his postlapsarian coinages, Lacan's thinking on the sinthome recasts fallen-ness as an opening. We can respond to it in a variety of ways (just as Derridean hospitality allows for any number of possible reactions); therefore, it places us in a position of responsibility. I will now consider the *Wake*'s interlinking of responsibility, discourse-formation, imperfect readability, and postlapsarian history by examining another theological motif that Joyce refers to: *Felix Culpa*, the fortunate fall.

Felix Culpa

The traditional concept of the fortunate fall goes back to St. Augustine. It interprets original sin as the Felix Culpa (Latin: "happy fault" or "happy fall") on the basis that a postlapsarian world occasions greater proof of divine mercy than would be possible if humankind had not fallen. The inflection given to the term by *Finnegans Wake* is a different one. Two of Joyce's sources, Vico and Freud, converge on the view that the state of innocence and perfection is not to be considered as the beginning of human history, but as excluded from this history, given that humanity begins with the Freudian horde's patricide (as discussed in Chapter 2) or with the Viconian giants' flight from the thunder god (as discussed in Chapter 3).

When Vico asserts that "*The civil world is certainly the creation of humankind*" (§331), he is not saying that we ourselves have brought about a fall from grace that resulted in our present state. Rather, Vico is claiming that the creation in question has always taken place in the absence of divine grace. Bishop comments that, in Vico, "history is made by men descended from animals, and not always well" (*Joyce's Book* 177). If the "civil world" we have created is not always well made, this should hardly surprise us, for we are inheritors of a natural history *sans* teleology. The "creation of humankind" Vico is concerned with is thus similar to Lacan's symbolic creation as quite separate from divine creation. The point is that, for human beings, no perfect language or ideal social organization has ever existed and subsequently been lost. Much like the accounts by Derrida and Lacan outlined above, Vico holds that certain intrinsic conditions of human perception and interaction locate us in a state of fallibility. Human activity has to make do with means that are anything but the ideal ones we attribute to superhuman beings such as the god of thunder.

While opposing the historical reality of ideal states, Vico also captures our tendency to invent such ideals. Consider the following sentence from the *Wake*, already mentioned in Chapter 3: "Now their laws assist them and ease their fall!" (579.26). I have read this as positing fallen-ness as a starting point, and procedures of discourse-formation as a response to that start. This dynamic is linked to Vico not only by its logic of historical progress, but also by the term "laws." As Klaus Reichert notes, Vico's giants, in responding to the rumbling of thunder, learn "something like self-restraint which in its turn leads to some form of natural law which Vico claims to be already present in the name of Jupiter (*Jovis – Jous – ius*)" (51). This etymology of "ius" derives the term from the name of a law-giving figure who embodies the conditions of the law's invention. In this explanation, the figure of Jupiter serves not as a merely convenient fiction, but as a necessary fiction covering over an absence. Authority itself is fictional in Vico: authoritative to the extent to which it is constructed. Jupiter can serve as the origin of the law, and thus of the law's name, only as the figure whom the giants hypothesize upon hearing thunder. "The figure of Jupiter was so poetic – that is, popular, exciting, and instructive – that its inventors at once believed it, and they feared, revered, and worshipped Jupiter in frightful religions" (§379). Without being invested with this fictional ideality, the noise in question would never become what the *Wake* calls the "last word of perfect language" (424.23–4). It would remain a meteorological phenomenon, incapable of giving rise to legal structures. What actually precedes these structures is not a perfect language or any other ideal state, but rather, as Reichert puts it, that "human beings in the first phase are still in a status [sic] of animal-like savageness" (49). Ideality as a concept emerges simultaneously with the giants' fall into culture, at which point they conceive of their own situation by construing a fictional ideal from which they describe themselves as excluded.

We can see this logic as Lacanian in its similarities to middle Lacan's paternal metaphor, which marks the symbolic authority from which we are inevitably barred. We can also call it Derridean with a view to Derrida's proposition that "The sign and divinity have the same place and time of birth. The age of the sign is essentially theological" (*Of Grammatology* 14). Divinity – e.g. Jupiter's frightful language – is retrospectively posited as the guarantor of a transcendental meaning whose loss is "in truth the loss of what has never taken place, of a self-presence which has never been given but only dreamed of" (112). Like the *objet petit a* or the trace as non-origin, Jupiter's language in Vico is the marker of an ideality that is only ever encountered as a retrospective projection.

Similar to how Derrida, Lacan, and Vico thus describe human activity as always taking place in a state of fallen-ness, the *Wake* casts the prelapsarian state as a phantasmatic one outside both history and its own narrative. For all its repetitions of the motif of falling, the *Wake* does not present us with any scene that corresponds to the moment of Eve and Adam's original transgression and that divides the *Wake* into a part set before the fall and a part set after it. The entirety of the *Wake* takes place in a postlapsarian world, within the horizon of a certain belatedness. The origin of such a state of affairs necessarily remains outside this horizon. In creating its narrative world, one of the opening gambits of *Finnegans Wake* is not to answer in a univocal way the question: "What then agentlike brought about that tragoady thundersday this municipal sin business?" (5.13–14). Instead, we are told: "There extand by now one thousand and one stories, all told, of the same" (5.28–9). Although the fall's manifestations are versions "of the same," the very frequency with which it is evoked, its repetition and division, transport the text away from the one all-decisive move from a prelapsarian to a postlapsarian condition, emphasizing instead a problem of falling and fallibility more generally speaking. The *Wake* could be said to be taking place "Ofter the fall" (589.20), in a time after the fall when, far from being over and done with, falls occur quite often.

In place of any pre-human or superhuman realm of (spiritual, linguistic, social, etc.) perfection, we encounter the already fallen creation remarked upon by James Atherton and spelt out by Joyce in I.4: "Let there be fight? And there was" (90.12–13). Conflict is with us from the word go ("let there be light"). At the beginning of "Haveth Childers Everywhere," we find descriptions of cultural activity already steeped in postlapsarian aggression. In the first paragraph, McHugh annotates "Shitric Shilkanbeard" (532.8) as "Sitric Silkenbeard" (532), leader of the Danes at the Battle of Clontarf, and "MacAuscullpth the Thord" (532.9) as "Ausculph Mac Torcall" (532), the Irish king under whose rule Dublin came under English control. Based on these historical allusions, Rabaté proposes that "the foundation of Dublin sends us back to Genesis, less to Adam than to Cain, killer, sinner, and builder" (*James Joyce* 179). HCE's account of city-building, that is, unfolds as part of a history in which Eden is replaced with a belligerence harking back to the first fratricide. HCE may even be identified with Cain who, having killed his brother, goes east of Eden, where "he built a city" (Gen. 4.17).

Later in the city-building section, HCE makes reference to "my stavekirks wove so norcely of peeled wands and attachatouchy floodmud, now all loosebrick and stonefest, freely masoned arked for covennanters and shinners' rifuge" (552.2–5). Although there is a sense of development (from "wands"/"once" to "now"), the description is not progressivist. There is a cultural history here leading from the catastrophe of the flood ("floodmud" and "arked") to the building of structures that serve as a refuge for sinners – i.e. for humankind in general. This marks the already familiar connection between biblical notions of the fall and social organization as a remedy. Yet, interestingly, the remedy in question is only half "stonefest" (as solid as stone, from German "fest"), being also "loosebrick." HCE's account of his cultural achievement thus takes into consideration the theme of history's precariousness. If HCE's city is something like the *Wake*'s shorthand for the history of human civilizations, what I find crucial is that HCE uses whatever imperfect means are at his disposal. He operates in a world in which builders – like Cain or Tim Finnegan – have fallen. Which is to say that *no amount of construction will do away with the potential for failure* that is the very definition of the postlapsarian condition.

There is another narrative choice which reinforces the sense that in the *Wake*, the state of fallen-ness is to be worked with, rather than lifted or transcended. Notwithstanding the various resurrections the text rehearses, the *Wake* does not stage a second coming – nor any equivalent from outside Christian myth – a moment of judgement and redemption that puts an end to worldly existence. Instead, the *Wake* ends in as postlapsarian a mode as it begins, with one cycle ending and another beginning. Its closed textual loop – "A way a lone a last a loved a long the [...] riverrun, past Eve and Adam's" (628.15–3.1) – sends us not to a realm beyond the text but back to the start, drawing us into the fallen world of the text once more. The process continues, with no end in sight: that is, without approaching a state of wholeness or completion.

It makes sense, then, that when Joyce alludes to the phrase "Felix Culpa" itself, a motif that returns throughout the text, the reference's context often signals that fallibility is not about to be canceled out by divine intervention. For instance, the fortunate fall can be related to HCE's crime in Dublin's Phoenix Park ("If you want to be felixed come and be parked," 454.34). Over the course of I.3 and I.4, HCE, who may or may not be a scapegoat, is tried for misconduct towards two girls and three soldiers in Phoenix Park. It appears that at one point in the proceedings, HCE is killed, or buried alive, and subsequently comes back to life: "There was a minute silence before memory's fire's rekindling and then. Heart alive!" (83.4–5). At this point, HCE has moreover already featured as a "foenix culprit" (23.16). His burial and resurrection make him, the suspected culprit in the Phoenix Park case, an avatar of the phoenix, the mythological bird that dies and is reborn from its ashes. This demonstrates HCE's ability to "rise afterfall" (78.7); yet this Christological feature is bestowed on a character of whose many flaws and possible crimes we are only too aware. The pattern of fall and redemption, that is to say, is playing out in a register that is decidedly less than divine. And whereas the traditional understanding of the fortunate fall refers to mercy afforded by a divine judge, HCE's case reimagines mercy as the possibility of escaping the verdict of other people.

Another form this escape may take is that of HCE's rehabilitation in the eyes of others, which is the goal that ALP can be seen working towards in some of her manifestations. Her letter is referenced throughout the book in connection with attempts to shed light on the events in the park. It is worth noting, then, that in the version of this letter found in Book IV, she writes: "When he woke up in a sweat besidus it was to pardon him" (615.22–3). Part of the letter's message seems to be ALP's attempt to exonerate HCE. This, too, would be a fall and rise quite different from the conventional notion of Felix Culpa. It involves not divine forgiveness, but the possibility of being forgiven by others, potentially by one's "fellows culpows" (363.20), that is, fellow culprits: people who are as caught up in culpability and fallibility as oneself, and whose forgiveness operates within that postlapsarian condition. In these narrative strands, rising after the fall is something to be achieved through human activity, the same activity of whose exposure to fallibility the recurring "Felix Culpa" motif so insistently reminds us. It is a mode of forgiveness more fraught with risk – palpable also in the distinct possibility that HCE may be undeserving of lenience – but also more attuned to accountability than the potentially solipsistic (occasionally psychotic) direct link between human individual and divine Other. What is more, just as we never definitively learn whether or not HCE is guilty, we never get to know whether he and ALP succeed in clearing his name. His rise is not a foregone conclusion, a mercy already granted. It is, at most, the continuation of getting another chance, about whose outcome *Finnegans Wake* remains silent. Although Book IV invokes the beginning of a new day, it does not provide a scene that undoes the fall by reinstating HCE in society or by otherwise redeeming him.

What are we to make of the notion of Felix Culpa within the confines of a narrative world that is always already imperfect, and stubbornly devoid of a more-than-human capacity to overcome imperfection? My suggestion is that in such a context, the fortunate fall is best understood along the lines of the Lacanian model. The fortunate fall is an affirmation that aims to inhabit the world in all its complexity. It is a fall because it ceases to avoid our postlapsarian state; it is fortunate because it strives to better understand what this state entails. Falling into the postlapsarian world confronts the true challenges of our situation and identifies certain transcendental ideals (like the god of thunder imagined by Vico's giants) as ultimately distracting inventions. This is how I would read the statement: "Ut vivat volumen sic pereat pouradosus!" (610.16). McHugh translates this as: "that the book may live let paradise be lost" (610). Understood as "that the book may live, let the fall from grace happen," this risks returning us to the ruthless calculation of a sacrifice, along the lines of: that we may have knowledge or freedom, let us give up on perfection, let us commit any misdemeanors and misreadings we want. But from a perspective of already inhabiting a world after the fall, it is possible to understand the phrase in a different way: as the affirmation and appropriation of a necessity. Let the fall from grace *have happened*, and let us accept and indeed affirm that it has happened; let, consequently, the paradise of an absolute interpretation of the book absent itself, so that the book may be the more alive, and we alert to its liveliness.

It should have become clear how the *Wake*'s meta-textuality can be related to this idea of the fortunate fall. The simultaneity of expressive power and risk features again and again in the *Wake*'s meta-textual narratives. It shapes the workshop of Shem the Penman. It is present in the language myths split between creation and destruction. It features as HCE's city, in which plurality is placed in close proximity to catastrophe and violence. And it is inscribed in Joyce's non-words, which make it more palpable than regular words that an iteration is always a ventriloquist vocalization producing specificity from excess. After all, any reading of a non-word activates only part of a Pentecostal plurality, and so constitutes a (potentially problematic) marginalization of alternatives. By calling all of this fortunate, I take Joyce's stance to be a humanist – verging on atheist – one which *prefers* flawed solutions to the kind of linguistic purity or cosmic eschatology in which all meaning knows only one goal (I discuss Mr Deasy's "one great goal" in the Concluding Remarks.) An actual interpretation may not be the one true interpretation, but its specificity can be seen to coincide with its relevance in a particular context. As Attridge has it, "we can still conduct meaningful and valuable discussions about rival frameworks – not in order to settle, once and for all, upon the right one, but to ascertain which are useful in which particular ways" (*Joyce Effects* 151). The usefulness of actual readings resembles that of HCE's city, whose achievements are decidedly less than perfect, but whose construction represents the sort of ongoing implementation of makeshift solutions that is possible in response to the challenges thrown up by postlapsarian life. We could say that the *Wake*'s various motifs of building – HCE's city, Tim Finnegan's fall, the Tower of Babel – cast both the postlapsarian condition and meta-textual reflections in pragmatic terms. The question is not how to return to perfection, but how to continue after collapse, how to make something out of chaos.

I want to underline again that none of this is a matter of choice. I do not take Joyce to be giving us a recommendation against returning to perfection. I take him to be saying that perfection is not an option. If Joyce keeps drawing attention to the simultaneity of production and destruction at the levels of both content and form, obsessively describing it, laying it open, it is thus for *didactic* reasons. He is trying to confront us with how we actually produce meaning in a postlapsarian world. Reading Joyce, Derrida, and Lacan side by side reveals similarities between them that perhaps make it easier to appreciate this aspect of *Finnegans Wake*. Their work converges on the idea that, confronted with the precarious plurality of possibilities, we should not look for a solution that would resolve all difficulty, neutralize the risk in iteration, and master any distortion of the symbolic. Those projects can only fail – and will moreover result in some version of Shaun's neurotic quest for certainty. Instead, the understanding of our postlapsarian condition shared by Derrida, Lacan, and Joyce can be subsumed under the motto: read without closure. Do not pretend that the actual meaning you construct is an essential meaning, something that came to you finished and unalterable.

This does *not* entail no longer reading at all. Nor is the result an endless deferral that forever avoids producing any actual reading. The goal of reading the text and doing it justice remains. Yet the imperfection of signification is such that we can only attempt to do justice through a responsive openness which cannot function unless it is also open to (whilst guarding against, but unable to quite foreclose) the risk of an injustice. We have to take this risk. Which does *not* mean, either, that anything goes. The absence of prelapsarian certainty Joyce, Derrida, and Lacan are concerned with results in responsibility, not inconsequential freedom. It is because our choices may be bad that we should do our best to make good ones. It is because there is no single mode of objective legibility that we need public discourse. It is because the excess of possibilities opened up by postlapsarian signification *requires* us to make a decision that there *necessarily* is responsibility for the decisions we make. Reading without closure means to encounter a text, realize that its secret constitutes an anxiety-inducing absence, and then go right through anxiety by making a decision and making some use of the plural possibilities which the text opens up.

The goal is to become a reader who does this to the best of their ability, and who remains invested in the decisions they make. Reading without closure requires only that one sees readings as depending on decisions, which also means that one suspends a final decision, the decision never to decide again, never to read again, never to reconsider one's perspective or consider a different one. As Eide puts it:

> Readers are asked to suspend decision, to entertain ambivalence, to place ourselves in a position between two options; that "place between" options is the ethical space of interpretation and, as Joyce suggests in these elliptical moments, the ethical space of subjectivity itself.
>
> (33)

Reading without closure means that I realize there are other takes than my current one: that I accept the partiality, the provisional nature, and the subjectivity of my response. Yet this subjectivity is not locked into some private space irrelevant to the public world. On the contrary, it is where we appeal to objectivity as the only approach possible that we seek to efface our contribution and evade responsibility for how we have positioned ourselves. Affirming that our contribution is partial, that it falls short of closure, also affirms agency and responsibility.

Here, Joyce's insistence on uncertainty encompasses more than a theory of literary exegesis. He provides us with a hermeneutic ethics of public work. This ethics rejects what may appear to be the reassuring stability of objectivity, tracing that assurance to a transcendental signifier, a dream of returning to essential meaning or a prelapsarian state. It is by rejecting this dream, focusing instead on the power of fallible human activity, that Joyce's hermeneutics succeeds in capturing the constructed and constructive nature of our discursive stances, including their transformative power and thus their real-life importance. Interpretations, languages, public realms, cities – these are all *made*, not given. Even inheritance is construction, since iteration is change. What is more, we can reject objective closure while remaining committed to communicability and public exchange. I don't take Joyce to be propagating an atomizing, individualist perspective in which the necessity of deciding for yourself is the freedom not to care about what anybody else thinks, feels, or needs (a definition of openness we encounter with alarming frequency in present-day debates). Openness should be thought as intrinsically linked to responsibility. The subject who affirms partiality already knows themselves to be in the presence of other subjects (you *will* encounter other readings of the *Wake*).

The plurality of possible constructions, being irreducible to a single synthesis, does not disperse into solitary projects either. It forms a public realm in which different subjectivities co-exist and interact. This ruins prelapsarian univocality, replacing it with a Pentecostal cacophony. In such a cacophony, the risk of making mistakes is very real. Yet this is a fortunate fall, insofar as constructions no longer bound to logocentric teleology are free to reread themselves and each other, to challenge, to inform, to transform and be transformed.

The *Wake* urges us to think a text's secret as that to which interpretation should strive to do justice, both in relating to the text and in relating to other interpretations. To acknowledge a text's secret is first of all to acknowledge the text's singularity, and therefore the need to adapt interpretative strategies to the elusive essence that is the only thing that can orient them. Yet, secondly, it is to acknowledge that this essence remains unassimilable, that the text keeps its secret and withdraws from our grasp, and that an interpretative process gives rise to a reading only through active decision-making. Finally, it is to realize that this active production of meaning from an excess of possibilities implies a plurality of readings. In the productivity spawned by the secret's absenting itself, any interpretative effort we may undertake will be one among many, gathered around the secret in a discursive space in which we continue to evaluate, compare, combine, and revise readings. *Hospitality towards the secret is hospitality towards other readings of it*, with all that the concept of hospitality implies about the need for careful assessment. It is in the resulting horizontal plane of simultaneity (the city) that the *Wake* achieves the kind of impact and resonance the vertical plane of uniformity (the tower) cannot hope to produce.

Concluding Remarks
The Uses of Difficulty

Over the course of this book, I have examined some of the ways in which the difficulty of *Finnegans Wake* is meaningful in its own right, forming part of Joyce's philosophy of language. It is not merely to accommodate his readers' penchant for free association, or his own ambition to dazzle for dazzling's sake, that Joyce confronts us with "variously inflected, differently pronounced, otherwise spelled, changeably meaning vocable scriptsigns" (118.26–8). Nor should we treat the *Wake* as a case in which the complexity of the subject matter requires difficult treatment, putting obstacles in the path of elucidation. Such an explanation posits that difficulty's strains and delays are superficial, orchestrated by an underlying principle that may eventually be revealed via processes of reduction and clarification. As I hope to have shown, the difficulty we encounter in Joyce's last work is of a different kind. It is itself the underlying principle.

Difficulty in *Finnegans Wake* can be read as an expression of alterity. Through its unique oddness, the *Wake* engages with the fact that there are moments in signification that resist appropriation. Both Joyce's non-language and his meta-textual reflections tell us that we can neither identify a signifier's unchanging essence (this is the argument of Chapter 1), nor limit its scope by isolating authorial intention (Chapter 2), that, consequently, interpretations are irreducibly plural, such that the possibility of one interpretation does not indicate the impossibility of others (Chapter 3), and that, ultimately, acceptance of this plurality is acceptance of the partial, imperfect, and to some extent provisional nature of each reading (Chapter 4).

Putting things this way, I have undoubtedly carried out what could be called a theoretical reading of Joyce. At the same time, I have tried to show that Joyce anticipates theoretical positions. It is important to acknowledge the tension between the idea of this anticipation and the argument I am making for the *Wake*'s unreadability. Insofar as Joyce's text remains opaque, the passages I cite throughout this study can only partly support any interpretation, including the meta-textual readings I develop here. The exegetical decision to be made in this regard is a fundamental one. If we take Joyce's distortions to be denying all meaning, then his writing should not be interpreted at all – not beyond an interpretation

DOI: 10.4324/9781003361411-6

of the effects of unreadability itself. My wager, however, is that one of these effects is Joyce's manipulation of our desire: a manipulation that transports his text away from anything like a pure denial of meaning. Unreadability still involves a notion of reading. It manifests not as the absence of referentiality, but as a referentiality without reference (one would not think to speak of unreadability where reading and referentiality are not at stake; the chair you are currently sitting on can hardly be called unreadable). Unreadability is not an absolute breakdown or denial; it leaves a promise in place. As Derrida has it, "The unreadable is not the opposite of the readable but rather the ridge [*arête*] that also gives it momentum, movement, sets it in motion" ("Living On" 95–6). The unreadable can function as the Derridean secret that makes inheritance possible, or as the real that in Lacan not only constitutes the realm outside symbolic and imaginary sense-making – delineating a silence beyond the speakable and the productive – but also acts as a transformative force *within* the symbolic: the unreadable stain that, in its very transgression of meaning, opens on a reinvention of meaning.

With unreadability operative as a productive force, we can see how applying interpretative frameworks to Joyce's obscurity might not be entirely beside the point. If the *Wake* denies simplistic claims to legitimate interpretation, I propose that it equally undoes the argument that a reading of its non-words is absolutely *illegitimate*. One of the things that the *Wake* allows such a reading to articulate – in a ventriloquized voice no longer fully intrinsic or fully extrinsic to the text – are meta-textual reflections on just this conflation of voices. In this view, Joyce appears as not only a favorite case study of that strange entity, literary theory, but as one of its exponents. The *Wake*'s difficulty is an example of how theory, for all its notorious inaccessibility, comes down on the side of openness, plurality, and decentralization. If *Finnegans Wake* can be called a work of theory, one reason is precisely that theory is difficult to access – not because of bad presentations obscuring an underlying simplicity, but because of a programmatic interest in productive alterity. In the introduction, I define theory by referring to the impossibility of *definitively* defining it. Miller writes that "it may be the essence of literary theory to resist definition" (*Topographies* 318), and he proposes that "To translate theory is to traduce it, to betray it" (319). As with the non-words of the *Wake*, emphasis cannot be on one particular formulation, on one particular translation or interpretation. The context of each new reading instils in it a partiality that makes it one in a series of possibilities.

With regard to Derrida, Nicholas Royle suggests that "reading Derrida means meddling *with* Derrida [...]. His texts call to be read differently, anew, every time: they affirm the open-endedness of the *or again*" (47). Consider my own use of Derrida's and Lacan's work in a synthetic approach neither of them can be said to have anticipated, let alone prepared. If I hope to draw on certain strands of their thought and to present these in language perhaps more approachable than Derrida's and

Lacan's own, it is clear that I do so at the cost of suppressing some of the original complexity. I offer a reading – an act of spectral ventriloquism – that I believe to be rigorous, yet this can only ever be *one* reading. It will have to be accompanied, or replaced, by other readings (carried out by myself or by others) that return to Lacan's and Derrida's productive strangeness, which in turn will give way to other thought.

I will presently address in more detail this notion of transience and the questions it raises about the validity of our constructs. For now, I want to emphasize that theory's reasons for rereading itself in this manner are akin to the reasons Joyce gives us for rereading *Finnegans Wake*. Or, to put it more summarily still, *Finnegans Wake* and literary theory are difficult for similar reasons. Each finds that knowledge is not coextensive with stability; each introduces complexities in order to make the point that there are elements in any system of knowledge that escape assimilation. To object that this is where theory, or indeed *Finnegans Wake*, shows an unwillingness to adopt a consistent, meaningful position (thus making things arbitrary, inconsequential, ultimately *less* difficult) is not a convincing argument. It is a bout for clarity that unduly conflates the meaningless, boundless malleability of a strawman postmodernism or poststructuralism with the difficult, infinite plurality of discourses as they actually present themselves to us.

As Robin Valenza and John Bender note, when difficulty is opposed to seriousness, usefulness, relevance, etc., "The operative belief [...] is that common speech embodies common sense and that anything worth saying can and should be said in broadly accessible terms" (36). This is not a belief theory shares, given its analysis of how accessibility is generated through a *dissimulation* of the instability of interpretative codes: that is, through a logocentrism that bestows the title of obviousness, objectivity, or common sense on an outlook whose partiality and contextual formation are henceforth no longer to be questioned. A critique of theory – and here, again, think of *Finnegans Wake* as a work of theory – that condemns difficulty and reasserts the primacy of understanding merely repeats this gesture. Complaining that theory's/Joyce's difficulty does not make sense, cannot be read, should not be taken seriously, such critique does not prove theory's/Joyce's analysis wrong or insubstantial, but simply fails to engage with it, thus masking "deeper structural divergences that such thinking refuses to acknowledge" (34). Theory/Joyce articulates just these divergences, takes issue with dissimulation, and aims to transform a debate's operational framework. By contrast, an out-and-out rejection of transformation risks denying productivity and indeed the conceptual sharpness of our tools in the name of handy stability.

The observation that, when theory, including the *Wake*, is returned to the logocentric procedures with which it explicitly breaks, much of what it does in excess of logocentrism, or in opposition to it, takes on the appearance of inconsistency, obscurity, and purely rhetorical effects – such an observation does not tell us much that was not already given in the gesture of that break. On its own terms, however, this break quite clearly delineates its hermeneutic upshots. It finds that there is no intrinsic homogeneity to any signifying gesture and that logocentrism can uphold the clarity and stability to which it lays claim only at the cost of problematic processes of exclusion. The "structural divergences" that are masked by a rejection of difficulty thus hinge on the question of whether or not you find that, in representing to ourselves certain parts of the world (for instance, certain works of literature), our hermeneutic enterprises are lent sufficient scope and depth by such methodologies as achieve transparency within the existing discursive frameworks. If so, then a break with these methodologies will resemble nothing if not a break with the world, or at least with sensible ways of communicating about the world. If not, however, then it becomes apparent that such a break attempts to articulate the possibility of the world itself undergoing change in ways not anticipated by the current frameworks – but *under such conditions, articulation is precisely the problem.*

If there has ever been a literary text embodying the breaking of extant articulation, it is *Finnegans Wake*. In my opinion, this renders self-defeating those critical approaches that hold, implicitly or explicitly, that in order to count as successful, a reading of this text should do away with uncertainty and anxiety. Now, it could be argued that the price paid for a deviation from existing structures is too high: that a writer or speaker who challenges the existing frameworks of intelligibility thereby fails to communicate whatever vision of alternatives they may have. We certainly recognize in this a reproach that has been leveled at *Finnegans Wake*, and there are discussions to be had about what kind of balance should be struck. But Joyce has put forward his answer to this question, and our interpretation of *Finnegans Wake* should try to do justice to his answer's radical nature. It is possible to argue Joyce has gone too far, but this is surely not to say that undoing his excess is in keeping with his intention.

All of this brings us back to the question of why it is so crucial to conceptualize articulation as changeable – crucial enough for Joyce to sacrifice readability. The answer is of course that discourse is not a self-contained realm, but permeates the building of social and political worlds. An axiomatic insistence on stability excludes unruly gestures (that is: an exploration of their merit or lack thereof) not just in the sense of experiments in poetics, but more generally in the sense of other ideas, other ways of speaking, other ways of living. Derrida notes that "the order of intelligibility depends in its turn on the established [social] order which it serves to interpret. This readability will then be as little neutral as it is nonviolent" ("Force of Law" 270). To counteract the violence of unquestioning, unreflecting continuation – and replace it, not with automatic success, but with at least the *possibility* of responsibility – postlapsarian world-builders have to review the assumptions that lend stability to their constructs. Our discourses are frameworks affording us agency and openness to ethical work only where we manage to realize they are not how the world naturally is.

Derrida calls this ongoing destabilization the *auto-immunity* of social systems, and he asserts that "no community <is possible> that would not cultivate its own auto-immunity [...]. This self-contesting attestation keeps the auto-immune community alive, which is to say, open to something other and more than itself" ("Faith" 51, editor's insertion). We recognize here the logic identified by Hägglund. If to be "alive" is to be "open," this is also to say: at risk. The community that lives already incorporates "more than itself." It is not quite itself, in the sense of a stable identity; it is always already in progress. Hence Derrida's term *democracy-to-come*, which despite what the name may suggest is a configuration of the here and now. "Derrida is arguing, not for some utopian future, but for a certain anticipation of openness to the other" (Wood 52). To make possible the political and social sphere in the here and now as, precisely, a social, intersubjective, interactive one, there has to be, at the very heart of the public, an element that escapes the public, a possibility of change not yet calculated, knowable, or symbolized: a secret.

The meta-textuality of *Finnegans Wake* can be read as being concerned with this dimension of the secret. As I hope to have demonstrated, Joyce anticipates the thought, found in both Derrida and Lacan, that the spheres of the public and the private cannot be conceptualized using a neat division between the monolithic, universal, secure and the disconnected, individualistic, ultimately inconsequential. The *Wake* stages the precariousness of the public in terms of both signification (seen in ALP's letter and its examination, in Shem's writing, in Shaun's ventriloquism, and in the book's various language myths) and co-inhabited space (seen in HCE's city). These scenes dismantle the notion that what is communal or shared is also stable, self-evident, and free of construction. The point is reinforced by the double commandment of Joyce's non-words. Our interpretations, for all their participation in various public realms, produce meaning only through active decision-making, which is to say: construction. In turn, the secret that withdraws from any and all such decisions is not an empty or superfluous element, which a truly public exegesis could or should somehow do without. It is precisely because of the unpredictability of each response to the alterity of the *Wake* that the text's public dimension is structured the way it is, presenting itself as a plurality of differently situated, differently relevant readings.

With regard to my own text, that plurality of readings should have us wonder whether there is perhaps any self-contradiction involved in my arguing that this hermeneutical position is articulated by *Finnegans Wake* (rather than simply by myself). A number of readers have probably asked themselves this question at some point over the course of *Joyce as Theory*. How can I possibly announce the openness of all texts to construction while also presenting an interpretation which claims to base itself on this particular text? The answer I suggest is that the sense of contradiction arising here results from a perspective that opposes (private) construction to (a public mode of) being based on. This opposition is precisely what we should reject, since, as we have seen, *construction is the only mode we have of basing-on*: of responsiveness, of rigorous and meaningful interpretation, of accountability to shared codes. Active iteration, iteration with a (potential) difference, is the only iteration there is. As I argue in both chapters 2 and 3, this is not to say that we cannot form opinions about whether a given iteration has successfully responded to a signifying gesture. Such opinions, however, are themselves *constructed* in response to those iterations, and in being shared, the opinions are opened up to further responses in turn. This process replaces the idea of an objective, transcendental criterion of correctness (not linked to construction in any way) with the test of a reading's public communicability.

There is no self-contradiction involved in asserting the necessity of construction while also holding that responsiveness is something we can evaluate, or arguing my reading's responsiveness to the text (which is to say that I believe my own reading here to be well-constructed and that my interpretation includes critiques of other interpretations with which I disagree). Self-contradiction would occur in an attempt to declare my reading the *only* possible one, or to declare it *stable*. As I put it above, my reading here will be accompanied or replaced by others. Ask me again in ten years, and I myself will probably want to put some things differently. The crucial point is that this transitory nature of meaning cannot be avoided and does not indicate the presence of error. Error would mean that in the future, I share my present categories, as if operating on a universal grid of thought, but come to recognize some inconsistency in their application. Instability means that the differential network of my categories will itself have shifted in subtle ways, no longer allowing for such binary evaluations as agreement or disagreement with my former position. I think this is a more common experience than we care to admit (especially in academia). Nor, and I cannot stress this enough, does such a future scenario detract from the seriousness of the present position, from how earnestly I am advancing my interpretation here. As John Maynard Keynes famously quipped, in the long run, we are all dead. Yet the horizon of entropy's triumph does not excuse us (unless you commit to radical nihilism) from doing the work that presents itself here and now, even if that means doing it with postlapsarian, notably imperfect tools.

The lack of definitive answers does not have to lead to the postmodern malaise of a disaffected subject who, having dissected the discourses they live by, is left paralysed: any rallying-cry, any ethical or political project, indeed any serious act whatsoever impeded by its now evident lack of "authenticity." Such an outlook amounts to an unliveable refusal of anything less than perfection. By contrast, if Joyce, Derrida, and Lacan dismantle apparently safe solutions, they also encourage us to get invested in more flawed, more complex, more problematic and critically self-aware undertakings. The ethical program we derive from reading Joyce,

Derrida, and Lacan in conjunction can be summarized as: go through anxiety. Make a decision and take a stance, and know that all stances, yours and others', are thus constructed, but also stand by your decision, if you believe it to be a good one. The element of constructedness should draw our critical attention, but it should not have us believe that a final step towards permanence or seriousness is yet required.

In different ways, the works of Derrida, Lacan, and Joyce all show us that there is no final level beneath or beyond construction. Which does not mean that nothing matters; it means that we desperately *need* our constructions and that even what matters most involves history and negotiation (in short, différance). Joyce's depiction of HCE as a pure name or legal fiction, for instance, is directly opposed to the idea that for someone to fulfill a certain symbolic function, they have to authentically embody it. The function resides not with the person, but with the name. Given the binding nature of legal fictions, it is clear that such "inauthentic" constructs cannot be cast aside. That is, once we see constructs for what they are, the next step is not to start searching for the real thing, but *to recognize the significance and power of constructs*. This corresponds to what Lacan aphoristically expresses in the title of his unpublished twenty-first seminar: *Les non dupes errent* (punning on "les noms du père" – the names of the father). Those who are not duped are mistaken; refusing to take constructs seriously, they err by missing the seriousness that lies, not in some hidden truth, but rather in constructs themselves. There are social constructs, discursive conventions, etc. on which even those who pride themselves on not being duped inevitably rely (just think of money). As Žižek comments: "What a cynic who 'believes only his eyes' misses is the efficiency of the symbolic fiction, the way this fiction structures our experience of reality" (*Ticklish* 390).

Once we acknowledge these constructs *as* constructs, we begin to see the stakes in their changeability, their ongoing negotiation. Much depends on at all realizing that a negotiation is taking place. The power of textual difficulty, in this view, is not to let itself be resolved too quickly. Breaking with the monotony of the seemingly self-evident, natural, and unpolitical, difficulty reminds us of our readings' constructedness, of their partiality, and of their indebtedness to particular assumptions. The obscurity of *Finnegans Wake* interrupts our interpretative activity, hampering the creation of an appropriate, relevant reading. But in doing so, difficulty also challenges us to address the question of what kind of reading we hold to be appropriate and relevant, and why. We could say that difficulty is a nuisance, but that it is a nuisance in much the same way noise outside your window is a nuisance when you are trying to concentrate on your work. Interrupting an activity that may feel self-contained, it reminds you that this activity is taking place in a context, and that much of its usefulness ultimately consists in how it newly inscribes you in this context. The partiality of meanings, rendered explicit, *reinforces* the ties between world and discourse, discourse and world.

With this said, let us get distracted for a moment and consider that as I am writing this, there are children outside my window, yelling and playing a game of football. Hearing the noise, I do not get up, but concentrate on the voices, attempting to be hospitable to a sound that enters my room unbidden and distracts me from my work. The children shout, sometimes in triumph, sometimes in anger. Occasionally, one breaks into song. It occurs to me that they are playing a game: they are applying rules, they are teaching themselves, and each other, the application of rules. They probably invent the rules at times. In more than the athletic sense, this is training, and if I describe it here, it is because I believe that their game, informal as it may be, and my writing, confined as it may be to a narrow section of cultural space, partake in the same activity: discourse-formation, the making of conventions and constructs. I hope that this example can go some way towards showing that discourse-formation is not some activity of Promethean dimensions. The point is rather that the world we experience and inhabit is not an inert container for our lives to take place in, but consists of these lives, down to their smallest events. This line of thought can be brought into dialogue with the moment in *Ulysses* when Stephen, perhaps exasperated with Mr. Deasy's declaration that "All human history moves towards one great goal, the manifestation of God" (2.380–1), opposes to this vision the sheer chaotic actuality of "A shout in the street" (2.386). In this scene, too – which my real-life event might be accused of plagiarizing, although in doing so, one would merely demonstrate the power of Joyce's "filiation machine" to wield fictional authority over reality itself – the noise in question is that of children playing a game: "Hooray! Ay! Whrrwhee!" (2.384).

These shouts contrast with behavior Stephen attributes to the same children only moments earlier. Sitting in his classroom shortly before their game of hockey begins, they produce remarks that he internally classifies as "A dull ease of the mind" (2.15). Before the hockey match, these children enact a conservative discursive style, looking for nothing but authoritative clarifications. Eide proposes that Stephen is trying to counteract this attitude by means of a teaching method which stimulates what little unorthodoxy it can find in his pupils' ideas: "thus cultivating creative thought processes and promoting [...] curiosity," whilst destabilizing "a codified distinction between fact and error" (65). The shout in the street can be seen in much the same light. Stephen enlists it as an alternative to Deasy's idea of an ultimate goal, of a code making sense of the totality of existence. The children's inarticulate expression of joy, precisely insofar as it breaks with the school-day's discipline and thus forms a contrast to Deasy's reductive belief in the creation of one meaning, can be classified as unreadable. It aligns itself with difficulty as I describe it here. By interrupting sense-making, it serves as a reminder of what lies beyond the discursive framework of Stephen's discussion with Deasy: a reminder of the value of the unruly and the unexpected.

What about the possibility, then, that difficulty's interruptions may become destructive? Am I saying that alterity is always good, and that the faster change happens, the better? On the contrary. We should keep in mind the problematic affinity of Joyce's language with HCE's city, which risks collapsing into a chaos that *threatens* the city's inhabitants. In view of this threat, the present account of difficulty requires one final line of thought. The shout in the street – heartily unconcerned with Deasy's one great goal – opposes itself not only to solidified codification's dull ease, but also to its hasty instrumentalism: what Attridge calls the effort of "the too full, excessively goal-oriented consciousness" (*Singularity* 123). Difficulty replaces this potentially reckless haste with a slowness that is purposely uneasy.

In *Stupidity*, Avital Ronell ventures that there are types of intelligence that lay claim to great efficiency through sheer velocity and agility – that is to say, ultimately, through ease – but whose operations are "smooth and unproblematic in terms of the results they yield" (300). Her conclusion is that "It could be that fast is slow, where mind hasn't stopped or been stopped, made to give pause over some imponderable or stumped by an effect of paradox" (300). Great ease may look impressive, but its refusal to be tripped up by the unexpected leads to shallow thought. Conversely, I would argue that slowness can be very fast indeed – that is to say, productive – while also remaining alert to the destructive chaos that waits just on the other side of paradox and Pentecostal richness. Against the very real danger of a collapse into yet another kind of inertia (the white noise of entropy), such slowness taps into the power of being stumped. It mobilizes the careful decision-making of hospitality towards a secret.

In other words, I take Ronell to be postulating an alternative understanding of productivity which closely resembles that put forward by Joyce: a productivity not tied to quantities of speed, volume, or density, but to a *quantity of interaction*, of stopping and problematizing. As Alessandra Pomarico has it in her contribution to an essay collection titled, appropriately enough, *Slow Reader*: "An ethos of care and compassion propagates, tensions unfold and may stay unresolved: we learn in that tension, maybe not to judge, but to expose and share, to discuss without being prompted to react or provide a solution" (216). This form of productivity is opposed to the goal-oriented mind-set that wants its knowledge in neat units and therefore equates uncertainty with ignorance. Against this push for certainty, the productivity of interaction is one for which a solution should not distract from the complexity of the problem and for which the result of a successful internalization of this complexity is a remainder of uncertainty or doubt. Based on my readings of Joyce's unreadability, I submit that this is one way to describe the attitude towards knowledge-production expressed in *Finnegans Wake*.

I would like to finish by emphasizing that we can hardly overestimate the significance of Joyce's position at the current moment, at which socio-economic and didactic trends organized around notions of *efficiency* exert vast influence over our understanding of knowledge and skillfulness. To adapt a suggestion Beckett makes apropos of *Finnegans Wake*, "The danger is in the neatness of identifications" (3). To this danger, Joyce opposes the slowing down of unreadability. It is as if Joyce, confronted with the reprimand that there are neater and better ways of conveying your message, ways that target a greater demographic and make a bigger impact by being more easily digestible, asserts his obstinate preference for doing things his way. Joyce resists the commodification of knowledge. In doing so, he illustrates for us the creative and political value of discourses that are shockingly inefficient.

Clarity and functionality are at present weaponized by neoliberal discourses that aim to outflank politicization and to make sheer speed and quantity of processing the necessary priority – i.e. the only possible or thinkable priority – even in matters of knowledge, thought, and communication. In this climate, we can well appreciate the provocation constituted by Joyce's interest in the secret, which throws a spanner into the works of apolitical information and of knowledge measured by its capacity to travel quickly and easily. As Byung-Chul Han remarks: "Secrets do not sit well with the regime of information and communication" (*Non-things* 65). Elsewhere, he argues that "transparency is an ideology; it is a neoliberal dispositif. It violently drags everything out into the open in order to transform it into information" (*Capitalism* 29). Secrets, then, are an affront to the neoliberal imperative to make things work, to keep everything smart and efficient while never asking *why*. They remind us that where we do make something work, we are not acting out a program to which "there is no alternative," but making decisions for which we are responsible.

The importance of the secret to Joyce's work is not necessarily bad news for interpretation. The more a text escapes appropriation, the more it interrupts any towering project and instead locates debates on a horizontal plane where they can generate meaning by growing into multiple habitats, separate or interlocking but always without an absolute center, and by executing such shifts as escape any teleology. At the same time, these debates will work on a *resistance*, on a difficulty that slows them down to a pace at which they do not gloss over complexity, but reveal both complexity and the accountability generated in the interpretation of complexity. Difficulty ensures that the democratic *openness* of a debate does not collapse into destructive limitless *acceleration* or into a *simplicity* that is merely some dominant perspective masquerading as the neutral, unmarked case. If such simplicity is what is sometimes leveraged against the scandalous alterity of theory, it is also what *Finnegans Wake* opposes – both in its own hermeneutic theory and in its form.

The chief rationale of the *Wake*'s unreadability, in this view, is to enact the *Wake*'s hermeneutics at the level that has the single greatest impact on the text's readers: the level of reading's materiality. If materiality is not legibility, then meaning is not expended in intuitive accessibility, and negotiation is constituted by neither dull stability nor destructive acceleration. *Finnegans Wake* is difficult for a reason. Its difficulty makes palpable that where a discursive space is to be built, it is with difficulty.

Works Cited

Aland, Barbara, Kurt Aland, and Eberhard Nestle (eds.). *Novum Testamentum Graece*. 28th rev. edn. Stuttgart: Deutsche Bibelgesellschaft, 2009.
Atherton, James S. *The Books at the Wake: A Study of Literary Allusions in James Joyce's Finnegans Wake*. Carbondale: Southern Illinois University Press, 2009.
Attridge, Derek. "Introduction: Criticism Today – Form, Critique, and the Experience of Literature." *The Work of Reading: Literary Criticism in the 21st Century*. Ed. Anirudh Sridhar, Mir Ali Hosseini, and Derek Attridge. New York: Palgrave Macmillan, 2021.
———. *Joyce Effects: On Language, Theory, and History*. Cambridge: Cambridge University Press, 2000.
———. *Peculiar Language: Literature as Difference from the Renaissance to James Joyce*. New York: Routledge, 2004.
———. *Reading and Responsibility: Deconstruction's Traces*. Edinburgh: Edinburgh University Press, 2010.
———. *The Singularity of Literature*. New York: Routledge, 2004.
———. *The Work of Literature*. Oxford: Oxford University Press, 2015.
Attridge, Derek, and Daniel Ferrer (eds.). *Post-Structuralist Joyce: Essays from the French*. Cambridge: Cambridge University Press, 1984.
Baden, Joel S. *The Composition of the Pentateuch: Renewing the Documentary Hypothesis*. New Haven, CT: Yale University Press, 2012.
Beckett, Samuel. "Dante... Bruno. Vico.. Joyce." *Our Exagmination Round his Factification for Incamination of Work in Progress*. New York: New Directions, 1972. 1–22.
Beckett, Samuel et al. *Our Exagmination Round his Factification for Incamination of Work in Progress*. New York: New Directions, 1972.
Benjamin, Roy. "Room in the Kirkeyaard: *Either/Or* and the Heinousness of Choice in *Finnegans Wake*." *Joyce Studies Annual* (2014): 215–35.
Bennington, Geoffrey. *Not Half No End: Militantly Melancholic Essays in Memory of Jacques Derrida*. Edinburgh: Edinburgh University Press, 2010.
Benstock, Bernard. "Concerning Lost Historeve: Book I, chapter v." *A Conceptual Guide to Finnegans Wake*. Ed. Michael H. Begnal and Fritz Senn. University Park: Pennsylvania State University Press, 1974. 33–55.
Benstock, Shari. "The Letter of the Law: *La Carte Postale* in *Finnegans Wake*." *Philological Quarterly* 63.2 (Spring 1984): 163–85.
———. "Nightletters: Woman's Writing in the *Wake*." *Critical Essays on James Joyce*. Ed. Bernard Benstock. Boston, MA: G. K. Hall, 1985. 221–33.

Berressem, Hanjo. "The Letter! The Litter! The Defilements of the Signifier in *Finnegans Wake*." *Finnegans Wake: Fifty Years*. European Joyce Studies 2. Ed. Geert Lernout. Amsterdam: Rodopi, 1990. 139–64.

The Bible: Authorized King James Version with Apocrypha. Ed. Robert Carroll and Stephen Prickett. Oxford: Oxford University Press, 2008.

Bishop, John. *Joyce's Book of the Dark: Finnegans Wake*. Madison: University of Wisconsin Press. 1986.

———. "Joyce's Last Word: Thoughts on the Last Paragraph of *Finnegans Wake*." Paper presented at the James Joyce Research Colloquium, University College Dublin, 18 April 2009. Unpublished.

Borges, Jorge Luis. "Joyce's Latest Novel." Trans. Eliot Weinberger. *The Total Library: Non-Fiction 1922–1986*. Ed. Eliot Weinberger. London: Penguin, 2001. 195.

Boucicault, Dion. "The Colleen Bawn." *Nineteenth Century Plays*. Ed. George Rowell. Oxford: Oxford University Press, 1972. 175–231.

Bristow, Daniel. *2001: A Space Odyssey and Lacanian Psychoanalytic Theory*. New York: Palgrave Macmillan, 2017.

———. *Joyce and Lacan: Reading, Writing, and Psychoanalysis*. New York, Routledge, 2017.

Brivic, Sheldon. "The Daughter in the Father: The Revolutionary Aspect of III.3." *Joyce's Allmaziful Pluralibities: Polyvocal Explorations of Finnegans Wake*. Ed. Kimberly J. Devlin and Christine Smedley. Gainesville: University Press of Florida, 2015. 255–71.

———. *Joyce Between Freud and Jung*. Port Washington, NY: Kennikat Press, 1980.

———. [Shelly]. *Joyce Through Lacan and Žižek: Explorations*. New York: Palgrave Macmillan, 2008.

Brown, Wendy. *Undoing the Demos: Neoliberalism's Stealth Revolution*. New York: Zone Books, 2015.

Butler, Judith. *Bodies That Matter: On the Discursive Limits of "Sex."* New York: Routledge, 2011.

———. "Values of Difficulty." *Just Being Difficult? Academic Writing in the Public Arena*. Ed. Jonathan Culler and Kevin Lamb. Stanford, CA: Stanford University Press, 2003. 199–215.

Campbell, Antony F., and Mark A. O'Brien. *Sources of the Pentateuch: Texts, Introductions, Annotations*. Minneapolis: Fortress Press, 1993.

Campbell, Joseph, and Henry Morton Robinson. *A Skeleton Key to Finnegans Wake: Unlocking James Joyce's Masterwork*. Ed. Edmund L. Epstein. Novato, CA: New World Library, 2005.

Cavender, Anne L. "The Ass and the Four: Oppositional Figures for the Reader in *Finnegans Wake*." *James Joyce Quarterly* 41.4 (Summer 2004): 665–87.

Chaitin, Gilbert D. *Rhetoric and Culture in Lacan*. Cambridge: Cambridge University Press, 1996.

Cheng, Vincent J. *Joyce, Race, and Empire*. Cambridge: Cambridge University Press, 1995.

Colangelo, Jeremy. "Textual Authority and Diagnostic Joyce: Re-Reading the Way We Read the *Wake*." *Joyce Studies Annual* (2016): 66–83.

Conley, Tim. "'Oh Me None Onsens!': *Finnegans Wake* and the Negation of Meaning." *James Joyce Quarterly* 39.2 (Winter 2002): 233–49.

Crispi, Luca, and Sam Slote (eds.). *How Joyce Wrote Finnegans Wake: A Chapter-by-Chapter Genetic Guide*. Madison: University of Wisconsin Press, 2007.
Critchley, Simon. *The Ethics of Deconstruction: Derrida and Levinas*. 3rd edn. Edinburgh: Edinburgh University Press, 2014.
Culler, Jonathan. *Literary Theory: A Very Short Introduction*. Oxford: Oxford University Press, 2000.
Deane, Seamus. "Introduction." *Finnegans Wake*. By James Joyce. London: Penguin, 2000. vii–l.
Derrida, Jacques. "Afterword: Toward An Ethic of Discussion." Trans. Samuel Weber. *Limited Inc*. Ed. Gerald Graff. Evanston, IL: Northwestern University Press, 1988. 111–54.
———. *The Animal that Therefore I Am*. Ed. Marie-Louise Mallet. Trans. David Wills. New York: Fordham University Press, 2008.
———. *The Beast & the Sovereign: Volume II*. Ed. Michel Lisse, Marie-Louise Mallet, and Ginette Michaud. Trans. Geoffrey Bennington. Chicago: University of Chicago Press, 2011.
———. "The Deconstruction of Actuality." Trans. Elizabeth Rottenberg. *Negotiations: Interventions and Interviews, 1971–2000*. Ed. Elizabeth Rottenberg. Stanford, CA: Stanford University Press, 2002. 85–116.
———. "Des tours de Babel." Trans. Joseph F. Graham. *Psyche: Inventions of the Other. Volume I*. Ed. Peggy Kamuf and Elizabeth Rottenberg. Stanford, CA: Stanford University Press, 2007. 191–225.
———. "Dialanguages." Trans. Peggy Kamuf. *Points…: Interviews, 1974–1994*. Ed. Elisabeth Weber. Stanford, CA: Stanford University Press, 1995. 132–155.
———. *L'écriture et la différence*. Paris: Éditions du Seuil, 2014.
———. *Edmund Husserl's "Origin of Geometry": An Introduction*. Trans. John P. Leavey, Jr. Lincoln: University of Nebraska Press, 1989.
———. "Faith and Knowledge: The Two Sources of 'Religion' at the Limits of Reason Alone." Trans. Samuel Weber. *Religion*. Ed. Jacques Derrida and Gianni Vattimo. Cambridge: Polity Press, 1998. 1–78.
———. "For the Love of Lacan." *Resistances of Psychoanalysis*. Trans. Peggy Kamuf, Pascale-Anne Brault, and Michael Naas. Stanford, CA: Stanford University Press, 1998. 39–69.
———. "Force of Law: The 'Mystical Foundation of Authority'." Trans. Mary Quaintance. *Acts of Religion*. Ed. Gil Anidjar. New York: Routledge, 2002. 228–98.
———. *Given Time: I. Counterfeit Money*. Trans. Peggy Kamuf. Chicago, IL: University of Chicago Press, 1992.
———. "Literature in Secret: An Impossible Filiation." *The Gift of Death & Literature in Secret*. Trans. David Wills. Chicago, IL: University of Chicago Press, 2008. 117–58.
———. "Living On." *Deconstruction and Criticism*. London: Continuum, 2004.
———. "The Night Watch (over 'the book of himself')." Trans. Pascale-Anne Brault and Michael Naas. *Derrida and Joyce: Texts and Contexts*. Ed. Andrew Mitchell and Sam Slote. Albany: State University of New York Press, 2013. 87–108.
———. *Of Grammatology*. Trans. Gayatri Spivak. Baltimore, MD: Johns Hopkins University Press, 1976.

———. "Plato's Pharmacy." *Dissemination*. Trans. Barbara Johnson. Chicago, IL: University of Chicago Press, 1981. 61–171.

———. *The Post Card: From Socrates to Freud and Beyond*. Trans. Alan Bass. Chicago, IL: University of Chicago Press, 1987.

———. *Rogues: Two Essays on Reason*. Trans. Pascale-Anne Brault and Michael Naas. Stanford, CA: Stanford University Press, 2005.

———. "Signature Event Context." Trans. Samuel Weber and Jeffrey Mehlman. *Limited Inc*. Ed. Gerald Graff. Evanston, IL: Northwestern University Press, 1988. 1–23.

———. *Specters of Marx: The State of the Debt, the Work of Mourning and the New International*. Trans. Peggy Kamuf. New York: Routledge, 2006.

———. *Spurs: Nietzsche's Styles*. Trans. Barbara Harlow. Chicago, IL: University of Chicago Press, 1979.

———. *Theory & Practice*. Ed. Geoffrey Bennington and Peggy Kamuf. Trans. David Wills. Chicago: University of Chicago Press, 2019.

———. "This Strange Institution Called Literature: An Interview with Jacques Derrida." Trans. Geoffrey Bennington and Rachel Bowlby. *Acts of Literature*. Ed. Derek Attridge. New York: Routledge, 1992. 33–75.

———. "Two Words for Joyce." Trans. Geoffrey Bennington. *Derrida and Joyce: Texts and Contexts*. Ed. Andrew Mitchell and Sam Slote. Albany: State University of New York Press, 2013. 22–40.

———. "Ulysses Gramophone: Hear Say Yes in Joyce." Trans. François Raffoul. *Derrida and Joyce: Texts and Contexts*. Ed. Andrew Mitchell and Sam Slote. Albany: State University of New York Press, 2013. 41–86.

———. *Writing and Difference*. Trans. Alan Bass. Chicago, IL: University of Chicago Press, 1978.

Derrida, Jacques, and Anne Dufourmantelle. *Of Hospitality: Anne Dufourmantelle Invites Jacques Derrida to Respond*. Trans. Rachel Bowlby. Stanford, CA: Stanford University Press, 2000.

Devlin, Kimberly J., and Christine Smedley. "Introduction: The Prodigal Text." *Joyce's Allmaziful Pluralities: Polyvocal Explorations of Finnegans Wake*. Ed. Kimberly J. Devlin and Christine Smedley. Gainesville: University Press of Florida, 2015. 1–13.

Devlin, Kimberly J., and Christine Smedley (eds.). *Joyce's Allmaziful Pluralities: Polyvocal Explorations of Finnegans Wake*. Gainesville: University Press of Florida, 2015.

Eagleton, Terry. *Literary Theory: An Introduction*. Anniversary Edition. Malden, MA: Blackwell, 2008.

Eco, Umberto. *The Search for the Perfect Language*. Trans. James Fentress. London: Fontana Press, 1995.

Eide, Marian. *Ethical Joyce*. Cambridge: Cambridge University Press, 2002.

Ellmann, Maud. "The Ghosts of *Ulysses*." *James Joyce's Ulysses: A Casebook*. Ed. Derek Attridge. Oxford: Oxford University Press, 2004. 83–102.

Ellmann, Richard. *James Joyce*. New and rev. edn. Oxford: Oxford University Press, 1982.

Epstein, Edmund Lloyd. *A Guide through Finnegans Wake*. Gainesville: University Press of Florida, 2009.

Evans, Dylan. *An Introductory Dictionary of Lacanian Psychoanalysis*. New York: Routledge, 1996.

Fink, Bruce. *The Lacanian Subject: Between Language and Jouissance*. Princeton, NJ: Princeton University Press, 1995.

Fordham, Finn. *I Do I Undo I Redo: The Textual Genesis of Modernist Selves in Hopkins, Yeats, Conrad, Forster, Joyce, and Woolf*. Oxford: Oxford University Press, 2010.

———. *Lots of Fun at Finnegans Wake: Unravelling Universals*. Oxford: Oxford University Press, 2007.

Freud, Sigmund. *The Standard Edition of the Complete Psychological Works of Sigmund Freud, Volume XIII (1913–1914): Totem and Taboo and Other Works*. Ed. James Strachey. Trans. James Strachey, Anna Freud, et. al. London: Vintage, 2001.

———. *The Standard Edition of the Complete Psychological Works of Sigmund Freud, Volume XX (1925–1926): An Autobiographical Study, Inhibitions, Symptoms and Anxiety, Lay Analysis and Other Works*. Ed. James Strachey. Trans. James Strachey, Anna Freud, et. al. London: Vintage, 2001.

Fuse, Mikio. "The Letter and the Groaning: Chapter I.5." *How Joyce Wrote Finnegans Wake: A Chapter-by-Chapter Genetic Guide*. Ed. Luca Crispi and Sam Slote. Madison: University of Wisconsin Press, 2007. 98–123.

Gallop, Jane. *Thinking Through the Body*. New York: Columbia University Press, 1988.

Gauthier, François. "Trouble dans le Genre et Grandeur d'une Philosophe: À propos de Judith Butler." *Revue du MAUSS permanente*, 26 August 2015. Web. 22 September 2015. www.journaldumauss.net/?Trouble-dans-le-Genre-et-Grandeur

Gibson, Andrew. *Joyce's Revenge: History, Politics, and Aesthetics in Ulysses*. Oxford: Oxford University Press, 2002.

Gilbert, Stuart. "Prolegomena to *Work in Progress*." *Our Exagmination Round His Factification for Incamination of Work in Progress*. New York: New Directions, 1972. 47–75.

———. *Reflections on James Joyce: Stuart Gilbert's Paris Journal*. Ed. Thomas F. Staley and Randolph Lewis. Austin: University of Texas Press, 1993.

Gordon, John. *Finnegans Wake: A Plot Summary*. New York: Syracuse University Press, 1986.

Hägglund, Martin. *Radical Atheism: Derrida and the Time of Life*. Stanford, CA: Stanford University Press, 2008.

Han, Byung-Chul. *Capitalism and the Death Drive*. Trans. Daniel Steuer. Cambridge: Polity Press, 2021.

———. *Non-things: Upheaval in the Lifeworld*. Trans. Daniel Steuer. Cambridge: Polity Press, 2022.

Harari, Roberto. *How James Joyce Made His Name: A Reading of the Final Lacan*. Trans. Luke Thurston. New York: Other Press, 2002.

Harpham, Geoffrey Galt. *Shadows of Ethics: Criticism and the Just Society*. Durham, NC: Duke University Press, 1999.

Hart, Clive. *Structure and Motif in Finnegans Wake*. Evanston, IL: Northwestern University Press, 1962.

Heath, Stephen. "Ambiviolences: Notes for reading Joyce." *Post-Structuralist Joyce: Essays from the French*. Ed. Derek Attridge and Daniel Ferrer. Cambridge: Cambridge University Press, 1984. 31–68.

Josephus. *Vol. IV: Jewish Antiquities, Books I–IV*. Loeb Classical Library edition. Trans. H. St. J. Thackeray. Cambridge, MA: Harvard University Press, 1957.

Joyce, James. *Dubliners*. Ed. Margot Norris. New York: W. W. Norton, 2010.
———. *Finnegans Wake*. Ed. Robbert-Jan Henkes, Erik Bindervoet, and Finn Fordham. Oxford: Oxford University Press, 2012.
———. *A Portrait of the Artist as a Young Man*. Ed. John Paul Riquelme. New York: W. W. Norton, 2006.
———. *Ulysses*. Ed. Hans Walter Gabler, Wolfhard Steppe, and Claus Melchior. London: The Bodley Head, 1986.
Kiberd, Declan. *Ulysses and Us: The Art of Everyday Life in Joyce's Masterpiece*. New York: W. W. Norton, 2009.
Kitcher, Philip. *Joyce's Kaleidoscope: An Invitation to Finnegans Wake*. Oxford: Oxford University Press, 2007.
Lacan, Jacques. "The Direction of the Treatment and the Principles of Its Power." *Écrits*. Trans. Bruce Fink. New York: W. W. Norton, 2006. 489–542.
———. "The Function and Field of Speech and Language in Psychoanalysis." *Écrits*. Trans. Bruce Fink. New York: W. W. Norton, 2006. 197–268.
———. "The Instance of the Letter in the Unconscious: or Reason Since Freud." *Écrits*. Trans. Bruce Fink. New York: W. W. Norton, 2006. 412–41.
———. "Lituraterre."*Autres écrits*. Paris: Éditions du Seuil, 2001. 11–20.
———. "On a Question Prior to Any Possible Treatment of Psychosis." *Écrits*. Trans. Bruce Fink. New York: W. W. Norton, 2006. 445–488.
———. "Le séminaire sur 'La Lettre volée'." *Écrits I: Texte Intégral*. Paris: Éditions du Seuil, 1999. 11–61.
———. *The Seminar of Jacques Lacan, Book II: The Ego in Freud's Theory and in the Technique of Psychoanalysis*. Ed. Jacques-Alain Miller. Trans. Sylvana Tomaselli. New York: W. W. Norton, 1991.
———. *The Seminar of Jacques Lacan, Book III: The Psychoses*. Ed. Jacques-Alain Miller. Trans. Russell Grigg. New York: W. W. Norton, 1997.
———. *The Seminar of Jacques Lacan, Book V: Formations of the Unconscious*. Ed. Jacques-Alain Miller. Trans. Russell Grigg. Cambridge: Polity Press, 2017.
———. *The Seminar of Jacques Lacan, Book VII: The Ethics of Psychoanalysis*. Ed. Jacques-Alain Miller. Trans. Dennis Porter. New York: W. W. Norton, 1997.
———. *The Seminar of Jacques Lacan, Book VIII: Transference*. Ed. Jacques-Alain Miller. Trans. Bruce Fink. Cambridge: Polity Press, 2015.
———. *The Seminar of Jacques Lacan, Book X: Anxiety*. Ed. Jacques-Alain Miller. Trans. A. R. Price. Cambridge: Polity Press, 2014.
———. *The Seminar of Jacques Lacan, Book XI: The Four Fundamental Concepts of Psychoanalysis*. Ed. Jacques-Alain Miller. Trans. Alan Sheridan. New York: W. W. Norton, 1981.
———. *The Seminar of Jacques Lacan, Book XIX: … or Worse*. Ed. Jacques-Alain Miller. Trans. A. R. Price. Cambridge: Polity Press, 2018.
———. *The Seminar of Jacques Lacan, Book XX: On Feminine Sexuality, the Limits of Love and Knowledge*. Ed. Jacques-Alain Miller. Trans. Bruce Fink. New York: W.W. Norton, 1998.
———. *The Seminar of Jacques Lacan, Book XXIII: The Sinthome*. Ed. Jacques-Alain Miller. Trans. A. R. Price. Cambridge: Polity Press, 2016.
———. "Seminar on 'The Purloined Letter'." *Écrits*. Trans. Bruce Fink. New York: W. W. Norton, 2006. 6–48.
———. "The Signification of the Phallus." *Écrits*. Trans. Bruce Fink. New York: W. W. Norton, 2006. 575–84.

———. "The Subversion of the Subject and the Dialectic of Desire in the Freudian Unconscious." *Écrits*. Trans. Bruce Fink. New York: W. W. Norton, 2006. 671–702.

———. "Television." Trans. Denis Hollier, Rosalind Krauss, and Annette Michelson. *Television: A Challenge to the Psychoanalytic Establishment*. Ed. Joan Copjec. New York: W. W. Norton, 1990. 1–46.

Lacivita, Alison. *The Ecology of Finnegans Wake*. Gainesville: University Press of Florida, 2015.

Landuyt, Ingeborg. "Cain-Ham-(Shem)-Esau-Jim the Penman: Chapter I.7." *How Joyce Wrote Finnegans Wake: A Chapter-by-Chapter Genetic Guide*. Ed. Luca Crispi and Sam Slote. Madison: University of Wisconsin Press, 2007. 142–62.

Lawrence, Karen. *The Odyssey of Style in Ulysses*. Princeton, NJ.: Princeton University Press, 1981.

Lernout, Geert. "The *Finnegans Wake* Notebooks and Radical Philology." *Probes: Genetic Studies in Joyce*. European Joyce Studies 5. Ed. David Hayman and Sam Slote. Amsterdam: Rodopi, 1995. 19–48.

———. "James Joyce and Critical Theory." *Comparative Critical Studies* 1.1–2 (2004): 85–96.

Lewis, Michael. *Derrida and Lacan: Another Writing*. Edinburgh: Edinburgh University Press, 2008.

Lurz, John. "Literal Darkness: *Finnegans Wake* and the Limits of Print." *James Joyce Quarterly* 50.3 (Spring 2013): 675–91.

MacCabe, Colin. *James Joyce and the Revolution of the Word*. New York: Macmillan, 1978.

Mahon, Peter. *Imagining Joyce and Derrida: Between Finnegans Wake and Glas*. Toronto: University of Toronto Press, 2007.

McCarthy, Patrick A. "The Last Epistle of *Finnegans Wake*." *James Joyce Quarterly* 27.4 (Summer 1990): 725–33.

———. "Postlegomena to Stuart Gilbert's Prolegomena." *Joyce's Disciples Disciplined: A Re-Exagmination of the 'Exagmination' of 'Work in Progress'*. Ed. Tim Conley. Dublin: University College Dublin Press, 2010. 33–41.

McGee, Patrick. "Errors and Expectations: The Ethics of Desire in *Finnegans Wake*." *James Joyce and the Difference* of Language. Ed. Laurent Milesi. Cambridge: Cambridge University Press, 2003. 161–79.

———. "Joyce's Pedagogy: *Ulysses* and *Finnegans Wake* as Theory." *Coping With Joyce: Essays from the Copenhagen Symposium*. Ed. Morris Beja and Shari Benstock. Columbus: Ohio State University Press, 1989. 206–19.

McHugh, Roland. *Annotations to Finnegans Wake*. 3rd edn. Baltimore, MD: Johns Hopkins University Press, 2006.

Míguez-Bonino, José. "Genesis 11:1–9: A Latin American Perspective." *Return to Babel: Global Perspectives on the Bible*. Ed. John R. Levison and Priscilla Pope-Levison. Louisville, KY: Westminster John Knox Press, 1999. 13–16.

Milesi, Laurent. "L'idiome babélien de *Finnegans Wake*: recherches thématiques dans une perspective génétique." *Genèse de Babel: Joyce et la Création*. Ed. Claude Jacquet. Paris: Éditions de CNRS, 1985. 155–215.

Miller, J. Hillis. *The Ethics of Reading: Kant, de Man, Eliot, Trollope, James, and Benjamin*. New York: Columbia University Press, 1987.

———. *Topographies*. Stanford, CA: Stanford University Press, 1995.

Mitchell, Andrew J. "Meaning Postponed: *The Post Card* and *Finnegans Wake.*" *Derrida and Joyce: Texts and Contexts*. Ed. Andrew J. Mitchell and Sam Slote. Albany: State University of New York Press, 2013. 145–62.

Mitchell, Andrew J., and Sam Slote. "Derrida and Joyce: On Totality and Equivocation." *Derrida and Joyce: Texts and Contexts*. Ed. Andrew J. Mitchell and Sam Slote. Albany: State University of New York Press, 2013. 1–16.

Mitchell, Andrew J., and Sam Slote (eds.). *Derrida and Joyce: Texts and Contexts*. Albany: State University of New York Press, 2013.

Moran, Patrick W. "An Obsession with Plenitude: The Aesthetics of Hoarding in *Finnegans Wake.*" *James Joyce Quarterly* 46.2 (Winter 2009): 285–304.

Muller, John P., and William J. Richardson (eds.). *The Purloined Poe: Lacan, Derrida and Psychoanalytic Reading*. Baltimore, MD: Johns Hopkins University Press, 1988.

Mulvey, Laura. "Visual Pleasure and Narrative Cinema." *Visual and Other Pleasures*. 2nd edn. New York: Palgrave Macmillan, 2009. 14–27.

Naas, Michael. *Derrida From Now On*. New York: Fordham University Press, 2008.

———. *The End of the World and Other Teachable Moments: Jacques Derrida's Final Seminar*. New York: Fordham University Press, 2015.

———. "The Mother, of All the Phantasms..." *Derrida and Joyce: Texts and Contexts*. Ed. Andrew Mitchell and Sam Slote. Albany: State University of New York Press, 2013. 163–81.

Norris, Margot. *The Decentered Universe of Finnegans Wake: A Structuralist Analysis*. Baltimore, MD: Johns Hopkins University Press, 1976.

———. "Joyce's Heliotrope." *Copying With Joyce: Essays from the Copenhagen Symposium*. Ed. Morris Beja and Shari Benstock. Columbus: Ohio State University Press, 1989. 3–24.

———. *Joyce's Web: The Social Unraveling of Modernism*. Austin: University of Texas Press, 1992.

Ostler, Nicholas. *Empires of the Word: A Language History of the World*. New York: Harper Perennial, 2006.

Platt, Len. *Joyce, Race and Finnegans Wake*. Cambridge: Cambridge University Press, 2007.

Plutarch. *Moralia, Vol. V: Isis and Osiris. The E at Delphi. The Oracles at Delphi No Longer Given in Verse. The Obsolescence of Oracles*. Loeb Classical Library edition. Trans. Frank Cole Babbitt. Cambridge, MA: Harvard University Press, 1969.

Poe, Edgar Allan. "The Purloined Letter." *The Purloined Poe: Lacan, Derrida and Psychoanalytic Reading*. Ed. John P. Muller and William J. Richardson. Baltimore, MD: Johns Hopkins University Press, 1988. 6–27.

Pomarico, Alessandra. "Situating Us." *Slow Reader: A Resource for Design Thinking and Practice*. Ed. Ana Paula Pais and Carolyn F. Strauss. Amsterdam: Valiz, 2016. 207–24.

Rabaté, Jean-Michel. "A Clown's Inquest into Paternity: Fathers, Dead or Alive, in *Ulysses* and *Finnegans Wake.*" *The Fictional Father: Lacanian Readings of the Text*. Ed. Robert Con Davis. Amherst: University of Massachusetts Press, 1981. 73–114.

———. "The Fourfold Root of Yawn's Unreason: Chapter III.3." *How Joyce Wrote Finnegans Wake: A Chapter-by-Chapter Genetic Guide*. Ed. Luca Crispi and Sam Slote. Madison: University of Wisconsin Press, 2007. 384–409.

———. *Jacques Lacan: Psychoanalysis and the Subject of Literature*. Basingstoke: Palgrave, 2001.

———. *James Joyce and the Politics of Egoism*. Cambridge: Cambridge University Press, 2001.

Reichert, Klaus. "Vico's Method and Its Relation to Joyce's." *Finnegans Wake: Fifty Years*. European Joyce Studies 2. Ed. Geert Lernout. Amsterdam: Rodopi, 1990. 47–60.

Renggli, Gabriel. "Building Metonymic Meaning with Joyce, Deleuze, and Guattari." *Joyce Studies Annual* (2018): 122–46.

Reynolds, Mary T. "The City in Vico, Dante, and Joyce." *Vico and Joyce*. Ed. Donald Phillip Verene. Albany: State University of New York Press, 1987. 110–22.

Rice, Thomas Jackson. *Cannibal Joyce*. Gainesville: University Press of Florida, 2008.

Ronell, Avital. *Complaint: Grievance Among Friends*. Urbana: University of Illinois Press, 2018.

———. *Stupidity*. Urbana: University of Illinois Press, 2002.

Rose, Danis. *James Joyce's The Index Manuscript: Finnegans Wake Holograph Workbook VI.B.46*. Colchester: A Wake Newslitter Press, 1978.

Rose, Danis, and John O'Hanlon. *Understanding Finnegans Wake: A Guide to the Narrative of James Joyce's Masterpiece*. New York: Garland Publishing, 1982.

Roughley, Alan. *Reading Derrida Reading Joyce*. Gainesville: University Press of Florida, 1999.

Royle, Nicholas. *In Memory of Jacques Derrida*. Edinburgh: Edinburgh University Press, 2009.

Russell, Letty M. "Encountering the 'Other' in a World of Difference and Danger." *Harvard Theological Review* 99.4 (October 2006): 457–68.

Salih, Sara. "Judith Butler and the Ethics of 'Difficulty'." *Critical Quarterly* 45.3 (October 2003): 42–51.

Schlossman, Beryl. *Joyce's Catholic Comedy of Language*. Madison: University of Wisconsin Press, 1985.

Schotter, Jesse. "Verbivocovisuals: James Joyce and the Problem of Babel." *James Joyce Quarterly* 48.1 (Fall 2010): 89–109.

Senn, Fritz. "Joycean Provections." *Inductive Scrutinies: Focus on Joyce*. Ed. Christine O'Neill. Baltimore, MD: Johns Hopkins University Press, 1995. 35–58.

Shatz, Adam. "Introduction." *The Meaninglessness of Meaning: Writing about the Theory Wars from the London Review of Books*. London: London Review of Books, 2020. 1–6.

Shelton, Jen. *Joyce and the Narrative Structure of Incest*. Gainesville: University Press of Florida, 2006.

Slote, Sam. "Derrida's Joyce." *Understanding Derrida, Understanding Modernism*. Ed. Jean-Michel Rabaté. New York: Bloomsbury, 2019.

———. "An Imperfect Wake." *Errears and Erroriboose: Joyce and Error*. European Joyce Studies 20. Ed. Matthew Creasy. Amsterdam: Rodopi, 2011. 135–49.

———. *Joyce's Nietzschean Ethics*. New York: Palgrave Macmillan, 2013.

———. "No Symbols Where None Intended: Derrida's War at *Finnegans Wake*." *James Joyce and the Difference of Language*. Ed. Laurent Milesi. Cambridge: Cambridge University Press, 2003. 195–207

Soler, Colette. *Lacan Reading Joyce*. Trans. Devra Simiu. New York: Routledge, 2018.

Sollers, Philippe. "Joyce and Co." Trans. Stephen Heath. *Tel Quel* 64 (Winter 1975): 3–13.
Sullivan, Edward. *The Book of Kells: With 24 Colour Reproductions from the Original Pages*. London: The Studio Publications, 1955.
Synge, J. M. *The Playboy of the Western World and Other Plays*. Ed. Ann Saddlemyer. Oxford: Oxford University Press, 2008.
Thurston, Luke. "Introduction: Lacan's *pas-à-lire*." *Re-inventing the Symptom: Essays on the Final Lacan*. Ed. Luke Thurston. New York: Other Press, 2002. xiii–xx.
———. *James Joyce and the Problem of Psychoanalysis*. Cambridge: Cambridge University Press, 2004.
Tindall, William York. *A Reader's Guide to Finnegans Wake*. New York: Syracuse University Press, 1969.
Valenza, Robin, and John Bender. "Hume's Learned and Conversable Worlds." *Just Being Difficult? Academic Writing in the Public Arena*. Ed. Jonathan Culler and Kevin Lamb. Stanford, CA: Stanford University Press, 2003. 29–42.
Van Boheemen-Saaf, Christine. *Joyce, Derrida, Lacan, and the Trauma of History: Reading, Narrative, and Postcolonialism*. Cambridge: Cambridge University Press, 1999.
Van Mierlo, Wim. "Indexing the Buffalo Notebooks: Genetic Criticism and the Construction of Evidence." *Writing Its Own Wrunes For Ever: Essais de Génétique Joycienne / Essays in Joycean Genetic*. Ed. Daniel Ferrer and Claude Jacquet. Tusson: Éditions du lérot, 1998. 169–90.
———. "Reading Joyce In and Out of the Archive." *Joyce Studies Annual* (2002): 32–63.
Van Seters, John. *The Yahwist: A Historian of Israelite Origins*. Winona Lake, IN: Eisenbrauns, 2013.
Vico, Giambattista. *New Science: Principles of the New Science Concerning the Common Nature of Nations*. 3rd edn. Trans. David Marsh. London: Penguin, 2001.
White, Allon. *The Uses of Obscurity: The Fiction of Early Modernism*. London: Routledge & Kegan Paul, 1981.
Wood, David. *Time After Time*. Bloomington: Indiana University Press, 2007.
Žižek, Slavoj. *Enjoy your Symptom! Jacques Lacan In Hollywood and Out*. New York: Routledge, 2008.
———. *The Parallax View*. Cambridge, MA: MIT Press, 2009.
———. *The Sublime Object of Ideology*. London: Verso, 2008.
———. *Tarrying with the Negative: Kant, Hegel, and the Critique of Ideology*. Durham, NC: Duke University Press, 1993.
———. *The Ticklish Subject: The Absent Centre of Political Ontology*. London: Verso, 2008.
———. "Why Lacan Is Not a 'Post-Structuralist'." *Newsletter of the Freudian Field* 1.2 (Fall 1987): 31–9.
Zoellig, Marc-Roland. "Des catholiques s'opposent à la remise d'un doctorat honoris causa." *La Liberté* [Fribourg, Switzerland], 11 November 2014. Web. 22 September 2015. www.laliberte.ch/news/regions/canton/descatholiques-s-opposent-a-la-remise-d-un-doctorat-honoris-causa-262988#.VHI1EcnsvhQ

Index

act *see* decision
Adam *see* Eden
agency *see* decision
ALP 33–4, 74, 114–15, 164
ALP's letter 34, 46–50, 58, 66–71, 92–3, 112, 128, 148
alterity 13, 17, 23, 75, 151, 169–73
analysis *see* Lacan: analytic practice
anxiety 35, 66, 69–70, 74, 76–82, 86
Atherton, James 160
Attridge, Derek 9, 13, 16, 23, 139, 142, 149, 151, 154–5, 165, 177
Augustine 160
authorial intention 10, 14, 28, 99–104, 129–32, 134–41, 172
auto-immunity 173

Babel 35, 108–10, 118–22, 147
Bataille, Georges 88
Beckett, Samuel 109, 178
Beethoven, Ludwig van 134
Belinda the hen 112–13, 115
Benjamin, Roy 88
Bennington, Geoffrey 41
Benstock, Shari 58, 93
Berressem, Hanjo 67
Bishop, John 115, 117–18, 160
Book of Kells 112
Book of the Dead 114
Borges, Jorge Luis 143–4
Boucicault, Dion 113
Bristow, Daniel 25, 61
Brivic, Sheldon 26, 63, 94, 104
Brown, Wendy 28
Butler, Judith 4–5, 22, 32, 54–6

Cain and Abel 74–5, 88, 162–3
Campbell, Joseph 19, 111
cannibalism 94–6, 147
Carlos, Wendy 134

castration 30–1, 53–6
Cavender, Anne 105
Chaitin, Gilbert 54
Cheng, Vincent 23
city 144–7, 162–3, 165
Colangelo, Jeremy 82, 102
Conley, Tim 109
creativity *see* Shem
Critchley, Simon 11–12

decision 11–13, 32, 35–6, 61, 65, 81–2, 85, 101, 141, 144, 153–7, 159–60, 166–7, 172–3, 175, 178
Derrida, Jacques: on Joyce 24–5, 51, 88, 99, 107–8, 119, 122; on "illimitable" interpretation 136–7; ontology 40–1; not a relativist 10–11, 41–2, 79, 135–6; similarity to Lacan 29, 32, 44–5, 52–3, 57, 77–9, 97, 157–60; "There is nothing outside of the text" 5–6, 78
desire 21, 23, 37–8, 42–5, 48–50, 52–3, 56–7, 64, 79–80, 170
dictation 89, 93
différance 41, 43, 79, 174–5
difficulty 2–3, 11–12, 14–18, 21–3, 26–7, 31–2, 50, 62, 86, 100, 105, 122–3, 128–9, 138–41, 169–72, 175–9
distortions *see* difficulty
Dubliners 17

Eagleton, Terry 28
Eco, Umberto 111
Eden 68–9, 108–10, 157–8, 162
Eide, Marian 166, 176
Ellmann, Maud 98
Esperanto 125
essence *see* meaning: essential

ethics *see* reading: ethics of; theory: ethics of
Evans, Dylan 68, 77
Eve *see* Eden

fall: fortunate 159–60, 163–5, 167; into history 158–9, 161–5; linguistic 108–12, 116–17, 122–3, 158
fetish 68–9
fiction *see* legal fiction
Fink, Bruce 30
Finnegans Wake: as anti-fascist 23, 122; as self-deconstructive 18, 32, 50, 105; as similar to neurosis 63; as theory 1, 9, 16–19, 27, 105–6, 130, 140, 167, 170–1, 178–9
flood myth 35, 110–11, 113–15
Fordham, Finn 86
Freud, Sigmund 76–7, 94–6, 118, 160
Fuse, Mikio 48

genetic criticism 20–1, 132–3, 138–41
Gilbert, Stuart 144–5

Hägglund, Martin 43–5, 153–5
Han, Byung-Chul 178
Harari, Roberto 59–61, 63, 65, 158–9
HCE 33, 93–8, 103–4, 144, 152–3, 162–4
hospitality 148–55

imaginary (Lacanian order of experience) 55
infinity 137
Issy 33–4, 115, 152–3
iterability 39–40, 51, 84, 92, 103, 134–7, 174

Josephus, Flavius 121

Kafka, Franz 90
Keynes, John Maynard 174
Kubrick, Stanley 134

Lacan, Jacques: analytic practice 32, 59–61, 63; Joyce's influence on 24–5, 31–2, 50, 61–3; similarity to Derrida 29, 32, 44–5, 52–3, 57, 77–9, 97, 157–60; "the unconscious is structured like a language" 52, 59
Lacivita, Alison 148
Landuyt, Ingeborg 83
legal fiction 98–9, 175
legitimacy *see* authorial intention
Lernout, Geert 131–6, 138–40

Lewis, Michael 44
literary theory *see* theory
Lot 152–3
Lurz, John 21

MacCabe, Colin 20, 97
McCarthy, Patrick 47–8
McGee, Patrick 23–4, 27
Mahon, Peter 25, 49, 86
meaning: essential 42–5, 79–81, 86–7, 100–1, 104, 134, 136, 149–50, 167; production of 45–6, 48, 50, 58, 65, 72, 82, 99–103, 129, 131, 134–7, 141, 144, 155, 165–7
Messiaen, Olivier 134
Míguez-Bonino, José 121
Milesi, Laurent 124–5
Miller, J. Hillis 12, 149, 170
Mitchell, Andrew 14–15, 26, 92
Moran, Patrick 75
multilingualism *see* plurality
Mulvey, Laura 69–70

Naas, Michael 45, 99–101, 151
neoliberalism 28, 178
Noah *see* flood myth
non-word 37–9, 45–6, 49–50, 71, 85, 104, 106, 109, 128–30, 138–9, 143–4, 165, 170, 179
Norris, Margot 19–20, 50, 125
nudity 67–9, 74, 158

objet petit a 44, 56–7, 77–81, 150
Ostler, Nicholas 120

Paris, Matthew 89
paternity 95–100
Pentecost 35, 123–7
perfect language *see* fall: linguistic
phallus *see* castration
Phoenix Park 98, 163–4
Plato 89–91, 103
Platt, Len 24
plurality 111, 120–6, 128–9, 137–43, 171; as a problem 142, 146–7, 152, 165
Plutarch 66
Poe, Edgar Allan 28–9, 51–2, 67, 149–50
Pomarico, Alessandra 177
A Portrait of the Artist as a Young Man 17
Previn, André 134
private and public 131–6, 138, 148–50, 155, 166–7, 173–4

Quinet, Edgar 147

Rabaté, Jean-Michel 25, 94, 97, 145–6, 162
Rattle, Simon 134
reading: ethics of 11–13, 23–4, 133, 166, 175
real (Lacanian order of experience) 30–1, 55–7, 150, 158, 170
Reichert, Klaus 161
responsibility *see* decision
Rice, Thomas Jackson 94
Ronell, Avital 123, 177
Rose, Danis 133
Royle, Nicholas 7, 170
Russell, Letty M. 124

Salih, Sara 22
Schlossman, Beryl 126–7
secret 149–50, 167–8, 173, 177–8
Senn, Fritz 14
Shaun: attacking Shem 73–6; as medium 93–4, 96, 103–5; as postman 91–2; as the professor 72; as a writer 82–3
Shem 75–6, 83–6, 100, 147
Shem and Shaun 33–4, 86–8, 90, 92–3, 100, 102, 109
sinthome 60–1, 63–4, 157, 159
Slote, Sam 14–15, 20, 26, 48, 115, 122, 125, 142, 144
Socrates 89–91, 103
Soler, Colette 56, 62
Sollers, Philippe 23–4, 122
specter 90, 93–5, 101–4, 131

split narrative 35, 110, 113–15, 117–23, 127–8, 146, 152, 159, 164–5
symbolic (Lacanian order of experience) 29–31, 59–61, 81, 99, 156–9, 170, 175
Synge, J. M. 113

theory: bad reputation of 5–6, 9, 140, 148; definition of 3, 8–9, 170; ethics of 4–9, 13–14, 27, 167, 170–3, 175, 177–9; relevance of 27–8
therapy *see* Lacan: analytic practice
Thurston, Luke 26, 60–2, 81, 85, 88, 156–7
Tower of Babel *see* Babel
trace 40–2, 44–5, 57, 79–80, 101
transience 174

Ulysses 17, 80, 98–9, 147, 157, 176
uncertainty *see* difficulty
unreadability *see* difficulty

Van Boheemen-Saaf, Christine 25–6, 58, 65, 71
Van Mierlo, Wim 140–1
ventriloquism 90–1, 100, 102–4, 131, 141
Vico, Giambattista 35, 114–19, 160–2

writing 85–9, 91, 100–1

Žižek, Slavoj 5, 30, 57, 78–9, 158–9, 175